FROM MESOPOTAMIA TO MARS

THE SANITY OF SOCIETY IS A BALANCE OF A THOUSAND INSANITIES.

BHAVNA DAHIYA

This book is dedicated to all homo sapiens, existing within society.

The greatest discovery of my generation is that a human being can alter his life by altering his attitudes.

- William James

Contents

Preface

He who cheats the earth will be cheated by the earth.

Cielo

What is a society?

It is an abstract concept of social relationships.

Once a human is born, social upheaval starts its journey of shaping the person according to its own principles and hues. A society is formed by some significant pillars of Societal norms and conventions, concepts of hierarchy, discrimination, patriarchy, language and gender roles with respect to space and communication. With a new concept of gender neutrality, and the rise of the third gender, society is undergoing a metamorphosis. The once rigid rules are being reshaped and rewritten. Does it mean that society is being revolutionised? Even though India broke through the shackles of colonialism decades before, it still finds itself a prisoner of the neo-colonialism of mind.

Yearning from decolonisation is no longer just about freeing oneself from the grasp of Capitalistic endeavours or the established notions of ultramodernity but about freeing oneself from the notions of being entrapped. To release the mind from the constraints of our colonised selves and enable fluidity and fecundity of the intellect beyond the confines of our shrunken and compartmentalised imaginations, decolonization is a gradual, purposeful, and rigorous process that must be understood.

Decolonization was the biggest historical development of the 20th century. The primacy of Europe and America in literature may not have ended the century yet, but it has unquestionably finished. The countries of Latin America, Africa, and Asia are today at the epicentre of literary creativity, not Europe and America. Various intellectually fascinating and intriguing works are emerging from these nations, and the writers are taking the initiative. While writers from Latin America and Africa critique European and American literature in those very languages, writers from Asian nations like India advance decolonization primarily via the use of their own non-European languages. The Second World War expedited a trend that had already begun at the turn of the century in Latin America, Africa, and Asia. The literary theorists of Europe and America have periodically developed several theoretical formulations, referring to this new literary ground well as "Commonwealth Literature," "New Literatures in English," and "Post-colonial Literature." The most recent of these terms is "Third World Literature."

The idea of "Third World Literature" might be viewed as a modern interpretation of Goethe's earlier idea of "World Literature," although it is not nearly as innocent. In reality, it is really a cunning scheme to keep "First World Literature" in power, and if we look closely, the phrase "Third World

Literature" is nothing more than neo- "orientalism" from the post-colonial era. Evidently, Europe and America still want something "other" than themselves in order to identify themselves. The Third World must also require a "other" in order to identify itself, and who better than the West could serve as this "other," according to this Western notion. This, in my opinion, is the proper vantage point from which to assess 20ᵗʰ-century Indian society's representation and evolution.

It is difficult to seek a solution outside of a decolonization-focused lens, whether the problem is one of tradition and modernity, regional and national identity, artistic experimentalism, or the integration of indigenous forms. As a result, the first thing to consider is how informed and involved Indian authors are in the current decolonization process. Furthermore, unlike at our seminars and conferences, this subject is not only of intellectual interest. The answer to the query immediately corresponds to the expression of our creative force. And as of right now, I believe that among Indian writers writing after Independence, the decolonization mentality present in writers from a previous age has become weak and lax. And this is why the narrative grows weak and there is no scope for anti-thesis unless we change the thesis.

Are we spiritually free from colonialism? There are several communities for whom colonisation had varying meanings. For instance, the grandeur of the colonial empire had little effect on the indigenous inhabitants in the country's northeastern parts. Reminiscing India's illustrious history is insufficient. That past was ruthlessly vanquished. We need to consider what was previously lacking. There wasn't any political cohesion. We were united spiritually and culturally, but there was no political idea of an Indian state. The claim that ancient India was completely self-sufficient is unfeasible and false. However, discarding it won't be sufficient either. To create Indian society, we must incorporate many components from throughout the globe, including those from our own past.

This book has tried to outline the historiography of our Indian society and the one in the making. Even after gaining independence in 1947, India is still dominated by its previous colonisers and new colonial elites, albeit more or less indirectly through the influence of multinational businesses on the Indian government, which has aided the implementation of their policies. Arundhati Roy euphemizes this by calling it "building a healthy investment climate," but Kwame Nkrumah refers to it as "neo-colonialism." In other words, neocolonialism is a form of indirect enslavement that has existed for over fifty years, but it saw a surge in the 1980s with the introduction of corporate globalisation and its dominating ideology of neoliberal capitalism.

With the installation of neoliberal ideologues like Margaret Thatcher and Ronald Reagan as heads of the most powerful states, favourable conditions were created for the implementation of neoliberal economic reforms, such as market liberalisation, cuts in social service spending, deregulation, privatisation, and abolition of the concept of "the public good" or "community." This strategy was used all over the world, but especially in less developed nations like India, which were poor as a result of the structural crises of the 1970s and need help in the form of loans to reconstruct their wrecked economies. Nonetheless, loans were made exclusively on the precise observation and implementation of the standards of international financial institutions, resulting in debts that would never be repaid in those nations.

Thus, when confronted with images of abject poverty, growing slums, fascism disguised as nationalism, genocide, but also young call centre workers whose true identities are not wanted in the market, apathetic youth crowding shopping malls, depopulated rural areas and overpopulated cities, environmental disasters, and exploitation of natural and human resources in general, the question arises: how free does the free market make us people? And are the flawless credit rating and imperial elite awards really worth that much?

For people who love even water is sweet.

Acknowledgements

I would like to thank the insightful pool of resources left behind by the scholastic community, on whose shoulders I build my experience to present my opinions and arguments.

Prologue

In almost every sphere of social life, India provides remarkable variety. Indian society is divided into several ethnic, linguistic, regional, economic, religious, class, and caste groupings. There are also significant gender and urban-rural divides. Particularly in kinship and marriage traditions, there are considerable differences between north and south India. Indian society is complex in a way that may not be found in any other of the major civilizations of the globe; it is more akin to a region as diverse as Europe than to any other single nation-state. Rapidly developing developments that have different effects on different locations and socioeconomic classes have added to the diversity of current Indian culture. However, despite the complexity of Indian culture, universally recognised cultural motifs support peace and order in society.

There are many ways people influence our behaviour, but perhaps one of the most important is that the presence of others seems to create expectations.

We don't expect people to act haphazardly, we expect them to act a certain way in a particular situation. Every social situation brings its own specific expectations of what is the "right" behaviour. Such expectations may differ from group to group.

One way these expectations become apparent is when we

look at the roles people play in society. Social roles are the roles that people play as members of social groups. Each time you assume a social role, your behaviour changes to match what you and others expect from that role.

In the words of William Shakespeare:

The whole world is the stage

And all men and women are just players:

They have exits and entrances.

And a man of his time plays many roles.

These lines capture the essence of social roles. Think about how many roles you play in a day. Sons, daughters, sisters, brothers, students, workers, friends, etc. Each social role has expected behaviours called norms. Social norms are unwritten rules of beliefs, attitudes, and behaviour that are considered acceptable in a particular social group or culture. Norms provide expected concepts of how we behave and function in order to create order and predictability in society. For example, students expect to attend class and finish work on time. The concept of norms provides a key to understanding social influences in general and malleability in particular. Social norms are the accepted norms of behaviour of a social group. These groups range from friendship associations and working groups to nations. Behaviours that meet these norms are called conformance, and for the most part, roles and norms are powerful tools for understanding and predicting what people will do.

Each social group has norms that define appropriate behaviour. For example, in hospitals, students, neighbours, and patients know the code of conduct. And when you move from one group to another, your behaviour changes accordingly. Norms ensure social order. It is difficult to imagine how human societies function without social norms. We need norms to understand. These are some of the reasons why most people follow social norms most of the time. There is great pressure to adapt to social roles. Social roles are an example of social influence in general and adaptability in particular. Most of us follow guidelines for the role we play most of the time.

We meet the expectations of others, respond to their approval when we play our part well, and their disapproval when we play our part poorly. India offers amazing diversity in almost every aspect of social life. Ethnic, linguistic, regional, economic, religious, class and caste group diversity permeates Indian society, as well as significant urban-rural and gender differences. Differences between North and South India are of particular importance, especially in relation to kinship and the institution of marriage.

Indian society is multifaceted to a degree perhaps unknown to any other great civilization in the world. It resembles a region as diverse as Europe than any other single nation.Adding further diversity to contemporary Indian culture is the fact that different regions and socio-economic groups are affected in different ways. change is happening rapidly. However, in the complex Indian life, widely accepted cultural themes promote harmony and order in society.

Complex societies face the daunting task of matching members to the roles necessary for their survival. These roles should create as little conflict or confusion as possible. Some people will be happy to take on lower-ranking jobs (positions), while others will be higher-ranking. Your church has doctors, lawyers and teachers. Others collect garbage, direct traffic, and put out fires. Not all of these roles carry the same prestige, but there is little conflict in deciding who takes which role. Think of a role as a deck of cards. You and I trade many role cards in our lives. In fact, we are always playing multiple roles. Now you are dealt student role cards, but you also have other role cards in your hand, such as: B. Boyfriend, son or daughter, basketball player, cheerleader, drugstore clerk, etc. Many of your role cards are a result of your birth, age, or gender. Other cards you have won such as B. Honours or Basketball Captain.

In India, caste is a group of role cards, perhaps the most important one.A unique caste is assigned. That is, children inherit the status and functions of their parents. Indians receive a caste card at birth. This is far from what many people in the United States believe about "good company." Our parents, family members, teachers, and friends tell us in many ways that our success in life depends on our efforts.

Many of us think that all societies follow the same rules, or at least try to do so. However, it is important to remember that no society exists where individual effort is the sole criterion of status.

Caste is a very important set of role cards, but Indians, like Americans, also use class (economy) cards. Both caste and class work at the same time. A very low caste person, like a cleaner, can get a good job unrelated to cleaning and save some money. With this wealth, sweepers can build luxurious homes and raise children. Children become doctors, lawyers, and government leaders. This type of role is usually fulfilled, although some inherit wealth.

In India, there is the possibility of attaining political power as well as class and caste status. Those of lower caste may be better at winning elections and becoming members of the central government. A member of the Dulit (former untouchables) caste, Jajivan Ram has held many ministerial positions during his political career. This system of gaining status is based on strength. Power is usually a position achieved rather than a role given at birth. Indians participate in caste games, class games and power games.

In India, castes are ranked, and caste members in a given region can identify castes above and below them. Caste hierarchies are based on cleanliness and contamination, which are often related to the functions of the human body. The roles associated with the head, such as thinking, speaking, teaching, and learning, are considered pure. Activities involving waste, feet and skin are considered environmentally hazardous. Thus, Brahmins, at the pinnacle of the measure of purity, were traditionally scholars who taught and guided religious functions. At the bottom of the scale, the Untouchables cleaned up human excrement, picked up trash, cut hair, skinned animals, and washed clothes. Because their occupation primarily dealt with humans, animals, and social waste, society believed that contact with the Untouchables was extremely unfriendly.

Food preparation and sharing shows how the castes are classified. Food cooked in oil and prepared by Brahmins can be accepted and eaten by any of the castes below. Food cooked in water is usually accepted by members of their own caste or lower castes. . Leftover food leftovers are mostly consumed only by very low castes. Foods that can be eaten raw are the most freely distributed and acceptable to any caste of any caste. Additionally, Prasad, the blessed food left over from religious offerings, is given to all people, regardless of caste.

There are also many pure and impure foods. Vegetables and grains are purer than meat and eggs. Fish is the purest non-vegetarian food, followed by chicken, goat, pork and buffalo. The most impure is beef. Sweet pastries fried in fat are one of the most widely accepted foods of all castes. By observing how food is prepared and with whom it is shared, we can rank the caste groups involved on a measure of cleanliness and contamination.

Social change can be caused by many factors. Population growth can make a difference. innovation – i.e. new ideas and objects can produce a new relationship. It is also possible for societies to borrow ideas and things from other societies. It can lead to fluctuations in social relationships. There are other factors related to social change in India. As we know all societies are subject to change. In some cases these can be radical. I feel that some social systems may be replaced by new ones. or there may be significant changes in the existing social system. For example, on-site nuclear family dominance Traditional family communities have changed the family as a social institution. Aside from that, there are other institutions that no longer exist. For example, if a society is based on slavery when replaced by feudalism, the social system of this slave society could also disappear. if we are observing a society over a period of time (i.e. historically) shows that change is taking place throughout. In some cases, these may be phased. In others they can be fast.

CHAPTER I

Caste has divided us. It is a notion; it is a state of the mind.

In India, a caste system is a unique form of social stratification. In fact, social change has always existed within the caste system. Certain changes have taken place in the social system since British colonialism and modern education. It has caused social and cultural changes in Indian society. Various sociologists and Anthropologists have tried to explain the social change in the context of India. Various factors act on society and bring about changes in society. Some of them may be outside the social system. For example, changes caused by economic changes or production conditions. In modern society, industrialization brings about social change. For example, changes in family composition post Industrialization. Nuclear families are more adaptable to the nature of industrial society. Shared families are suitable for pre-industrial, predominantly agricultural societies. and at the same time, there are also actors who bring about change in society

M.N Srinivas developed the Sanskritisation concept to understand social change in India. In his book Religion and Society Among the Coorgs of Mysore (1952), he states the Caste system dynamics in Indian society. He used the term to describe the process as A study of cultural fluidity in the traditional social structure of Indian society. The concept of Sanskritization is that "the ‘lower’ castes, tribes, or other groups of Hinduism change habits, rituals, ideologies, ways of life to higher, more often, twice their Birth caste". According to Srinivas, lower-caste Hindus adopted the rituals and practices of the higher castes to improve their social status in the caste hierarchy.

The caste system is a rigid system of social stratification that defines the position of each caste Transfer between hierarchies is possible only for those who have the dual affiliation of an intermediate caste or hierarchy of birth. Low-caste individuals take a generation to change their position only by adopting vegetarianism and Sanskritization of their rituals, or two. Sanskritization is therefore seen as an imitation of Brahman practices and opposition to lower caste manners. As Srinivas pointed out, "the different models of mediation of Sanskritization by the locally dominant caste emphasises the importance of caste in the process of cultural transmission. Of course, local dominant Castes have their own ideas of Brahmin, Kshatriya or Vaishya models. "

This observation indicates variation and diversity in the mobility or caste change system. To substantiate his observations more strongly and empirically, he cites K.M. Panickers who think that All Kshatriyas Enter and Exit through the seizure of power by the lower castes and hence it is the role of the Kshatriya in the social hierarchy. Srinivas goes on to say that all non-dominant castes, especially castes that are not low-caste or double-caste, want Sanskritization, but the ones with improved economic and political situations succeed. For example, the Ejawa tribe of Kerala also tried this for the social rise.

Ezhavas were traditionally toddy tappers. They were led by Sri Narayanangru and he formed an association called S.N.D.P. Yogam and Shri Narayana and Guru Dharma Pariparayan. The Society was founded in the late 19th century and it started the activity of Sanskritizing Ezhava norms and practices. It embarked on a secular program such as the establishment of schools and cooperatives. Ezhavas also joined hands with Christians and Muslims to achieve their goals. Culturally, however, the distance between tribes and upper castes is very high and the indigenous peoples were ecologically and socially isolated. They had developed their own traditions, customs, habits and way of life. Sanskritization of tribes began with opening tribal areas to the outside world. One of the most common effects of Sanskrit tribal communities is that it leads to the Integration of segments of tribal societies into broader caste structures and their assimilation into Wider Hindu folds. There are many examples of this type of integration or cultural assimilation. Bhumija of East India, Raj Gond of Central India, Pateria of India and The West Indies are examples of such integration into caste structures. This integration cannot be understood only by rituals and changes in lifestyle, but also by indigenous peoples more fully integrated into the big picture of the economic system. Sanskritization is not the one-way process that local cultures seem to go through to get more than they give.

As Srinivas put it, "This is something to remember. Throughout Indian history, local elements have entered the body of the Sanskrit faith. Myths and customs, and her elements of travelling across India, Sanskrit culture has undergone various transformations in different cultures. festivals like Dasara, Deepavali, and Holi definitely have certain things in common across the country, but they also have important regional characteristics. Some festivals only in the name are common across India and differ in everything else. They have the same name but different meanings for people from different regions. Similarly, each region has its own folklore about heroes. The story of the Ramayana and Mahabharata, often with epic events and characters, are related to the salient features of the local geography. And in every part of India are to be found Brahmans who worship the local deities which preside over epidemics, cattle, children's lives, and crops, besides the great gods of all-India Hinduism. History of India, Sanskrit and Hinduism incorporate local and folk elements and their existence.

Regardless of its established nullification in 1950, the act of "distance"- the burden of social handicaps on people by reason of birth into specific standing remains parts a lot of a piece of the country India. Addressing north of one-6ᵗʰ of India's populace or about 160 million individuals Dalits persevere close to finishing social alienation. "Untouchables" may not go too far in separating their piece of the town from that involved by higher stations. They may not utilize similar wells, visit similar sanctuaries, or drink from similar cups in tea slows down. Dalit youngsters are every now and again made to sit at the rear of study halls. In what has been referred to India as' "covered up politically-sanctioned racial segregation," whole towns in numerous Indian states remain totally isolated by standing.

"Untouchability" is built up by state assignment of assets and offices; separate offices are accommodated in separate standing-based areas. Dalits frequently get the more unfortunate of the two, assuming that they get any whatsoever. In numerous towns, the state organization introduces power, disinfection offices, and water siphons in the upper-position segment, however, fails to do likewise in

the adjoining, isolated Dalit region. Essential conveniences, for example, water taps and wells are likewise isolated, and clinical offices and the better, covered rooftop houses exist solely in the upper-position settlement. As uncovered by the contextual analysis beneath the seismic tremor in Gujarat, these equivalent practices turn out as expected even in the midst of extraordinary cataclysmic events.

On January 26, 2001, a staggering seismic tremor shook the northwest Indian territory of Gujarat. Promptly after the nation's most awful catastrophic event in late history, no less than 30,000 were proclaimed dead and north of 1,000,000 were left destitute. In the months since the seismic tremor, occupants of the territory of Gujarat have been blockaded by a man-made calamity: rank and shared separation in the dissemination of help and recovery, defilement in the treatment of help, and political quarrelling that has done close to nothing to help the quake's neediest casualties.

A month and a half after the seismic tremor, Basic liberties Watch visited the towns of Bhuj, Bhijouri, Khawda, Anjar, and Bhachau in Kutch, the state's most crushed locale. In all areas visited by Common freedoms Watch, Dalits and Muslims lived independently from upper-station Hindus. A few occupants and survivors told us, "we are enduring the manner in which we lived, that is the reason we are in discrete camps."

While the public authority has dispensed equivalent measures of financial remuneration and food supplies to individuals from all networks, Dalit and Muslim populaces didn't have similar admittance to satisfactory safe houses, power, running water, and different supplies accessible to other people. This was obvious in a few urban communities close to Bhuj, including Anjar and Bhachchau, where the public authority had given infinitely better sanctuary and fundamental conveniences to upper-standing populaces.

The consideration is presently moving to the course of restoration and reproduction of homes. As of this composition, it still needed to be worked out whether the public authority would build incorporated lodging and give impact to its 1950 established nullification of "distance."

India's rank framework normally tracks down conclusions in different pieces of the sub-mainland, including Nepal, Pakistan, Sri Lanka, and Bangladesh. Inside the Dalit people group of Nepal, there are eight significant rank gatherings and 25 recognized sub-standings. A few NGOs gauge the Dalit populace at 4.5 million, or 21 per cent of Nepal's populace. In spite of their huge numbers, they keep on being misled by reason of their position.

Nepal's 1990 constitution disallows separation based on rank (alongside religion, race, sex, and philosophy). Notwithstanding, an exemption was made for Hindu strict practices. Subsequently, Dalits can and most frequently are legitimately rejected from Hindu sanctuaries and customs. They are likewise frequently held back from entering lodgings, shops, or homes, and are even barred from cowsheds because of the conviction that they will contaminate the draining cows. In a high profile case in 2000, named the "Gaidakot Milk Embarrassment," the upper positions of the Gaidakot Multipurpose Milk Creation Co-usable Foundation Restricted would not sell milk from a creature raised by a Dalit. Solely after fights and the intercession of NGOs and common freedoms associations were Dalits permitted to offer their milk to the helpful.

As in India, the public authority has subscribed to creating approaches focused on the social and financial headway of the Dalit populace. In 1998, the Autonomous Discouraged and Abused People group Gathering was framed with the goal of planning approaches and administering projects to help Dalits. Nepal's 10ᵗʰ Five-Year Plan likewise took on a few explicit strategies and projects for Dalit financial improvement in the space of schooling, well-being, sterilization, preparation and abilities upgrade, and work. On August 16, 2001, the top state leader of Nepal declared that the public authority would ban the victimization of lower-rank Hindus and vowed to pass new regulations to condemn unapproachability rehearses and uphold the previously established restriction on standing segregation. At this composition, explicit regulation still couldn't seem to be proposed.

Dissimilar to India, which diligently contends that "the strategies of the Indian Government connecting with Planned Standings and Booked Clans don't go under the domain of Article 1 of the Show [on the End of All Types of Racial Discrimination]," Nepal has given point by point records of the country's concerns with rank segregation in a few of its reports to CERD. In its fourteenth occasional report under ICERD, the public authority honestly recognized that "for a mind-boggling greater part of individuals the rank framework keeps on being a very remarkable element of individual personality and social connections and, somewhat, decides admittance to social open doors." It further expressed that:

[R]acial segregation in the general public, particularly in provincial regions, is still in present. Alleged untouchables couldn't actually go into the places of individuals of supposed higher and working-class standings. On one hand,

they are socially smothered by the privileged societies and, then again, they experience the ill effects of neediness; the power of destitution is by all accounts higher in socially in reverse individuals.

At the Asian Territorial Preliminary Gathering for the World Meeting Against Prejudice, Racial Separation, Xenophobia and Related Narrow mindedness held in Tehran in February 2001, the Nepali government additionally pronounced that the issue of station segregation ought to be tended to at WCAR.

Inside Sri Lanka's greater part Sinhala people group, the Rodiya were generally rejected from towns and networks, constraining them into road asking, rummaging, and meandering. Besides, Rodiya could wear station-explicit clothing; were limited from schools and public offices; isolated at gravesites, and made to drink out of expendable coconut shells from nearby teashops so as not to sully the glasses of others. A background marked by rejection has conveyed forward into present-day rehearses Rodiya keep on dwelling in isolated networks with practically no cooperation with upper ranks.

As indicated by the U.N. Subcommission on the Advancement and Assurance of Common liberties' functioning paper on work and plunge-based segregation:

In Sri Lanka, there are two position frameworks, one for the Sinhalese and the other for the Tamils. Despite the fact that the two of them have their starting point in India, the Sinhalese standing framework isn't connected to the Hindu varna. It was a part of a medieval society that isolated individuals "as per Drop and Blood" or as indicated by their genetic jobs and works. The station framework was a common hierarchy.... Social distance was drilled yet the thought of contamination scarcely existed. As an American researcher closed, "The shortfall of the Hindu idea had delivered the Sinhalese position framework gentle and helpful when decided by Indian principles."

The exemption is the position of Rodiyas or Rodi (signifying "rottenness") from early times. Numerous legends encompass their starting point, all concurring that they were ousted for terrible wrongdoing and sentenced to an existence of asking or, all the more precisely, requesting donations. They were denied land and work and exposed to many burdens and corrupting treatment.

Position separation happens in both of Sri Lanka's really Tamil people groups (those plummeted from ranch labourers of Indian beginning brought to Sri Lanka by the English pilgrim government, as well as those with predecessors in Sri Lanka). Marriage bars endure, as do other social boycotts. Rank-based segregation is some of the time applied to non-Hindus-including Tamil Christian and Muslim proselytes, and individuals from other minority gatherings. These strains are exacerbated by struggle driven dislodging, which can put gatherings of shifting position foundations in nearer closeness to another

Rank contrasts between Indian origin Tamil manor labourers additionally stay noticeable. Higher-standing labourers will frequently decline to contact food proposed to them by "untouchables." "Untouchables" are likewise made to perform explicit assignments during Hindu ceremonies that are specific to their low-position status.

Position-based divisions of work are vital to a few ethnic gatherings in numerous West African nations, including the Fulani, Mandinka, and Wolof people groups. Different U.N. common freedoms settlement checking bodies have made passing reference to rank-based qualifications in Burkina Faso, Mali, Cameroon, and Mauritania. Beyond West Africa, rank in Burundi and Mauritius has likewise been noted. While this report restricts its conversation in West Africa to Mauritania, Senegal, and Nigeria, notwithstanding the nations referenced above, rank frameworks can likewise be found in Guinea, Guinea Bissau, the Ivory Coast, Gambia, Sierra Leone, and Liberia.

However caste frameworks exist inside a few ethnic gatherings in Senegal, this report limits itself to the Wolof people group, the country's biggest ethnic gathering. In July 2001, an alliance of Senegalese nongovernmental associations held a public studio on issues looked by rank networks in the country. The one-day meeting was in anticipation of the World Gathering Against Bigotry. Among the members was notable humanist Abdoulaye Bara Diop, who has composed widely on rank frameworks among the Wolof of Senegal. He commented: "When we talk about ranks we consider India where the position situation unbendingly structures all of society. Sub-Saharan African likewise knows ranks, among which the griot are the most notable." He proceeded to add that stations can be characterized as inherited, endogamous gatherings that are appointed explicit occupations and administered by severe various leveled connections. All such qualities can be found among the Wolof who are primarily split between the geer and the neeno.28

The Senegalese constitution declares the right, all things considered, to rise to insurance of the law paying little mind to race, religion, sex, or beginning, a reference to one's station foundation (article 1), and restricts all demonstrations of racial, ethnic, and strict separation (article 5). In spite of these sacred securities, the degree to which neeno standings approach the courts for lawful change on separation claims is irrelevant.

Inside the Igbo people group of southeastern Nigeria, the minimization of those that have been ordered as Osu apparently remains to a great extent unchecked.29 The expression "Osu" generally applied to people who were held to be "claimed" by deities.30 Like position qualifications in different social orders, the qualification of Osu is consequently passed on by legacy and drop and can't by and large be survived. Osus can't be recognized from others based on their actual appearance or their speech.31

However Osu share similar legitimate status as different Nigerians-the Osu framework was prohibited with the entry of the Osu Framework Regulation and the Laws of Eastern Nigeria in 1956 und 1963-individuals from the Osu people group are as yet disregarded as outcasts and denied social equality.32 Generally landless, Osu can customarily just wed inside their standing, and are covered in isolated cemeteries.33

Oppression Buraku, now and again known as estimated time of arrival (differently characterized as "contamination bountiful" or "messy") perseveres in Japan. Academic agreement today holds that the assessed 3,000,000 Buraku who live in Japan today can follow their family to the people who became associated with occupations remembered to be messy during Japan's primitive Tokugawa time in the seventeenth hundred years. These occupations included cowhide making, an errand disregarded by Shintoists and Buddhists who felt that anything which included the taking of life was messy. The then-government classified such victimization Buraku when it expressly considered specific gatherings recognized by their occupations to be estimated time of arrival and hinin ("nonperson"). These recently framed lower standings were then additionally constrained into explicit occupations. The etas had to discard dead cows or accept fill in as conceal leather treaters and other cowhide related creates, while the hinin became safety officers and killers. Starting in the mid 1700s, the Japanese government laid out unambiguous principles restricting the sorts of garments and hairdos that Buraku could wear, delivering them effectively recognizable. Buraku were frequently disallowed from entering towns around evening time or regularly visiting specific strict sites.34 Their headstones were likewise set apart with names interfacing them to servitude or cattle.35

The Buraku framework was authoritatively abrogated by the Liberation Proclamation of 1871, however oppression Buraku endures right up to the present day. Following the decree, laborers revolted in fight at being positioned as equivalents to Buraku, burning down Buraku towns in western Japan and it be denied to request that the declaration. In advanced Japan, numerous Buraku actually live in isolated networks in urban areas around the nation, including significant urban communities like Kyoto, Osaka, and Kobe. Burakumin keep on being portrayed as "grimy" and "improper" to connect with. They are even supposed to be of an unexpected drop in comparison to most of Japanese individuals despite the fact that they are racially unclear from the remainder of the populace.

Today, the Buraku public are the objectives of obnoxious attack and prompting to savagery, frequently as spray painting or messages posted on the Web with trademarks like "Kill Buraku Individuals" or "Eliminate Buraku

Individuals." Hostile messages are habitually shipped off NGOs dynamic on Buraku issues, like the Buraku Freedom Development.

Isolation likewise keeps on being a lifestyle for the Buraku nation in country regions in Japan, however in metropolitan places many have effectively coordinated with non-Buraku people group.

Frequently, unbending accepted practices of virtue and contamination are socially authorized through severe forbiddances on marriage or other social association between stations. While financial and social pointers other than standing have acquired in importance, permitting intermarriage among upper stations, in numerous nations solid social hindrances stay set up against marriage among lower and higher ranks.

In India the judgment can be very serious, going from social exclusion to reformatory brutality. On August 6, 2001, in the north Indian province of Uttar Pradesh, an upper-rank Brahmin kid and a lower-station Jat young lady were hauled to the top of a house and freely hanged by individuals from their own families as many observers looked on. The public lynching was discipline for declining to cut off a between position friendship. Between position relationships can likewise prompt enormous scope assaults on lower-rank networks. In May 2000 in Hardoi region in Uttar Pradesh, a police constable rankled by his girl's union with a Dalit was joined by different family members in shooting and killing four individuals from his child in-regulation's loved ones. Dalits who wed high-standing people in Nepal at times allegedly have been detained by neighborhood specialists in light of misleading arguments recorded against them by individuals from the upper-rank families. Dalits are frequently prohibited from performing marriage or burial service customs in open regions or, in certain areas, from addressing individuals from upper positions.

In both the Tamil and Sinhala people group of Sri Lanka, intermarriage between upper-station and lower-position people is still socially deterred. Marital advertisements in Sri Lankan papers set by Tamils and Sinhalese both regularly determine the station foundation of the match that the family is looking for.

In Japan marriage stays an essential wellspring of separation for Buraku individuals today. Doubts that an individual is of Buraku drop frequently lead to private examinations concerning their family foundation. These record verifications are not difficult to lead since family libraries are effectively realistic, and Buraku names are unmistakable and conspicuous. After finding that the expected lady or lucky man is of Buraku plunge, the marriage plans are frequently purportedly dropped or denounced.

Relationships are as yet expected to fall along station lines for the Wolof social orders of Senegal; a geer who weds somebody from the lower ranks might be segregated. Indeed, even among the neeno, marriage inside one's own station is liked, especially among the griot local area. In pieces of southeastern Nigeria, union with an Osu by a non-Osu is exceptionally deterred and, surprisingly, censured by society, while offspring of such an association are probably going to be segregated and abused.

Assignment of work based on station is one of the principal fundamentals of numerous rank frameworks, with lower-

standings commonly confined to errands and occupations that are considered as well "disgusting" or "contaminating" for higher-position networks.

Among the Wolof of Senegal, the idea of standing is established on word related gatherings, and in like manner separates Wolof Senegalese into one of four classes, every one of which are either genetic or accepted upon marriage. The "prevalent" class of the geer was customarily included ranchers, angler, fighters and animal raisers they are as yet considered society's noblest. They generally can wed inside the gathering, and are not permitted to rehearse the conventional callings of the lower positions. Albeit the lower-standing callings are split between three unmistakable positions, they are all in all named neeno and are hence recognized from the geer.

The neeno are additionally partitioned into subcastes: the jeff-lekk are contained craftsmans while griots and entertainers comprise the sab-lekk. A third class of the noole, who are moderately very few, make up the workers and mistresses. The craftsmans are additionally isolated into four sub-ranks, specifically metal forgers or gem specialists, shoemakers, woodcutters, and weavers. Underneath the neeno is the classification of jaam or slaves-they are considered to be outside the position framework. Over the long haul, the movement of Wolofs to urban areas and bigger towns has prompted more noteworthy admittance to instructive and proficient open doors for neeno ranks, however difficult issues remain.

Sterilization occupations including road cleaning and the treatment of human waste and creature bodies are works solely performed by Dalits in India, Sri Lanka, Bangladesh, and Nepal.

Dalits in Bangladesh-who initially relocated from India under English rule and stayed after the parcel of the subcontinent in 1947-work chiefly as metropolitan cleaners and homegrown specialists, modest positions that are avoided by the country's larger part Muslim Bengali populace. In the nation's capital, for instance, Dalits make up most of the 5,500 cleaners working for Dhaka City Enterprise. They live in little, dirty quarters furnished by the city enterprise without any gas or power and are paid a little over U.S. $1 every day.

Dalits additionally breed pigs for Dhaka's minority Hindu and Christian populace and work as merchants and cart pullers.

Indian-beginning Tamils in Sri Lanka keep on confronting extreme social separation. For a large number of the country's minority Tamils, little has changed occupationally since the eighteenth century when individuals from lower-standings from southern India were brought to Sri Lanka as hostage work to deal with manors and as city cleaners. Right up to the present day, the conventional division of work keeps on being propagated. At the lower part of the rank order in the Indian Tamil people group are three unapproachable stations. While Pallas and Nalavas can deal with upper-station land for compensation, Paraiyars are overwhelmingly taken part in "messy" disinfection work. Manor workers additionally remain underestimated from financial, instructive, and social open doors, and experience the ill effects of chronic weakness care and a powerlessness to take part in political life.

As per the subcommission's functioning paper on work and plummet based segregation:

A new claim of segregation in view of plunge is that made by Tamils of Indian beginning utilized for the most part as tea bequest laborers in the slope country. As to compensation, lodging, disinfection, wellbeing and instructive offices, they were a mistreated gathering. Enhancements have gradually been made because of government arrangements and strong worker's guild activity. Coordination with the remainder of society is more troublesome inferable from bias, yet this is separating. There are indications of up versatility through training and non-prejudicial regulations. Station differentiations exist among themselves and protests have been made that laborers (generally Dalits) are kept out of worker's organization office by high rank bosses.

The Sri Lankan government's turn of events and social government assistance programs have additionally neglected to coordinate the Rodiya into standard society, passing on numerous to depend on humble compensation work as sterilization laborers and clinic specialists.

Most Dalits in India likewise keep on living in outrageous destitution, without land or valuable open doors for better business or training. Except for a minority who have profited from India's strategy of quantities in schooling and government occupations, Dalits are consigned to the most humble of errands as removers of human waste and dead creatures, cowhide laborers, road sweepers, and shoemakers. Dalit youngsters make up most of kids auctions into servitude to take care of obligations to upper-rank lenders.

As per government measurements, an expected 1,000,000 Dalits in India are "manual foragers" (a greater part of them ladies) who clear defecation from public and confidential toilets and discard dead creatures; informal evaluations are a lot higher. Treatment of human waste is a station based occupation, considered as well "dirtying and foul" for anybody yet Dalits. Manual scroungers exist under various rank names all through the country, like the Bhangis in Gujarat, the Pakhis in Andhra Pradesh, and the Sikkaliars in Tamil Nadu. Individuals from these networks are perpetually positioned at the actual lower part of the rank order, and, surprisingly, the progressive system of Dalit sub-standings. Utilizing minimal in excess of a brush, a tin plate, and a crate, they are made to clean defecation off of public and confidential restrooms and convey waste to unloading grounds and removal destinations. However lengthy prohibited, the act of manual searching go on in many states.

In November 1999, after a twister banged into India's eastern territory of Orissa, killing thousands and delivering millions destitute, the public authority got 200 Dalit manual foragers from New Delhi, and wanted to bring 500 more from different pieces of Orissa, to stack creature corpses onto hand-drawn trucks and remove them to be scorched. Government authorities had allegedly offered neighborhood upper-rank occupants more than the day to day the lowest pay permitted by law for every creature consumed yet they declined, refering to the rotted states of the cadavers and the way that the undertaking was underneath them: they had "some confidence left." As seen with the tremor in Gujarat, even in the midst of catastrophic event, the laws of "immaculateness and contamination" win and the public authority's activities frequently build up the bias.

Oppression Buraku endures in Japan's economy. In a high profile case in 1998, as per Buraku social equality gatherings, more than 700 organizations were found to have recruited private examiners to uncover work candidates' Buraku beginnings, ethnic foundation, identity, belief system, religion, and political connection. Subsequent to figuring in every trademark, a candidate was positioned from "brilliant" to "prudent not to recruit." Be that as it may, an individual found to be of Buraku beginning was not evaluated and therefore not employed.

As of now years prior, in 1975, the act of selling "Buraku records" had been uncovered. Likewise assembled by analytical organizations, these rundowns remembered data for the names and areas of Buraku families and were promoted to privately owned businesses for the motivations behind screening position candidates and to families looking to orchestrate and endorse relationships. Some case that the rundowns were utilized to counter the Buraku freedoms development, which effectively lobbied for a standard request for employment for secondary school understudies, and for the preclusion of the oppressive utilization of family registers to be lawfully ordered. Such records were accounted for to be available for use as of late as 1996

The unfortunate compensation of manual searching, agrarian work, and different types of low-position business frequently force groups of lower standings or rank like gatherings into servitude. An absence of requirement of important regulation disallowing obligation servitude in the greater part of the nations concerned considers the training to proceed unabated.

An expected forty million individuals in India, among them exactly fifteen million kids, are working in slave-like circumstances to take care of obligations as fortified workers. Because of the exorbitant loan costs charged, the businesses' command over records, and the appallingly low wages paid, the obligations are only sometimes settled. Fortified workers are much of the time low-station, unskilled, and incredibly poor, while the banks/bosses are normally higher-standing, educated, nearly well off, and moderately more remarkable individuals from the local area.

The Reinforced Work Framework (Nullification) Act, 1976 cancels all arrangements and commitments emerging out of the fortified work framework. It expects to set all workers free from subjugation, drop any remaining obligation, deny the making of new servitude arrangements, and request the monetary recovery of liberated reinforced workers by the state. It likewise rebuffs endeavors to force people into subjugation with a limit of three years in jail and a Rs. 2,000 (U.S.$43) fine. In any case, moderately scarcely any reinforced workers have been distinguished, delivered, and restored in the country.

In Pakistan the obligation servitude framework is most common in the rural regions of southern Punjab and Sindh. Most workers around there are minority Hindus from lower ranks. In an example like that rehearsed in India, the charging of extravagantly exorbitant financing costs guarantee that credits from landowners never get reimbursed. While the credit arrangement is many times made between the landowner and the male top of the laborer family, the work to take care of the advance is performed by the whole family, including ladies and youngsters. Ladies have additionally been held in care via landowners when reinforced male individuals from the family leave the land or region, and have even been sold into marriage or prostitution should the male relative neglect to return. As in India, kids frequently acquire their families' obligations and stay caught in a pattern of obligation bondage.

An upsetting impression of the servitude of hundreds of years past is the legitimate act of binds up or fastening fortified workers to impede their break. Of the 7,500 fortified workers answered to have gotten away or been delivered beginning around 1995 in the southern Sindh territory, basic freedoms associations report that "few hundred" of them were found "restricted or in chains." Comparatively, in 1991 the Pakistani armed force purportedly directed a strike that uncovered the unlawful detainment of 295 workers, including 132 kids, every one of whom were shackled every evening. Most were just given flour and stew peppers as food and had no admittance to plumbing offices or clinical consideration. Public regulation in Pakistan forbidding these practices allegedly has done close to nothing to kill them. Commonplace states answerable for their requirement still can't seem to lay out instruments to try them

As per the Unified Country Advancement Program's "Nepal Human Improvement Report 1998," in spite of legitimate declarations running against the norm, reinforced work has not been annihilated in Nepal. The report adds:

In the mid-western and far western slopes, the obligation reinforced horticultural workers, haliyas, basically from "unapproachable" ranks, work under this framework. The Abolitionist Servitude Global and INSEC73 in 1996 seldom noticed haliyas from among individuals from the high position groups.... Their report likewise uncovered that in the districts noted above, individuals from "unapproachable" families were charged exceptionally high paces of revenue - as high as 10%/month - on credits sent by their property managers, while individuals from "high station" families were by and large charged just 2-3 percent/month. Such segregation was intended to keep alive and strengthen the arrangement of obligation servitude. The "low standing" Tarai bunches like Musahar, Dusadh, Dom, Chamar, and so forth deal with a comparative issue: reimbursement of credits is effectively put by the property managers down (on the same page.). Since the essential premium of the property manager lies in proceeded with development of his territory and in ordinary confirmation of work supply, his loaning isn't coordinated towards making revenue in money (NRB 1988).

The tradition of bondage as a type of rank and plummet based segregation in Mauritania is an issue the public authority should accomplish other things to address. While President Maaouiya Ould Sid'Ahmed Ould Taya has carried public thoughtfulness regarding advanced subjugation rehearses all through the nation and keeping in mind that the public authority indicates to have executed significant training and agrarian changes its record on upholding bondage explicit regulation, and regulation advancing the social liberties of previous slaves, is frail.

Both the Bedouin and Afro-Mauritanian gatherings have long recognized local area individuals based on rank, and both incorporated a standing like assignment of "slave" inside these frameworks. Right up 'til now a previous "slave" differentiation especially for the Haratines, Arabic speakers of Sub-Saharan African beginning actually conveys huge social ramifications. Best case scenario, individuals from higher and lower positions are deterred from intermarrying. In Soninke people group, individuals from the slave position are likewise covered in isolated graveyards. Even from a pessimistic standpoint, in any case, there is a boundless arrangement of neglected bondage expected of networks whose individuals still self-distinguish as slaves. However the public authority has long banned slave-like qualifications and practices, it has found a way couple of ways to uphold these regulations. A feeble economy likewise leaves previous slaves with not many choices other than staying with the groups of bosses who possessed their progenitors. Station frameworks like those found among the Wolof of Senegal can likewise be found among Soninke, Halpular, and Wolof Afro-Mauritanians.

Huge financial and educational abberations persevere among lower and higher-standing networks in the nations featured in this report. Lower-station networks are much of the time tormented by low proficiency levels and an absence of admittance to medical care and training. An absence of formal instruction or preparing, as well as segregation that successfully bans them from many types of work, and the nonenforcement of defensive regulation, propagates station based business and keeps its innate nature alive.

Starting around 1997, there were apparently just two Dalit clinical specialists and fifteen Dalit engineers in Nepal. The future pace of Nepal's Dalits is five years shy of the public normal of 55. Kids face a higher frequency of hunger and everyone needs admittance to clean drinking water or legitimate wellbeing administrations.

Nepal's 1998 Human Advancement Report uncovered that improvement pointers firmly followed rank lines. Without a solitary exemption, the lower the rank, the lower the future, the education rate, long stretches of tutoring, and per capita pay. In 1999, Nepal's fourteenth occasional report to CERD likewise honestly and usefully featured the monetary variations that keep on enduring among low-and high-standing populaces:

[A]wareness creation, pay age, training and wellbeing offices programs were executed to resolve the issues of the regressive networks. Be that as it may, the hole between alleged higher and lower positions has not restricted. There have barely been any progressions in the general public or the expectation for everyday comforts of poor people. Thus, individuals of in reverse networks have felt victimized and could hardly imagine how the Public authority was doing anything for their government assistance and advancement. The principal purposes behind this are: absence of coordinated programs, powerless execution and manageability, inability to standard in reverse networks and curbed individuals into the public advancement process, focus situated/based programs as opposed to local area based/participatory projects, little consideration regarding human asset improvement and absence of support to the turn of events and modernization of conventional occupations and abilities, absence of viable institutional systems, and so on.

Admittance to Education
High quitter and lower education rates among lower-position populaces have rather straightforwardly been portrayed as the regular results of neediness and underdevelopment. However these rates are somewhat owing to the requirement for low-station kids to enhance their family compensation through work, more tricky and less factual is the oppressive and harmful treatment looked by low-position youngsters who endeavor to go to class, because of their instructors and individual understudies.

More than a long time since India's protected commitment of free, necessary, essential schooling for all youngsters up to the age of fourteen-with exceptional consideration and thought to be given to advance the instructive advancement of planned standings ignorance actually torment close to 66% of the Dalit populace when contrasted with around one-half of everybody. The proficiency hole among Dalits and the remainder of the populace fell a meager 0.39 percent somewhere in the range of 1961 and 1991. The greater part of the public authority schools in which Dalit understudies are selected are lacking in essential foundation, homerooms, educators, and educating helps. A larger part of Dalit understudies are likewise signed up for vernacular schools whose understudies experience serious hindrances in the gig market when contrasted with the people who learn in English-talking schools.

Notwithstanding state help with essential training, Dalits additionally experience the ill effects of a disturbing drop-out rate. As per the Public Commission for Booked Standings and Planned Clans' 1996-1997 and 1997-1998 Report, the public drop-out rate for Dalit kids who frequently sit toward the rear of homerooms was a stunning 49.35 percent at the essential level, 67.77 percent for center school, and 77.65 percent for optional school.

Rodiya kids in Sri Lanka seldom concentrate on past rudimentary levels, if by any stretch of the imagination. All things being equal, their folks expect them to understand their pay procuring possible even as small kids, and frequently rashly remove them from school.87 Lower-station Tamil ranch laborers of Indian beginning in Sri Lanka likewise have low education levels. As per a Sri Lankan lobbyist just 65% of estate laborers can peruse or compose, contrasted with a high 90 percent public normal. Higher drop out rates among offspring of estate laborers stems halfway from the work of these youngsters as homegrown specialists, inn laborers, or disinfection cleaners.

The Buraku of Japan additionally experience the ill effects of lower levels of advanced education than the public normal, and higher dropout rates than the more extensive society. Specifically, Buraku ladies report lower levels of proficiency, secondary school and college enlistment, and work. Exceptional grant programs that reinforced public midpoints of Buraku training are supposed to be deliberately eliminated by Walk 2002, in spite of the impressive achievement they had in spanning the schooling hole among Buraku and non-Buraku.

In Nepal, the education rate for Dalits is horrifyingly low at 10% for men and 3.2 per cent for ladies, contrasted with a public proficiency rate that surpasses 50%. As per the public authority's own fourteenth intermittent report under ICERD, "The most reduced education is among the word-related standings. Ladies comprise multiple-thirds of the unskilled people.

Most Dalit casualties of maltreatment in India are landless farming workers who structure the foundation of the country's agrarian economy. In spite of many years of land change regulation, more than 86% of Dalit families today are landless or close to landless. The people who own property frequently own tiny. The land is a great resource in country regions that decides a singular's way of life and economic well-being. Likewise, with numerous other low-standing populaces, the absence of admittance to land makes Dalits financially defenceless; their reliance is taken advantage of by upper-and centre-rank property managers and considers many maltreatments to slip by everyone's notice. Landless horticultural workers all through the nation work for a couple of kilograms of rice or Rs. 15 to Rs. 35 (US$0.32 to $0.75) a day, well beneath the lowest pay permitted by law recommended in their state. Numerous workers owe obligations to their bosses or different moneylenders.

Indian regulations and guidelines that deny estrangement of Dalit lands, set roofs on a solitary landowner's property, or dispense surplus government grounds to planned stations and booked clans have been to a great extent disregarded, or more regrettably, controlled by upper ranks with the assistance of locale organizations.

Albeit a significant number of Nepal's horticultural workers are Dalits, Dalits likewise have a startlingly low pace of land possession just 3.1 per cent of Dalits own more than 21 ropanies of land and on the whole, Dalits own around 1% of Nepal's all out cultivable land. In addition, 90% of Nepal Dalits live below the neediness line, contrasted with 45% of the general populace. Their per capita pay adds up to a measly U.S.$39.60 while the remainder of Nepalese normal U.S.$210 per year.94 Nepali Dalits are among the world's most unfortunate poor people.

India's approach of "reservations" or rank-based portions is an endeavour by the focal government to cure past treacheries connected with low-position status. To consider the corresponding portrayal in a specific state and bureaucratic establishments, the constitution holds 22.5 per cent of national government occupations, seats in state councils, the lower place of parliament, and educational organizations for planned standings and booked clans.

Lower-standing ladies are independently situated at the lower part of position, class, and orientation progressive systems. To a great extent uninformed and reliably paid not exactly their male partners overall they constantly endure the worst part of double-dealing, segregation, and actual assaults. Sexual maltreatment and different types of brutality against ladies are frequently utilized by landowners and the police to incur political "examples" and squash contradictions inside the local area. Lower-standing ladies likewise endure lopsidedly as far as admittance to medical services, training, and resource compensation when contrasted with ladies of higher stations.

Dalit ladies in India and Nepal make up most of the landless workers and foragers, as well as a huge level of the ladies constrained into prostitution in country regions or sold into metropolitan massage parlours. Thusly, they come into more prominent contact with property managers and requirement organizations than their upper-rank partners. Their subordinate position is taken advantage of by people with significant influence who complete their assaults without any potential repercussions. Episodes of assault, stripping, and marching ladies bare through the roads, and causing them to eat waste are wrongdoings well-defined for Dalit ladies in India. Sexual viciousness is additionally connected to obligation subjugation in India, Pakistan, and Nepal.

As per a Tamil Nadu state government official, the assault of Dalit ladies uncovered the lip service of the position framework as "nobody rehearses unapproachability with regards to sex." Like other Indian ladies whose family members are looked for by the police, Dalit ladies have likewise been captured and tormented in guardianship for the purpose of rebuffing their male family members who are stowing away from the specialists.

CHAPTER II

Who decides who is polluted and who is pure.

In India, the concepts of cleanliness and pollution are recognized by upper and lower castes across the country. The caste system in India is divided into four castes: Brahmins, Kshatriyas, Vaisyas and Sudras. Brahmins maintained social distance from the Sudras. Social distancing was maintained by upper and lower castes. The upper castes communicated and negotiated with the far-flung lower castes. The concept of social distancing indicated that the concept of purity and pollution was practised in ancient India.

In modern India, on the other hand, in modern India, the upper urban castes hire domestic helpers to perform various kinds of domestic chores. going. Communication takes place between individuals belonging to distant upper and lower castes. Social distancing is maintained by upper and lower castes as they were believed to be in a polluted state because of their caste and status. Maintaining social distancing shows the concept of purity and pollution being practised in modern India. About their education, skills, abilities and talents. Caste is determined by birth and individuals remain caste throughout their lives.

Brahmins believed in the concepts of purity and pollution. The shudras performed the duties of cleaning and sweeping the houses of the brahmins, and the brahmins were given separate chairs and food and drink were given on separate utensils (Purity, 2022). done in place. Brahmins maintained social distance from the Sudras. Social distancing was maintained by upper and lower castes. Social distancing determined that the concepts of purity and pollution were practised in ancient India.

The concepts of cleanliness and pollution are key features of the caste system. These concepts are evaluated according to different aspects. H. Conduct, dress, language, occupation, diet. Filthiness is characterised by participation in occupations such as alcohol consumption, non-vegetarian diets, high-caste leftovers, leatherworking, removal of animal and bird carcasses, cleaning, and garbage hauling. Lower castes practice these occupations and are said to be in squalid conditions. Higher castes take the position that they are in a state of purity (Purity, 2022). They are engaged in professions such as education, administration and administration, which signifies their purity. On the other hand, the shudras performed their labour duties of cleaning and sweeping. These occupations were considered dirty. In some cases, the shudras were not given equal rights and opportunities. you have been discriminated against. The shudras lived according to their own norms and values. On the one hand, all castes lived according to their values.

The concepts of purity and pollution are practised in modern India. In modern India, the upper urban castes hire domestic helpers to perform various types of household chores such as sweeping, washing, sweeping, meal preparation, repairs, electrical work, painting, carpentry and plumbing. Domestic helpers and service providers visit the homes of upper caste people on a daily or irregular basis. Therefore, they pay special attention to clean hands when preparing food. Additionally, you need to make sure they are well informed about their professional duties and are appropriately dressed. Communication takes place between individuals in remote locations.

Upper castes maintained social distance from lower castes. Adherence to social distancing shows that the concepts of cleanliness and pollution are being put into practice in modern India.Domestic helpers and service providers are paid for their services. Apart from payment, you also receive clothes, food, blankets, bags, etc. Daily or occasional visits to upper caste homes provide food and drink. Another tool is used for this. When communicating, they sit on the floor or are given separate chairs. So in this way the concepts of cleanliness and contamination are put into practice in modern India.

Members of the upper caste rely on the services of domestic helpers and service providers to carry out their work. When older people have health problems, illnesses of any kind, or are unable to move, they should seek help from domestic helpers and service providers to perform routine household chores. However, most of the time communication takes place at a distance and food and drink are served on separate utensils. This signifies the spread of concepts of purity and pollution in modern India. Concepts of purity and contamination are determined by individual actions and deeds. In today's advanced world, individuals of all castes recognize the meaning and importance of education.

Getting an education facilitates the development of skills and abilities to engage in employment opportunities. Research studies show that among the lower castes, even if the individual is uneducated, their children are enrolled in educational institutions to receive an education. They enter college and go on to undergraduate, graduate and doctoral programs. Her parents are domestic helpers in upper caste homes and offices and Provide courteous communication and support as needed. However, communication takes place at a distance and food and drink are served on separate utensils. This point highlights the spread of concepts of cleanliness and pollution in modern India.

In March 1930 Dalit activist Dr. B.R. Ambedkar and social reformer B.K. Gaikwad held a protest in front of the KalaRam Temple in Nashik. Two prominent social activists and numerous other Dalit congregations called for lower caste members to be allowed entry to temples and shrines. In 2016, following a favourable ruling by the Bombay High Court, two women stormed the main temple of Shani Her Singapur village in Maharashtra. Previously, women were not allowed to enter the main hall of the temple.

In 2019, several Dalit women were denied entry to the local Chamadher Mandir in Khurja, Uttar Pradesh. In November of the same year, India's Supreme Court ruled to reconsider an order barring all women between the ages of 12 and 50 from entering the Sabarimala Temple in Kerala. This was perhaps the most heated debate on the issue of access to the temple.

The above headlines and news clips reveal that certain members of Indian society, especially menstruating women and members of lower castes, are traditionally denied access to sacred places such as temples. Ambedkar's protests against Dalit temple admission predate India's independence, but more than 70 years of democratic government have not changed public attitudes on the issue. Newspapers continue to report on the denial of entry of Dalits and women, sometimes resulting in violent conflicts and deaths.

The issue of untouchability is rooted in Hindu beliefs in purity and pollution. Some caste groups are outside of his four-tier hierarchical classification of the caste system (Brahmins, Kshatriyas, Vaishyas and Shudras) and are called untouchables. They performed simple tasks such as cleaning toilets and disposing of corpses. In Hindu tradition, animal and human corpses were considered the dirtiest. But the untouchables were treated equally impure, perfect for performing the crudest of tasks. Each higher subcaste refused to touch or be near touched objects. As a result, the untouchables were denied entry to temples, hospitals, markets, shops and other public areas. They lived in another part of the city, far from the village's communal well and the nearest school.

When upper caste members come into contact with things they cannot touch, a cleansing bath removes those impurities and restores them to a pristine state. I do not eat food from caste members. They argued that touching, receiving, or receiving anything from lower caste members, including food and water, would contaminate them, and is therefore based on the assumption that it should not come into contact with food or drink. Some other caste restrictions are based on misconceptions of purity. An example is endogamy who marry within their own caste or clan. Some tribes or caste groups believe that marrying a member outside their own caste, especially a lower caste, can bring impurities to the tribe.

Even today, concepts of purity and pollution determine the lives of millions of people in India.But Hinduism is more than a rigid caste system. Hinduism also emphasises tolerance and acceptance and teaches its followers to include all religions.This openness and acceptance must be extended to followers of the same religion. The concept of purity of Manusumurity is discriminatory and disgusted. Access to public facilities and venues should not be denied. The Constitution of India lists freedom to practise religion as a fundamental right. Visiting temples and worshipping deities is a way of practising one's religion, and thus this basic right cannot be denied to anyone based on superfluous caste practices.

The same principles of purity and contamination applied to menstruating women. In India and around the world, societies share prejudices about discussing menstruation, menstrual cramps, and sanitary napkins. Public recognition and implementation of contemporary discourse was considered taboo. Some of these taboos still exist today.

Although the menstrual cycle is a natural event of female sexual and reproductive health, society views its occurrence as an impurity. When a woman begins her menstrual cycle, she is automatically considered unclean or unclean. Therefore, many Hindus believe that she should not be allowed to enter sacred places or participate in religious ceremonies. It was also considered a sin for a woman to participate in celebrations and rituals during her menstrual period. The spurt of her blood polluted the sacred atmosphere, desecrating both the purity of the tradition and the divine beings to which it was dedicated.

For this reason, many temples forbade women from entering the sanctuaries and sacred shrines within the premises. Women can choose not to attend religious events while on their period, but prohibiting attendance limits autonomy and makes menstruation taboo. A former education minister who campaigned to ban women from entering the Sabarimala temple said that menstruating women "defile" places of worship because menstrual blood is polluted and impure. By banning menstruating women, temples and shrines demonstrate that this natural process is disgusting, filthy, and deplorable. However, it is important to understand that menstruation is associated with fertility.

This is also a sacred concept that many people, especially farmers, pray to a female goddess for fertility and prosperity.

Temple worship is perhaps one of the greatest manifestations and controversies surrounding the concept of purity, but there are many other unsubstantiated notions of impurity and contamination. Access to safe drinking water, good food and sanitation should be granted regardless of caste status. People should not be excluded or isolated from society because of their caste status. Efforts are needed to integrate the lower castes into the larger society and to understand their trials and tribulations. It is unethical and inhumane to use ancient Hindu texts to discriminate against those who are members of our society.

India's population, now over 1 billion, has grown by more than 18 million annually over the past decade, rivalling Australia's. The most populous state of Uttar Pradesh has grown by over 25% in his decade to reach about 166 million, or 60% of the US population. India is about one-third of the US population and supports more than 3.5 times the US population. Although the population growth rate is gradually declining due to the growing popularity of family planning, by 2050 India's population will reach about 1.5 billion, making India the most populous country.

In India's vocal democracy, various groups are increasingly demanding their share of scarce resources and profits. Forests, rangelands and water tables are declining as new crops and technologies increase productivity. As competition intensifies, political, social, ecological and economic issues are hotly contested. Equity in issues of class, gender, and access to desirable resources remains an elusive goal.

India is just one of many countries facing these critical problems, and it is not the only country seeking solutions. For centuries, the people of India have been adept at shaping complexity into manageable order, promoting harmony among people with diverse interests, and treating each other as close relatives and friends. It has brought together widely separated groups in structured efforts for the benefit of the wider society that knows. We trust one another, assign different tasks to those with different abilities, and strive to do what is morally right in the sight of God and the community. These are some of the great strengths that Indian society can rely on to meet the challenges of the future.

CHAPTER III

Patriarchy is a phrase, a name, a stereotype.

When the chief executive officer of Twitter, Jack Dorsey, held up a placard that read "Smash Brahminical Patriarchy" while meeting a group of feminists during a visit to India in November 2018, it created a huge uproar in the media, forcing him to apologise. Brahminical/Brahminism has been narrowly equated with the Brahmin caste, and even so-called "liberals' ' began to attack the Twitter CEO for being party to this casteist slogan that targeted one particular community, excluding all others.

Other than the small academic circle, the words ``Brahminism" and "Brahminical" are widely used in political circles while fighting for the rights of marginalised communities. The usage clearly signifies the attitude of dominant sections that obstruct the rights of marginalised communities rather than indicate/target any particular caste. Understanding the real meaning of Brahmanical patriarchy, which cannot be narrowly confined to a particular caste, can offer a holistic perspective in understanding the status of women in India. Patriarchy generally refers to a hierarchical balance of power in which men are dominant and women are subordinate.

Women's subordination is evident in many ways, both in the private and public spheres where women are denied rights and denied access to many things readily available to men.As a concept/tool Patriarchy helps us critically understand the place of women in any society. manifests and institutionalises its dominance and extends its influence into the public sphere of society. Patriarchies have commonalities across societies, but they behave differently in different societies and are connected to other dominant structures. In India, this relationship between patriarchy and caste has historically been found to be exploitative and mutually nurturing.

Endogamy, the patriarchal practice of marrying within a caste, has long been a functional element in maintaining the purity and hierarchical exclusivity of the caste system. Controlling female fertility through These norms continues to play an important role in Indian society, as female sexuality is a gateway for interference in the destabilisation of the caste system. Dr. B.R. Ambedkar's influential work entitled 'Indian Caste: Its Mechanisms, Origins and Development' remains a relevant source for understanding contemporary Brahman patriarchy today. In his work, Ambedkar identified endgamy as a distinct caste trait that hierarchically segregated the population, and mixed races were severely punished. , and sannyas (asceticism) and child marriage were prescribed to solve the problem of excess males. These practices, which acted as a bulwark against men and women marrying outside the caste system, were first developed in the Brahmin community and later practised in other communities.

Such strict rules were seen as necessary to protect the purity of the caste system and to be able to enjoy the religious, political and economic rights associated with it. The caste system also allowed for anuloma (hypergamy), in which a man of a higher caste could marry a woman of a lower caste. However, the practice of platiloma (hypogamy), in which a higher-caste woman married a lower-caste man, or the practice of disrupting the patrilineal basis of patriarchy, was strictly rejected.

We see cases of murder. Additionally, other discriminatory patriarchal norms such as virginity and femininity (the practice of a married woman staying in her husband's home) to govern women's sexuality and protect the caste system through endogamy. was imposed. Such institutionalised norms not only regulated women's sexuality, but also degraded their status within the family and denied them all opportunities for self-expression. Moreover, these norms are magnified at the social level, making women inferior to men.

In his writings, Ambedkar identified Brahmanism as a denial of the spirit of liberty, equality and brotherhood. Brahmins as a community initially developed these patriarchal practices, but all other communities subsequently followed them to maintain their religious, political and economic dominance. Brahmanism is equated with a system of class equality that denies and exploits the rights of others as applied to most of the dominant communities of our time. Rather than targeting a particular community, Brahmin patriarchy is a conceptual tool for understanding discrimination against women in Indian society.

In April 2018, Human Rights Her Watch found that approximately 94.6% of rape suspects were known to the victim, based on 2016 government data. In 2016 there were 106 rapes in India every day. More than 30,000 rapes are reported in India each year, but the social stigma associated with it makes such crimes highly underreported.

Brahman patriarchy sees rape as a violation of the purity of a woman's sexuality and places a social stigma on the victim rather than the perpetrator. In fact, rape and other acts of sexual violence are among the underreported crimes in India, given patriarchal values related to women's sexuality and morality. Based on NFHS 2015-16 data and her NCRB data, it was estimated that her 99.1% of sexual violence incidents in India went unreported because they involved close relatives of the victims. rice field. Sexual violence against women by close relatives shows that women's sexuality is controlled by men and punished accordingly. Patriarchal social norms encourage men to violate women's sexuality, both privately and publicly, in order to control them.

The Brahmanic Patriarchal system works in all sectors of Indian society, managing women and their sexuality, and upholding the caste system and male dominance. Even after women's entry was declared a national law by India's Supreme Court, recent protests against women entering Sabarimala reveal that notions of patriarchy are pervasive in Indian society. In India, therefore, the emancipation of women cannot be separated from the struggle against the hierarchical caste system that maintains and strengthens

India's Brahman patriarchy.

We live in a society where our daily actions, thoughts and feelings are shaped by patriarchal ideas that permeate our social fabric. Women have been exposed to the ailments of a male-dominated society at every stage of their lives, even before they were born. Patriarchy is unique in that this oppression is pervasive throughout the world, yet so many aspects of it are subverted by society or hidden within its structure that no one is aware of it and is exposed to it. Especially in Indian society, patriarchal norms and values are also the result of the caste and religious inequalities that plague the society. Restricting women's access to the Sabarimala Temple in Kerala.

The transmission of patriarchal values and ideas from one generation to the next takes place during the process of socialisation. Socialisation is the process of internalising the norms and ideologies of society. During and at the end of the process, the individual, whether male or female, adapts to the socialised group or society and learns to behave in ways that are socially acceptable. It forms the basis for the normalisation of patriarchy. Attempts at sustainable and equitable social change must therefore begin with the socialisation process.

Socialisation occurs at two levels: primary and secondary.

In primary socialisation, a child accepts and learns a set of norms, values, and attitudes. For example, if a child sees a mother expressing hatred toward someone, the child may think this behaviour is acceptable and continue to harbour hatred toward the other person. In secondary socialisation, a child learns appropriate behaviour as a member of a small group in a larger society. Secondary socialisation occurs outside the home. Both children and adults learn how to act appropriately in situations. School demands very different behaviour than at home, and children must behave according to new rules.

The central social institution of the primary socialisation process is the family. Parents' actions have a great impact on their children. The idea in Indian society that the man is the breadwinner and the woman the stay-at-home mom is also a result of patriarchal norms. So is every child who sees his father go to work and his mother at work. Thus, the occupational segregation we see in the labour market is rooted in the family. By doing so, the child's ability to think critically about such ideas is not developed. This is a vicious circle. Socialisation processes lead to unequal labour markets, and unequal labour markets have the worst impact on socialisation processes.

Masculinity is not a uniform, monolithic structure. It is shaped by sociocultural forces like Caste/race, class, urban-rural divide, geopolitical divide, family, other environmental influences, etc. However, due to its prevalence, certain common trends can be seen across cultures in terms of Patriarchy. Many forms of sexism are fostered through the family process of socialisation. Playing with dolls, helping my mother, working in the kitchen with my sister and doing household chores are a few basic examples.

It's projected not to be a male arena, and the boys who rely on it aren't simply labelled as 'effeminate' not only by older men but also by peer group members. Boys are taught from an early age that expressing sadness and crying is not characteristic of a real man and boys are conditioned not to express themselves in terms of normal human emotions like fear and sadness, so the male mind must banish them with the armour born from kindness, sense of justice, and sensibility. There is a need for Boldness that radiates a feeling of alienation and loneliness. From there begins his quest for power and control to feel empowered. Competition for power leads to a vicious cycle of incompetence to build relationships and lose sight of their value.

Pantherides et al. (1995) showed in their study that most girls were given measurably less time than boy's free time. The modern women's movement helped identify and bring its focus on gender issues that affect women in different parts of the world. Violence against women is universal and manifests itself differently in different societies. Examples: dowry murder, genital mutilation, honour killings, etc. Women's studies do more than just make these "invisible" issues visible. It provided a robust and comprehensive alternative framework for analysing all "human" problems. From sexuality and gender relations to development, everything from a "woman's perspective". Roop Kanwar's Sati movement mobilizes feminists to raise voices against injustices made in the religious sense. The government responded and passed the Anti-Sati Act, which was repeated in the 1929 Act but had several shortcomings. The law blurred the distinction between compulsory and voluntary sati, defined sati as a crime against women, and forced others to participate in sati.

Domestic violence and patriarchy are sociological problems in Indian society from time immemorial, the laws of Manu fostered violence through a husband against his wife when she has been unfaithful. With the development of society, certain norms and practices that encouraged domestic violence, such as dowry, were punished with life imprisonment, but there are other forms of violence that make the life of one woman a hell. Most women become victims of violence by the age of 15. This is true when children grow up. Older people learn to resemble their fathers, and other male members, according to social learning theory.

The 21st century continues the unfinished agenda of the globalisation of democracy in a more vivid way. Given the continuing tendency of democracies to exclude or marginalise large segments of society, there is concern on many fronts about the achievement of representative democracy. This is especially true for women around the world. For democracy to be truly representative and inclusive, all citizens must have equal opportunities to participate in the democratic process. If these conditions are not met, the benefits of democracy for social and economic development are severely limited. They remain constrained by the institutional base and women still do not enjoy full and equal citizenship across the country.

Despite the progressive nature of the Constitution, traditional social structures that restricted women's participation in society were rapidly strengthened after India's independence. Excluded from the community decision-making process. Politics in particular has been promoted as a male domain, and in the last 60 years of democratic rule, women in India have been excluded from full participation in that democracy. The constitution guarantees women the right to vote, but women are largely excluded from political dialogue.

Moreover, traditionally, women have made uninformed voting decisions and have been influenced by the preferences of the male family members and voted along caste lines. However, this voting pattern changed after Indira Gandhi was assassinated in October 1984 and his son Rajiv Gandhi became prime minister. Against family and caste preferences, in December 1984, women across the country took effect to vote for Rajiv Gandhi's Member of Parliament. Underpinning this voting decision was a deep empathy for the history of the young Gandhi, India's youngest prime minister.

This was followed by a marked shift in women's perceptions of their role in politics. Today, young women are increasingly participating in politics as active politicians. They are engaging in political dialogue, being active in student politics, engaging in the media, and increasingly questioning the conditions and structures of traditional political frameworks. I voted more than that. In the 2009 general election, women made up her 54% of voters. Female voters also outnumbered male voters in the first half of 2013 national elections. In Tripura, which had record turnout in the 2013 elections, 93% of women voted against 90% of men.

The statistics are similar in Nagaland, where 91% of women voted, compared to 89% of men. In Meghalaya, women made up just over 50% of her total electorate. His last election in 2013, which took place in his four states of Madhya Pradesh, Rajasthan, Chhattisgarh and Delhi, saw a marked shift in male and female voter turnout. 72% of women exercised their right to vote, up from 45% of her 30 years ago. Male voter turnout was 74% for him, only slightly higher than females. Female voters outnumbered male voters in Rajasthan. Rajasthan is considered one of her most hit states in terms of gender ratio. Women's voting choices reflect this shift, with young women moving away from traditional voting patterns and making informed and independent choices about who they want to represent in politics.

The distribution of power in Indian democracy is based on a set of overarching traditional conditions that influence society's voting behaviour. Important determinants of the system are religion, caste, region and community. Choosing candidates on the basis of cultural equality obscures the motives behind democracy. However, these factors continue to have a significant impact on Indian voters. Real-time issues such as lack of development, corruption and women's issues have been pushed into the political background of India. But the country has recently witnessed a new wave. People are gradually waking up to a guilty conscience. Uprisings against corruption in the political space and calls for domestic women's safety are exciting phenomena.

However, the power of women voters is still underutilised and gender issues continue to be kept out of the political arena.

Women are grossly underrepresented in all major political parties, and the patriarchal nature of party structures marginalises and discriminates against women who choose to actively participate in politics against societal expectations.

The exclusion of women from political decision-making bodies has led to inadequate responses to women's issues and generally gender-neutral policymaking. Women's safety has been on the political agenda since the gang rape and murder of a 23-year-old woman in Delhi on December 16, 2012. But the government's approach is very patriarchal and patronising. Instead of emphasising women's right to live in a safe environment without fear of violence, governments have portrayed women as defenceless, vulnerable and in need of protection. This regressive approach focuses on female victims rather than male perpetrators, demonstrating the patriarchal and insensitive nature of the Indian Parliament to women's issues.

The exclusion of women from government institutions represents a growing imbalance between men and women across the country. The conservative and patriarchal mindset prevalent among elected officials and communities at large is a major reason for the continued opposition to women's political empowerment. Women's involvement in governance threatens the status quo in two ways. First, women's participation in politics makes women's voices more prominent and influential in governance processes. This will lead to more gender-sensitive policy and service delivery and a more gender-sensitive society.

Achieving gender equality inevitably goes hand in hand with a decline in the power imbalance of men and women in society. Therefore, this is not the desired result for many men. Second, most Indian leaders are male, and their status as leaders gives them power and prestige within their communities. threatening a position of power. In India's current political scenario, securing 33% of board seats for women means almost 33% of male leaders will lose their influence in shaping seats, jobs and destinies. Promoting women's political empowerment for male leaders is therefore often in direct conflict with women's personal and professional interests, explaining the lack of political will to address women's political marginalisation.

Full empowerment of women cannot be achieved unless women have the opportunity to contribute equally in all areas of society, including the political sphere. While women continue to be excluded from leadership positions, women's issues continue to be ignored. The Constitution gives women equal opportunities to participate in political debates, vote in elections, and hold leadership positions in local, state, and national governments. Women's full and equal participation in politics is also essential to achieving gender equality in our society. Increased representation of women will bring women's issues to the fore more frequently and will significantly change the way elected bodies are governed, especially their priorities.

Given the benefits of increasing women's political participation as voters, politicians, committed party members and elected representatives, it is important to take steps to enable equality in the political arena. is. One policy intervention that can speed up this process is the extension of reservations to state and federal politics. This will ensure women's participation in all political and decision-making bodies across the country. Women's groups and civil society are increasingly pressuring political parties to address gender imbalances in politics by increasing women's ticket sales and formulating and implementing quotas for women at the party level. Institutional interventions are therefore needed to overcome discrimination and marginalization of women in higher politics.

Women's political participation is a human right. It is also critical for overcoming widespread gender inequality and discrimination and achieving key development outcomes such as improved health and education. Women leaders have the ability to challenge and transcend the traditional and patriarchal social, cultural and political structures that hold India back from realising its potential as a global leader. Facilitating their participation in politics keeps them at the forefront of economic and social progress. Across India, male dominance in politics must be challenged. Women leaders hold the key to our future.

"*Money, muscle and misogyny have marred the political careers of women in this country.*"

Cielo

The provocation of the president of the West Bengal BJP sector at Mamata Banerjee is a testament to the crude nature of Indian politics, given the recent uproar caused by Dilip Ghosh against the backdrop of the 2021 general elections underway in West Bengal. Not only that, no matter how powerful a woman is, she will ultimately be judged by her body.

Dilip Ghosh on the background of the 2021 West Bengal election campaign says it's inappropriate for women in sarees to show their legs, Bermuda must wear her shorts if they want to show their legs. According to him, her bare skin offended the atmosphere of Bengali culture.The 'Bengali Asmita' - Bengali culture and its honour - is carried on the shoulders of Bengali 'Bhadra Hira'. Bengali Bhadra Hira is the epitome of endurance and politeness. But to Ghosh, Mamata Banerjee was not acting like Bhadramahira. Rather, it was 'Unsanskari' and not suitable for Bengali culture. This comment shows the dissatisfaction of the entire Indian political culture. Banerjee is known for being outspoken and is currently fighting hard against the BJP in the ongoing campaign in West Bengal. Ghosh's commentary points to the fact that capricious women in India are a threat to society and the only way to subdue them is to shame them. In short, women are meant to be "dominated".

Gauche's comments bring up the notion of "honour" for women. The body becomes a common property of society. Women's honour here is the "collective honour" of society. It subdues women. V Spike Peterson and Laura Parisi, in Human Rights Fifty Years on: A Reappraisal, edited by Tony Evans, use culture as an ideological tool for the oppression of women when used to justify the objectification of women. claims to be. In her "Social Hierarchies as Systems of Power", Peterson sees social hierarchies such as gender and race as interlocking systems of power.

Groups at the bottom of the social hierarchy face not only subordination but also the kind of comments politicians make about women who have naturalised ruling power. Men represent a direct or indirect form of female oppression that sits at the top of the social hierarchy and further reproduces negative stereotypes. His comments further imply that it is inappropriate for society to respect women who are immoral and do not know how to take care of their bodies. It also shows the patriarchal nature of Indian political culture. The problem isn't with political parties per se, but with the way society thinks it's okay to make such comments about women, and do so with moral authority without fear of repercussions.

And when such statements come from an influential figure, it not only renders women's safety laws useless, but it sends the wrong message to society by giving them moral authority to judge women. The impact of such statements by influential people permeates and shapes the mindset of ordinary people.

One such contemporary example is the "Love Jihad" law. The law often had civilians act as vigilantes and increased surveillance over women's bodies and their choices. The law targeted Muslim men under the pretext of luring and converting Hindu women. It also shows that the state and the private sector share the responsibility of protecting women and making decisions on their behalf, thereby depriving them of the power and ability to choose their partners, thereby causing serious harm to women. also turned out. This creates a vicious circle, creating an unfair society for girls, women and all other marginalised groups. The constitutionally guaranteed right of all individuals to equality and equal treatment will cease to function on its own. Because if men are judged by their talents and achievements, and women by their dress, they judge people unequally. Mamata Banerjee is the founder of the All India Trinamool Congress and the first female Prime Minister of West Bengal. She also became the first woman to serve twice as Minister of Railways.

Coal, human resource development, resource development, youth issues, sports, women and children development. in the Cabinet of the Government of India. Among her various development activities is the 'Kanyashree Project', a targeted and conditional cash transfer program to promote girls' education, also endorsed by the United Nations in 2017. Her 'Sabooj Sathi' program, which aims to provide free bikes to all students from grade 9 to her 12th grade, has proven particularly helpful in reducing school dropouts.

According to The World Summit on the Information Society (WSIS), Sabooj Sathi was voted as the best system in the e-government sector. Naturally, it doesn't matter what a woman wears. Because she should be valued for her work, not her body. But comments like Ghosh's make us understand why our laws are becoming more and more protectionist. The state has come to act as a "Big Brother" in pursuit of sisters. for women. This kind of protectionist policy makes women themselves responsible for their own safety when they fail to "protect" their wives.

An example of this is Madhya Pradesh's so-called women's security proposal. This requires all working women to register with the local police station and be charged for their safety. This type of politics is not only inherently regressive, it stems from the idea that women need to be protected. This policy gives room for "moral policing" where women's bodies and sexuality must be protected by the male state. Rather than ensuring that the streets are lit up, that women's helplines are working properly, that perpetrators of street harassment are held accountable, and that women feel comfortable reporting their problems, the proposed guidelines will ensure that women need It expresses the patriarchal mindset of the society. Monitored.

In politics, such comments are made simply because they understand the far-reaching effects of patriarchy on women, and thus become a deliberate ploy to divert the tide of politics. One such example comes from a recent comment on women by Uttarakhand Chief Minister Thiras Singh Rawat. He said that women wearing ripped jeans and showing their knees are uncultural and therefore fail to give children the proper value to be recognized. It not only shifts all the responsibility of teaching values to children at home onto women, but also shows how our political representatives perceive women and their bodies. supersedes her talents and merits. She is reduced to her own body. To her, a woman's body is immovable, and anyone can make it their own by making comments or suggestions. is determined by

It is dangerous for Indian political representatives to make such statements. Because their words shape the way Indian society thinks. It works in two ways. The first is that the words of politicians reflect the morals of society, and the second is that the statements of politicians firmly shape society's consciousness. Therefore, we must remain vigilant and challenge patriarchal thinking and the privilege of political representatives and society at large, creating just and just spaces for the marginalised

CHAPTER IV

Some people only hear what they want to hear.

'*Hasbunallahu wa ni-aamal wakeel*'

'*Om trayambakam yajaamahe sugandhim pushtivardhanam*

Urvaarukamiva   bandhanaan   mrityor   muksheeya maamritaat'.

'*Saachaa naam salaaheeai saachae tae tripat hoe.*'

'*Lord Jesus Christ, you are the name above every other name. Your name is like a fortified tower in which I can find safety and security. When I am troubled, I can find peace in your name.* '

What is the difference?

Is this what we call Religion?

Whether I am making a dua or chanting Maha Mritunjay Mantra; what is the difference anyway?

Religion has become the overcoat that all of us need to get through the harsh winters. It is the oar that we need to row the boat to get through the cold sea and reach the hospitable shore.

Religion is the identity that people behold.

It is a veil of social customs that seek to humanise humans.

Religion, put simply, is just 'sharing'. We follow religion when we share ideas, faith and meals with our fellow members of the community.

But, a question that comes to my head is then, why is religion just meant for humans ?

If it is just about sharing a meal, humans are not the only ones who share a meal. Neanderthals are documented to pool resources including for meals. Bonobos are believed to have shared food not just within their social groups but even outside the conventionally-organised group.

Researchers from the MPI-EVA observed natural food sharing behaviour of the chimpanzees of the Tai National Park, Ivory Coast, and found that chimpanzees are very selective in who they share desirable food items, like meat, honey or large fruits, with. They show that chimpanzees were more likely to share food with their friends, and that neither high dominance status nor harassment by beggars influenced their decision. This complement results from another study by the same team published last month that examined meat sharing after group hunting of monkeys. There they found that chimpanzees in possession of meat after successful hunts were likely to reward other hunters by sharing with them.

Why isn't religion applied to them in that case ?

Is it just 'sharing of meals' that defines a religious community ?

Is defining religion this easy ?

The complications of the matter have been penned down by Frans de Waal, a primatologist, who noted that if we ever start defining religion in a room full of people 'half the audience would have angrily stomped out of the room'.

But, ofcourse, shared experiences play a key role in defining religion as the 'unite humans into one single moral community'.

Religion is also a way of being. It is also a feeling that emerges within a human in examples of peace, serenity, loyalty, satisfaction etc.

Cielo

Émile Durkheim, on the other hand, argued in 'The Elementary Forms of Religious Life', that the heart of religion was not its belief system or even its moral code, but its ability to generate collective effervescence: intense, shared experiences that unify individuals into cooperative social groups.

Religion is a kind of social glue.

Cielo

Feelings of faith and loyalty to beliefs unite people, evident in followers of the Nazareth Baptist Church who climb the Nhlangakazi Holy Mountain to foster the feeling of unification. Evening namaz of Isha at Kaaba unite Muslims in feelings such as awe, loyalty, and love. Buddhist monks launch a sky lantern during the Yee Peng Festival in Chiang Mai. The ritual symbolises the release of kindness and goodwill.

History of religion is not about the evolution of an individual's religion but it is about 'our' evolution. Human religion emerges out of this increased capacity for sociality, to promote bonding.

But, feelings are often complex.

Feeling of awe is often a mixture of fear and happiness as evident in the practice in which Jewish men take part in the Tashlich ritual, during which sins are cast into the water to the fish.

Having discussed the complex terminology of religion, the chapter will focus on analysing the prospects of ancient religion's relevance with the modern religion.

The present study would include the possibility of the application of the concept laid out by Akbar; ' Sulh-i-kul' in the 21ˢᵗ century

Is there a possibility that Sulh-i-kul could have been the answer to all problems that the nation faces today ?

Would it be the right choice when it comes to a legitimate acceptable religion ?

Before analysing this proposal, I will mention what Sulh-i-kul as a concept is.

What is it ?

What is it about this concept that I found it suitable to mention it in the chapter ?

Is it really a magnum opus of its times that it might be a successful endeavour in the contemporary times ?

Muhammad Abdul Baki, in his history of Akbar's reign, states: "Akbar extended toleration to all religions and creed, and would recognize no difference between them, his object being to unite all men in a common bond of peace.

Sulh-i-kul as a concept, was introduced by the third Mughal ruler of India, Jalaluddin Muhammad Akbar (1556 - 1605). Akbar is said to have experienced religious ecstasy when he was barely fifteen. His mind delighted in listening to the philosophical discourses of sufis and saints.

In A.D. 1582, he, while referring to the discord among the diverse creeds, proclaimed his new order, Din-i-Ilahi, emphasising the necessity of bringing all religions into one in such fashion that they should be both 'one' and 'all' with the great advantage of not missing out what is good in any one religion while gaining whatever is better in another.

Sulh-i kul is an Arabic term literally meaning "peace with all," "universal peace," or "absolute peace," drawn from a Sufi mystic principle. It described a peaceful and harmonious relationship among different religions. In keeping with efforts to mesh the diverse populations of his realm, Akbar proposed unity and peace among all human beings – sulh-i kul. The concept implies not just tolerance, but also the sorts of balance, civility, respect, and compromise required to maintain harmony among a diverse population. The term was originally used during Akbar's reign and sometimes after him in the Mughal court and among some Sufi movements in India.

The reason that I took up this theme for a study was the deep connotations of the term and the positive possibilities of the term's application. Sulh-i kul was invented to describe universal peace, specifically with regard to interfaith tolerance and equal treatment for all, regardless of religious beliefs. Given continuing religious conflicts matched to the reality of cultural pluralism, it seems useful to resurrect this historic term as a modern tool. The concept also has potential for discussions of such concrete contexts as managing a multicultural workforce.

Sulh- i-kul was to become his method of judging what was legally right or wrong within his empire and was created because Akbar understood that he was trying to build political institutions for predominately non-Muslim society. Thus, in his empire, the beliefs and opinions of the orthodox mullahs were not to be the critical test for his rule because he wanted all of his subjects to be judged equally before the law.

Akbar established separation of state and religion and opened government positions to members of all religions. He abolished the jizya on non-Muslims and the forced conversion of prisoners of war to Islam. He converted the meetings of Muslim clerics into open discussions between Islam, Hindu, Parsi and Christian scholars and in 1579 issued an edict that made him the highest authority in religious matters.

In the civil courts Akbar abolished laws that discriminated against non-Muslims. He raised the Hindu court system to official status side by side with Muslim law and reformed the legislation with the aim to maximize common laws for Muslim and Hindu citizens.

To begin with, Akbar first freed himself from existing methods of kingship. He chose to adopt a style which maintained Muslim beliefs while uniting Muslim and Hindu systems of governance. This sort and synergetic approach had been adopted in other lands by his Mongol forefathers to great effect.

Having discussed the concept, it is also important to remember that the idea did not survive during that epoch and could not hold a firm ground.

Akbar, in my opinion, was the Enlightened Monarch just like we had Catherine of Russia, Joseph of Austria and Friedrich of Prussia, in the Eastern Europe. The only difference was that Akbar seems more enlightened than the latter.

An enlightened monarch, also known as a benevolent monarch, is a ruler with absolute power who embraces

Enlightenment ideals, such as the rights and liberties of individuals, and chooses to use their absolute power to better the lives of average citizens. This philosophy implied that the sovereign knew the interests of his or her subjects better than they themselves did. The monarch taking responsibility for the subjects precluded their political participation.

He seemed much more ahead of his epoch, evident in his approach towards religion and society. But his revolutionary ideal of Din-e-Ilahi could not survive the waters as it had no adherents except a handful of people who presumably converted to the new religion to try and win favours from the emperor. Din-i-Illahi is believed to have become extinct some time after the death of Akbar's son Jahangir. Sulh-e-kul, in its definition, is the elimination of friction and the creation of absolute harmony between man and man, man and God, as well as man and nature. It conceptualised a similar harmony on earth that exists in the cosmic order. It was meant to facilitate the essential mystical framework within which the peaceful co-existence of diverse ethnic and religious entities or communities could be made possible.

Now, I would move on to the prospects of application of Sulh-I-Kul and Din-I-Ilahi in the 21st century.

Is it possible that it would survive ?

Can it be a good solution given the highly surcharged intolerant environment that we are a part of ?

Religion generates critiques of inequality and capitalism while others invoke it to celebrate the free market and individual wealth. And, religious concerns shape views on policy issues as diverse as same-sex marriage, climate change, and government-sponsored healthcare. From challenges to evolution to debates on stem-cell research, religions juxtapose faith and modern science. Religions likewise factor prominently in various military conflicts around the globe and in the long-running debates over the proper relationship between religion and the state. All traditions - whether religious or secular - experience a struggle over authority, and this struggle seems to intensify with globalisation, as it has brought people around the world in closer contact with each other. In spite of the debate about secularisation or de-secularization, the existential-bodily need for religion is basically the same as always. What has been changed are the horizons within which religions are interpreted and the relationships within which religions are integrated.

'Status of Religion 'is a hotly debated topic that often divides opinion. Everywhere you look Religions & Religious Controversies are shaping our world. Because of the passions I inspire, religion is a topic that seems inherently given to controversy. Religion faces extraordinary challenges, (including those from Science), in the 21st Century. In history Religion will continue to be the most important world-wide shaping phenomena of the 21st Century. Religion now focuses on how religion, both as belief

systems and socio-cultural systems are interwoven in today's challenges'.

Cielo
Andre' Malraux

India is to remain Pluralistic as envisioned by Dr. B.R. Ambedkar. However, Religious polarisation is a pain. But when 'Faith' turns into Fanaticism, Religious Unity can look like Carnival and religious liberty can look like Funeral.

Man has faith in the supernatural power, which controls the most sacred future of the entire life and the universe or nature. In order to establish the closest personal or social psychic and mental relationship and unfolding of the methods and mode of conduct and behaviour can be defined as Religion.

God is one but wars in the name of Religion are being waged everywhere. Contractors are eager to convert themselves into God.

India's Culture teaches Politeness and Civility to the world. But in the same culture Babri Masjid is demolished and thousands of people die. Religion has divided us into Saffron, Green and White colours.

In the 21ˢᵗ Century, the winds blowing in the name of religion demonstrate that Today's Religion has acquired destructive and Anti Human forms.

The rituals and practices are crystallised over thousands of years and the 21ˢᵗ Century has no option but to accept the Reality. The cow slaughter ban law, evolving concept of Muslim terrorism, the connotations of the term 'love jihad', opening of Sabarimala temple, Citizenship Amendment Act, Ram temple in Ayodhya-Babri Majjid conflict and so many local and regional issues lead to conflicts and they cannot be stopped.

Internationally, less than 20% of the population is 'Unaffiliated' while the rest of the population follows the Religious divide. Therefore, some people are pursuing their own interests by sticking to their religion and riots are being fomented in the name of religion, social conflicts are being brought about. For politicians, religion is like a 'paris' (Philosopher's Stone which attracts Gold) of power. It is as if some politicians have been fully accustomed to Religious Mathematics to manipulate Elections. Subject of religion is slow poison, sowing seeds of hatred in the minds of the people is their business. The temples, places of worship of particular religions are given more importance than the hospitals, surgeries and treatments.

Whose health will be improved by building these temples?

The former communist bloc countries went from being officially atheist to experiencing a strong religious revival. It's impossible to mention Poland without mentioning the cultural importance of Catholicism there. Religion is also a common theme in any discussion of Russia, where the Orthodox Church has stepped in to provide a sense of Russian identity and become, for better or worse, given its alliance with the Putin regime; a key force shaping the country's culture.

The post-Enlightenment secular worldview tends to treat religion as nothing more than a private hobby. It rejects out of hand the notion that people's spiritual beliefs matter in a broader context. When evolution tells us we're just genes trying to spread, when economists tell us all we do is maximise our self-interest, when psychologists tell us we just want to fulfil our desires, we become convinced that humans act on nothing but narrow material desires. As a matter of fact, human beings are spiritual beings first, with a natural orientation toward transcendent realities. Religion has been the most intense worldview-shaping phenomenon in history, and it will continue to be the most important worldview-shaping phenomenon of the 21st century.

It is, in my opinion, way too naive of us to even imagine that Sulh-i-kul could hold ground in India.

If it would have been a part of our daily life today, our life would have been chaotic. Isn't it?

I came to this conclusion as we live in a country wherein even religion in itself is misunderstood. The terms that formed the basis of the religion are used for personal gains and petty wins in politics. Religion has been turned into the shoulder that is used by the government to shoot at the sanity of the citizens.

As we start to examine the above statement, I would like to state some examples from all religions about how the terms in themselves are being misunderstood.

CHAPTER V

I Question, But who believes the Answer?

"True joy and happiness lie in the simple enjoyment of what is good and not in the kind of false pride that enjoys happiness because others are excluded from it. Anyone who thinks that he is happy because his situation is better than other people's or because he is happier and more fortunate than they, knows nothing of true happiness and joy, and the pleasure he derives from his attitude is either plain silly or spiteful and malicious. For example, a person's true joy and felicity lie solely in his wisdom and knowledge of truth, not in being wiser than others or in others' being without knowledge of truth, since this does not increase his own wisdom which is his true felicity. Anyone therefore who takes pleasure in that way is enjoying another's misfortune, and to that extent is envious and malign, and does not know true wisdom or the peace of the true life."

–Benedict de Spinoza, Theological-Political Treatise, p.43

Cielo

If I call myself a Hindu, I face an inevitable dichotomy as to whether being a Hindu would refer to my nationality or religion ?

It is a secular nation, India. Therefore, it is improper to refer to her as a Hindu nation. Interesting enough, though not officially, India is still referred to as Hindustan, the land of the Hindus. She is also known as Hind—Jai Hind, Victory to Hind, has long been the clarion call to instil a sense of national identity and nationalism. The Hind people would obviously be referred to as Hindi, just as the Bengal's people are referred to as Bengali.

As alternative names for India, we have Bharata or Bharatavarsha, which we can set aside for the time being, as well as India, Hindustan, and Hind. India and Hindu are related etymologically, which means that they both originated from the same source. In this case, that source is Sindhu, the name of the river that runs through the northwest of India and Pakistan. The expression Hapta Hendu, which refers to the Sapta Sindhu, Seven Sindhu, land as one of the sixteen best, vahistem, places created by the prophet Ahura Mazda, can be found in the later Avestan Zoroastrian text of Vendidad, dated no later than the 8th century BC. This may be the earliest recorded use of the term Hindu.

Unquestionably, the phrase "country of the Sapta Sindhu" refers to the modern-day Punjab, and the "seven sindhus" are the Sindhu or Indus, its five tributaries, and the legendary Saraswati River.

It is unknown exactly how or when the Sapta Sindhu or Hapta Hindu religion came to be referred to as the Hindu land. The Persians eventually expanded the region that was originally known as the "land of the Hindus" to include the entire Indian subcontinent, or at least all of northern India, which has intermittently been united under one empire over the past two thousand years under different emperors beginning with Ashoka and ending with the Mughals.

It is not unusual to refer to a group of people or their home country by the name of a river.

Rha, an old Greek name for the Volga, is related to the Latin word ros, which means moisture, and the Indo-Iranian words rasa or raha. The Rig Veda contains a legendary river named Rasa. The Slavic terms vlaga and vologa, which signify moistness and humidity, are the source of the name Volga. Even today, a tiny number of individuals in the Volga basin who speak Mordvinic languages refer to the Volga as Rav, which is undoubtedly related to the word rasa. Rasa, the old name for the Volga, may still be included in the name Russia.

It may be noteworthy to note that the native population was not homogeneous even at the time of the Rig Veda, not later than 1500 BC, or roughly seven centuries before the name Hindu was first used to describe the inhabitants of the Indus valley. The present-day Punjab may have been populated mostly by Indo-Aryans who spoke Sanskrit during the early Rig Vedic period, circa 1700 BC, according to Professor Michael Witzel, a renowned historian at Harvard University. Para-Munda, Meluhan, and proto-Dravidian may have been the languages of the upper Indus valley and the southern Indus, respectively. All of these people were diverse ethnically. The next three millennia saw a rise in diversity.

Still, it was common to refer to them all as Hindus together with the other inhabitants of the entire subcontinent.

The physical isolation of the Indian subcontinent from Central Asia may have contributed to the decision to refer to a heterogeneous set of people who speak different languages and adhere to distinct rituals and practises under a single term. As a result, the term "Hindu" has always been used to describe a heterogeneous set of people who may have only had one thing in common: the seclusion of their native region.

The fact that even the Muslim emperor Aurangzeb was completely comfortable with the term Hindustan, by which the Indian subcontinent, especially the north Indian empires, would be mostly designated, shows that the term Hindu was never used to denote a particular religion or its adherents. The inhabitants of the Indian subcontinent have traditionally been identified as Hindu. Before the Indian subcontinent was subsequently united as a single entity during the British era, the inhabitants of the whole region were always referred to as Hindu and its cognates by the world at large.

What was the name of the religion practised by the great majority of Indians if Hindu was never the name of any religion?

Let's look at what the Indian word for religion has been in order to comprehend it. The closest Indian term to what is understood by religion, dharma, is etymologically unrelated to the word "religion." According to the Sanskrit dictionary by Monier Williams, the closest definition to "religion" is possibly "customary observance or regulated action." There has never been a singular dharma associated with the religion that is currently referred to be Hindu.

It would be nonsensical to include all of the diverse schools of religion or "ordered behaviour," which developed directly or indirectly from the Vedas, under one umbrella of religion. This includes Buddhism, Jainism, and Sikhism. And for just that reason, none of these schools ever received a single label.

Amartya Sen refers to Charvaka as "the crown jewel of the atheistic school" in his book The Argumentative Indian, where "in addition to the denial of God, there is also a rejection of the soul, and a statement of the material foundation of the intellect." This specific religious school, which falls under the umbrella of what is now known as Hinduism, is possibly more foreign to, say, the Vaishnava school, than Islam or Christianity is.

Tena tyaktena bhunjita, which translates as "you should take just that which is laid aside for you," is a well-known Ishopanishad maxim. It is the fundamental idea behind the phrase "enjoyment in renunciation," which is taught in most Indian religious institutions. The exact contrary, "bairagyo sadhone mukti, she amar noi," or "deliverance is not for me in renunciation," as said by Rabindranath Tagore is also a recognised school of thought. The Nirakarvadi school, which worships the Supreme God as a shapeless being, much like Islam, is wholly opposed to the Sakarvadi, who revere idols.

A Vaishnavite and a Shaivite would be hostile to one another, much as a Muslim and a Jew may be. Worship of Manasa, the snake goddess of West Bengal, is unquestionably an indigenous paganism. It is opposed to worship of Shiva in the same way as, for example, an Indian would be opposed to a Pakistani.

These are only a few instances of the orthogonally distinct features of the numerous schools of Indian religion that have all been sought to be grouped together under the umbrella term of Hinduism. That is irrational, because neither in the distant nor recent past has that ever been the case.

This also explains why all of these conflicting schools of religion, which coexisted peacefully for millennia, were never given a single name. However, it has long been fashionable to refer to everyone who practises competing "religions" as Hindu. This simply supports the idea that the term "Hindu" was never used in a collective sense. Instead, it has traditionally served as the commonality across India's many ethnic groups.

As can be seen, the word "Hindu" has Persian roots, and as would be expected, for a very long period it was never used in any Indian texts. The heterogeneous people of India lacked an indigenous label until recently, while outsiders traditionally perceived them as Hindus.

When was the phrase first used in an Indian text? There isn't a workable alternative to this. The word "Hindu" is said to appear in Gaudiya Vaishnava texts, which were written in Bengali between the 16th and 18th centuries, according to an interesting article titled "The Word "Hindu" in Gaudiya Vaishnava Texts," which was published in the 3rd edition of the 93rd volume of the Journal of the American Oriental Society in 1973. Only forty eight times do we find the term Hindu in the eighty thousand Bengali couplets we are considering.

It's vital to remember that Bengal was already under Muslim dominion. For the first time, outsiders were in charge of the indigenous population. It follows that the Muslim population, particularly the ruling elite, is frequently referred to as yavana, meaning aliens, and mlechcha, meaning hated individuals. Rarely is the collective word "Musalman " employed. The ethnic words Pathans and Turks are occasionally translated into Bengali to allude to the Muslim rulers. And the local population, as opposed to outsiders, is virtually generally referred to be Hindu.

It cannot be claimed that the Vaishnavites, whose religious books are under study, are the only ones to whom the word "Hindu" applies. It's most likely that the word refers to all inhabitants, not just Vaishnavites. However, it's unclear if the name "Hindu" also refers to the tribal people and converted Muslims. But it's obvious that the phrase was only used to forge a patriotic identity of the locals against the outsiders. It's interesting to note that in the past, the Greeks were also called yavanas. Therefore, the word "Hindu" also refers to a cohesive national identity among a diverse group of people with varied religious beliefs and ethnic backgrounds.

It's significant to notice that these books use the Bengali terms "Hindur dharma," which refers to Hindu religion, or "Hindur achar," which refers to Hindu rituals. Do you ever refer to Islam as "Muslim's Religion" or Christianity as "Christian's Religion"? However, you could instead use the terms "Religion of the Romans" or "Religion of the Turks."

Another interesting finding from these writings is that the Muslim or foreign ruling class members frequently refer to the indigenous people as Hindus in their discourse. The phrase is only sometimes used by indigenous in their speech.

This suggests that the phrase employed to describe the indigenous' uniting patriotic identity was more often used by outsiders and that the term itself was not widely accepted by the natives as a means of self-identification.

According to David N. Lorenzen's essay "Who Invented Hinduism," the Maithili poet Vidyapati used the term "Hindu" in his historical tale Kirtilata from the early fifteenth century.

Turkish and Hindu residents coexist nearby.

Each makes fun of the faith of the other.

It should be emphasised that Muslims are referred to as Turks in this instance based more on their ethnicity than their religion.

Therefore, Lorenzen's question on the origin of Hinduism remains unanswered. He noted in his study that W. C. Smith may have used the term "Hinduism" in the sense of a religion for the first time in 1829. In addition, he notes that Ram Mohan Roy's English publications from 1816 and 1817 contain references to hinduism. The usage of the phrase, referring to a religion, was probably already popular by the nineteenth century, even though this precedes W. C. Smith's mention of hinduism.

It's probable that the colonial British intentionally or inadvertently massively grouped the great majority of non-Christian and non-Muslim locals under the banner of the Hindus, turning an ethnically and geographically uniting national identity of the Indians into a communal one.

One may question why this should be a problem right now. Whatever the cause, secularists may argue that it is pointless to "polarise" the public after the name "Hindu" has come to be identified with a certain group of people. Polarisation or politicisation are not the issues. It's about attempting to forcibly build a new identity after completely rejecting one that dates back more than two millennia.

The foundations of cultures, countries, and civilizations are built on long-lasting identities. Even if the majority of Roman culture and history is linked to a single religion, calling it "Roman" without the word would be ludicrous. Contrarily, the Hindu civilisation or culture has never been one that is uniform. Instead, as has been previously demonstrated, there has always been a series of opposing civilizations that have coexisted peacefully for thousands of years. In contrast, the contemporary conception of the Indian country and culture does not enjoy the same illustrious history of secularism or harmonious cohabitation.

India, Hindi, and Hindu are all related terms, therefore it appears hypocritical that the term Hindustan is still in use while terms like India and Hindi are acceptable yet Hindu is not. One may contend that etymology by itself scarcely covers the whole variety of implications a word may have at a particular moment in a specific sociocultural environment.

Even if everything is grammatically sound, the terms "Hindustan" or "Hindu" carry with them emotional meanings that originate from the lived histories of those structures and might range from pride to paranoia, fairness to terror. Although "Hindu" as a religious designation is virtually useless, it is nonetheless a very potent indicator of identity. The phrase becomes a symbol for this actual line of separation between identities.

Following this, I now wish to delve deep into the term 'Hindutva' itself. The controversy started afresh after the release of a book "Sunrise over Ayodhya: Nationhood in our Times" authored by a very senior Congress leader, Salman Kurshid. It is reported in the media that a lawyer has filed a complaint with the Delhi police against the author for his remarks that, "Sanatan Dharma and classical Hinduism known to sages and saints were being pushed aside by a robust version of Hindutva, by all standards a political version similar to the Boko Haram which is a terrorist organisation based in Northern Nigeria, which is also active in Northern Cameroon. The similarity suggested has political implications.

Critics receive it as a serious allegation against their religion, but in Indian politics currently going on will not bring about a united Hindu reaction. It can only be used to polarise voters in Uttar Pradesh, where State Assembly elections are shortly due. The author distinguishes Hindutva from Hinduism.

"India is a Hindu nation, Hindutva its identity", said RSS chief, Mohan Bhagat, in 2014 while inaugurating the Golden Jubilee celebrations of the Vishwa Hindu Parishad.

He explained that the "cultural identity of all Indians was Hindutva and the present inhabitants of the country were descendants of this great culture". His point rests on the analogy that if the inhabitants of England are English, Germany are Germans, and the USA are Americans, then all inhabitants of Hindustan are to be known as Hindus. But, In the Constitution, our country is called India, that is, Bharat. Its inhabitants are known all over the world as Indians irrespective of their religion. What happens to the followers of the other faiths in that case ?

On 11 December 1995, a three-judge bench of the Supreme Court delivered a landmark judgement in a case challenging the validity of the election of some Shiv Sena-BJP candidates for Maharashtra Legislative Assembly for appealing to voters in the name of religion by using Hindutva. The Court held that the term "Hindutva" adopted as a poll plank could not be construed narrowly to mean an appeal to religion unrelated to the culture and ethos of the people of India. The judgement stated that the term ordinarily meant to denote a way of life and state of mind should not be understood as Hindu fundamentalism.

Hindutva is a combination of two words, 'Hindu' and the Sanskrit word tattva ('thatness' or 'essence'). Based on this, Hindutva is popularly translated as 'Hindu-ness' and a good many Hindus simply think of Hindutva as the idea and practice of living a life according to Hindu teachings or even just a descriptor of being Hindu. Others see it as an imminent global threat to freedom, equality, and democracy.

How can one word evoke entirely opposite concepts depending on who's using it?

The Supreme Court of India defines the term thusly: "Hindutva is understood as a way of life of state of mind and is not to be equated with or understood as religious Hindu fundamentalism...it is a fallacy and error of law to proceed on the assumption...that the use of words Hindutva or Hinduism per se depicts an attitude hostile to all persons practising any religion other than the Hindu religion."

Going back to the oft-described father of Hindutva, VD Savarkar wrote that Hindutva is more expensive than the religious aspects of Hinduism, encompassing the cultural, linguistic, political, and social aspect of the Hindu people — which he thought of as those people living within the historical boundaries of India, not strictly those who we'd describe as Hindus today. He also specifically said, writing prior to India gaining its independence from Britain, that "All citizens [of an independent India] should have equal rights and obligations irrespective of caste or creed, race or religion... The fundamental rights of liberty of speech, liberty of conscience, of worship, of association, etc., will be enjoyed by all citizens alike."

On the other end of the spectrum are those individuals and organisations that clearly see Hindutva as an irredeemably negative concept. They, like the organisers and allies of the Dismantling Global Hindutva (DGH) conference, see Hindutva and its supporters as insidiously dangerous. Savarkar chose the term 'Hindutva' to describe the 'quality of being a Hindu' in ethnic, cultural and political terms. He argued that a Hindu is one who considers India to be his motherland (mathrubhumi), the land of his ancestors (pitribhumi), and his holy land (punya bhumi). India is the land of the Hindus since their ethnicity is Indian and since the Hindu faith originated in India. (Other faiths that were born in India, like Sikhism, Buddhism and Jainism also qualified, in Savarkar's terms, as variants of Hinduism since they fulfilled the same three criteria; but Islam and Christianity, born outside India, did not). Thus a Hindu is someone born of Hindu parents, who regards India—'this land of Bharatvarsha, from the Indus to the Seas'—as his motherland as well as his holy land, 'that is the cradle-land of his religion.'

In 1939, Savarkar wrote the foreword to a book by the Nazi sympathiser and European-born Hindu revivalist who called herself Savitri Devi. Savitri Devi (1905–1982), born Maximiani Portas of mixed Greek, French and English parentage, was a remarkable figure who, among other idiosyncratic beliefs, considered Adolf Hitler an avatar of Vishnu. Her book, prophetically titled 'A Warning to the Hindus', is a passionate polemic about the need for Hindu reassertion. Savitri Devi asserted that 'Hinduism is the national religion of India, and there is no real India besides Hindu India'. Savarkar joined the author in arguing that 'In all walks of life, for a long time, the Hindus have been fed on inertia-producing thoughts which disabled them to act energetically for any purpose in life, other than "moksha," that is to say escape from this world where to? God knows. And this is one of the causes of the continuous enslavement of our Hindu Rashtra for centuries altogether'. Not for Savarkar the abstruse metaphysics of Advaita; what he and Savitri Devi were interested in was political power, here and now. For Savitri Devi, political power, defined as 'the power of law with organised military force' is 'everything in the world... We would like the Hindus to remember this, and to strive to acquire political power at any cost. Social reforms are necessary, not because they will bring more "humanity" among the Hindus, as many think, but because they will bring unity, that is to say power.'

Is it what Hindutva is ?

Well, it has been used in this respect for political gains but the debate carries on about whether the word has been interpreted correctly or not.

One question that arises here is then are the followers of other faiths not Indians ? It might be an utter disregard to the multiethnicity and secularism quotient mentioned proudly in our constitution in that case.

The DGH organisers quote that "Hindutva is a modern political ideology that advocates for Hindu supremacy and seeks to transform India, constitutionally a secular state, into an ethno-religious nation known as the Hindu Rashtra (Hindu nation)."

Is it a gap between lofty rhetoric and a purportedly grotesque reality that has caused such widely divergent views on the same word? Or is some other factor or factors at play such as politics in India, plain anti-Hindu bigotry, or the broadly human failing to judge an entire group of people by the actions of the worst amongst them and not the best?

Nowadays, words are easy to weaponize, people are easy to label, and misinformation is easy to spread. We consume information and form opinions from 30-second clips or 280 characters with little regard for context and perspective.

It is quite easy to accept what others say, but is it justified? Lakhs of Indians still turn a blind eye to the terms that are often misconstrued.

Nationalism is deeply embedded in gendered constructs. From lady liberty to Bharat Mata (Mother India), the idea of the nation as feminine, or even divine, and in need of external protection has been utilised throughout the world.

The need to protect the innocent feminine from a brute external threat serves as a mobilising force for many men and women supporters alike. Throughout the world, religious nationalist movements effectively implement exclusionary policies that frequently target minority religious groups. This protection is often done to protect some real or imagined, often feminised, version of the nation. In India, Christians and Muslims have been especially vulnerable.

CHAPTER VI

The Stone that is manipulated to kill all birds

Islam, meaning peace and submission to God, is a religion of ethics, obedience and harmony, and is based on a faithful belief system. Conversely, in various parts of the world, Islam is broadly represented as a religion of intolerance and killing. Muslims believe that God's messenger, Prophet Mohamed, was sent to the world as a 'mercy to mankind'. Prophet Mohamed is introduced in the Quran in these words: [And We have not sent you forth but as a mercy to mankind.] (Al-Anbiyaa':107)

Cielo
This shows that the Prophet's distinctive quality is being a blessing incarnate in word and deed, not to prompt killing and suffering.

Meanwhile, it is vital to delve into a common confusion and misinterpretation that slowly, but surely adds to the negative portrayal of Islam, the word 'Jihad'.

Contrary to the popular belief, Jihad is not a synonym for combat.

In Arabic language, the word 'Jihad' basically means to strive and exert your utmost effort for any given objective. Additionally, in Islam, Jihad can be classified into several realms; Jihad by the heart, tongue, hand and finally, by the sword.

Unfortunately, because of its widespread misconception and abuse by extreme Islamic groups for their own gain, the latter form of jihad is typically the one that receives the greatest attention and publicity.

It should be noted that in Islam, jihad that is combative refers to "the declaration of war against belligerent and aggressive non-Muslim powers or against fellow Muslim transgressors." However, jihad by the sword is not a decision that should be made carelessly in accordance with the tenets of Islamic law. "The interests of the people must be the driving force behind the actions of the leader, and in some circumstances, the interests of the collective take precedence over the interests of the individual."

As a well-known example, Prophet Mohamed only used the sword in Jihad when unbelievers declared war on him and his message and started a fight; there was no other option than to fight back. But for many years prior to that, he had solely used invitations that were made in a peaceful manner and the three other types of Jihad to accomplish his goal.

Combative jihad should be restricted in certain circumstances, such as when a military invasion of a sovereign state is taking place, when self-defense is necessary, and when retaliating against aggression.

Jihad does not declare war on other faiths. It is important to note that Jews and Christians are particularly mentioned in the Holy Quran as "people of the book" who need to be protected and revered. However, Islamic organisations like ISIS and Al-Qaeda have purposefully promoted this falsehood by brainwashing their supporters into joining them in order to further their own great cause of jihad.

These organisations profess religiosity, but their deeds simply demonstrate infidelity. For instance, it is well known that alcohol and drug use are forbidden in Islam.

"O you who have believed, certainly, drinking, gambling, [sacrifice on] stone altars [to gods other than Allah], and divining arrows are but filth from the work of Satan; shun it that you may prosper." (5:90)

However, ISIS is the primary drug cartel in the Middle East, according to the Russian Federal Drug Control Service. The Russian Federal Drug Control Service reported that "according to our estimations, IS makes up to $US 1 billion annually on Afghan heroin transported through its control."

Love Jihad. Since last summer, these two words have captivated the attention of Indians and have gotten extensive publicity in the regional media. In this so-called "War on Love," Indian Muslims are accused of attempting to marry off innocent Hindu females in order to convert them to Islam.

In August 2014, a Hindu girl vanished from her home in the village of Uttar Pradesh in northern India. She reappeared a week later and claimed to have been kidnapped, raped, and forced into becoming a Muslim by numerous Muslim males from her community. A national response was prompted by the occurrence.

Hindu fundamentalist organisations, who have become more vocal and powerful since the BJP took office, have given the "Love Jihad" myth a new lease on life.

Against the backdrop of emerging urban modernities, which offers women exposure to education, romantic choices and inter-religious marriages, employment in urban labour economies, and opportunities to experiment with religious ideologies and sexualities, tit is quite clear how the discourse of 'Love Jihad' was modified to act as a regulatory mechanism to control the choice and mobility of young urban women. 'Love Jihad' has been conceptualised in multiple nationalist sites, in order to shed light on the ways in which right-wing organisations attempted to realign the urban public sphere in accordance with a gendered Hindu civil order.

India is infamous for marital endogamy, especially caste endogamy, which maintains social control in an otherwise pluralistic society. Even during Nehruvian secularism, interfaith marriages, though allowed by the law, were not commonplace. Much of this had to do with society and parental emphasis on marrying not just within the same religion, but the same caste (jaati). The law of that generation also reflects this social control over marriage. The Special Marriage Act, 1955, allows individuals of different faiths to marry, but only after a month's notice period. The couple's personal details, address, intentions, etc., are widely publicised. It is almost as if the law was written by parents who needed some time to intervene and discipline their errant children.

Is that all to it ?

Let me put forward an example in this case to bring the complexities to light.

In June 2020, authorities in the district of Muzaffarnagar in north India's Uttar Pradesh state arrested a 22-year-old Muslim man on charges of fraud, sexual assault and forced religious conversion.

Officials claimed the complainant was Amandeep Kaur, a 24-year-old Sikh woman from the man's neighbourhood.

Constituting nearly 1.7 percent of its population, India is home to the largest number of Sikhs in the world. Despite repeated attempts by Hindu supremacist groups to club the community under a wider Hindu umbrella, the Sikhs maintain they are an independent religion.

"It was a case of love; they turned it into something called 'love jihad'," Kaur told Al Jazeera as she locked the doors of the small house she shared with her parents.

Love Jihad is a term used by the Hindu political and religious right to describe an alleged phenomenon where Muslim men lure Hindu women into marrying them and converting to Islam. Hindu groups claim, without evidence, it is a conspiracy of an organised racket.

Kaur's connection with Usman Qureshi became a public spectacle a year ago, and now she is afraid of unidentified people, including the media and anyone wanting to "help." But she stresses that Qureshi was her voluntary partner for more than two years, thus she is not a victim.

The couple's difficulties started in October 2020 when the Uttar Pradesh high court declared religious conversions made primarily for matrimonial reasons to be "unacceptable."

Days later, the saffron-robed chief minister of the state's BJP, Yogi Adityanath, who is notorious for his anti-Muslim policies and hate speech, issued an odd ultimatum.

Speaking to a gathering in Jaunpur district before by-elections for the state legislature, Adityanath vowed to defend the "honour and dignity of women," particularly from the phenomena of "love jihad... at any cost."

"I warn those who conceal their identity and play with our sisters' respect: if you don't mend your ways, your 'Ram Naam Satya' [a Hindu funeral chant] journey shall begin," he said.

Adityanath's administration passed the Prohibition of Unlawful Conversion of Religion Ordinance a month after his speech.

The legislation, which became a law in February 2021, made it illegal to convert to a different religion "by marriage, lying, coercion, or seduction." If found guilty, the offender could spend up to 10 years in prison.

Kaur's father was asked to go to the neighbourhood police station in June 2021. The 63-year-old retired sugar mill worker obeyed without understanding why.

"I discovered my father had been in the police station for more than two hours when I got home from work. I was aware that something was wrong. But I didn't realise this wasn't at all about him until I arrived there myself. It concerned me," Kaur said.

Concerned about the gathering, Kaur pulled out her phone to call her older brother who lives in New Delhi, the nation's capital. However, one of the men took her phone away before she could dial. Both sympathy and rescue-related feelings were repeated in the cacophony of voices. The men claimed they wanted to exact revenge for her former Muslim lover forcing her to change her name from Amandeep Kaur to "Jannat Qureshi.

A member of the Rashtriya Swayamsevak Sangh (RSS) in New Delhi who asked to remain anonymous responded to a question about Hindu right-wing groups purportedly targeting Muslim men in "love jihad" cases by saying, "I am not aware of any surveillance or involvement of Hindu organisations in such anti-conversion cases."

The BJP and the majority of other Hindu supremacist organisations in India are ideologically influenced by the RSS, which was founded in 1925 in the style of European Nazism. Prime Minister Narendra Modi is one of the organisation's millions of lifetime members. Kaur later discovered that a phoney Facebook account had been made with a picture of her and Qureshi and her new Muslim name.

"I was confused when a friend forwarded me the Facebook profile. Usman and I took the display photo together when we were dating, and he frequently referred to me as "Jannat" (heaven in Urdu). But neither of us ever wed, and there was no Jannat Qureshi either," she continued.

The Bajrang Dal men persisted in pressuring Kaur to accuse Qureshi. She rejected several times, claiming there was no case to be filed. She only wanted to call her mother and bring her elderly father home. However, the discussion quickly became combative, and the men's worries had morphed into threats. The men abused her and threatened to prevent her and her father from returning home until she made a report.

She agreed to write and sign whatever was necessary to leave because she was afraid of what they would do and because she could see how her father was doing.

She remarked, "I could see everything, but tears in my father's eyes.

A police complaint against Qureshi – with whom she had separated and who was now married to a Muslim woman – was her sole saviour in that situation.

The bogey of 'love jihad' is divisive, built on fake news, and designed to foster hatred and suspicion between religious communities.

Qureshi was detained a few days later. Three months later, the police submitted a charge sheet accusing him of rape, betrayal of trust, cheating, and forgery. Three of the five offences did not allow for bail.

Additionally, he was subject to two provisions of the Prohibition of Unlawful Conversion of Religion Act. Nadeem, Qureshi's older brother, is the subject of a separate criminal investigation. 'My life was altered the following morning. Everyone spoke to me differently, from my neighbours to my coworkers', said Kaur, an arts graduate who worked as an adviser for an insurance company.

She was forced to stay at home due to the fallout from a recent "love jihad" case in the communally charged town of Muzaffarnagar. It was suggested that she take a sabbatical from her job.

Kaur sought legal advice from many attorneys over the course of the following six months and visited the district court practically biweekly. She was compelled to rely completely on her resources and raced from pillar to post to establish the falsity of the accusations made against Qureshi and his brother.

"Women like Amandeep Kaur are victims of the state and patriarchal and communal standards that it upholds. According to journalist Pamela Philipose, "They are segregated and forced to fight a war to be heard under the guise of protection.

"My consent, agency and basic rights were violated. I do not think I can overcome the trauma and harassment I was subjected to, and I cannot imagine how many other women like me are out there. Our private lives were made political tools" - Kaur

Since the BJP came to power with a clear majority in parliament in August 2019, it has stripped the special provisions in the constitution that had granted a substantial degree of autonomy to Jammu and Kashmir – now a Union Territory, an arrangement in India's federal dispensation under the direct rule of the national government.

In 2019, the Indian government also passed the Citizenship Amendment Act, which eases the pathway to citizenship for a range of religious groups from India's neighbouring countries but excludes Muslims.

Now, in its latest move, India's most populous state, Uttar Pradesh, where about a fifth population consists of muslims and the state government is led by the BJP, has taken to policing the private lives of its citizens. In November, the state passed the first "love jihad" law in the country.

Known as the Prohibition of Unlawful Religious Conversion Ordinance, it requires couples from different religious communities to provide two months' notice to a district magistrate before getting married. A district magistrate is an official belonging to India's administrative services – a vestige of British colonial rule – who is in charge of the district, the basic unit of administration, and has legal as well as significant executive powers.

Under the terms of the ordinance, the presiding judicial official would have the discretion to decide whether the conversion was through compulsion; the offending person could then be denied bail and sentenced to 10 years in prison. The irony of this issue is that few individuals routinely choose to marry outside their religious affiliation.

Notionally, this law applies with equal force to all interfaith marriages. However, for all practical purposes this would affect Muslims, as Islamic personal law requires a non-Muslim to convert to sanctify the marriage. So far, enforcement has targeted only Hindu-Muslim marriages. Since its passage last year, as many as 30 Muslim men arrested in Uttar Pradesh are facing possible prosecution. It remains unclear at this stage what sanctions Muslim women marrying Hindu men might confront.

Conversion of any form has been strongly opposed, and this opposition dates back to British India. A Hindu revivalist movement known as "shuddhi" began to take shape in the 1920s. It aimed to win back individuals who had decided to follow other religions, most notably Islam. Interfaith unions were unusual at the time.

The movement's message was extremely patriarchal and depicted Hindu women as helpless prey to Muslim men's tricks. Although it had some support at first, this movement lost ground as other, more pressing social and political causes, such anti-colonial nationalism, took centre stage.

I contend that since India became independent, a fairly comparable enthusiasm has resurfaced. In addition to this legislative act, two other recent events deserve special attention.

The first involved a television advertisement for a high end jewellery chain that was launched on Indian television in October. The advertisement was from Tanishq, an affiliate of one of India's largest conglomerates, the Tata Group, and was titled "Ekatvam," or "unity" in Hindi.

The advertisement depicted a Hindu woman and a Muslim man preparing for a wedding. As soon as the advertisements were aired, some Hindu activists protested vigorously on social media. The company, fearing violence, withdrew the advertisement altogether.

The other episode took place in November when Netflix aired BBC's adaptation of the novel "A Suitable Boy" by the acclaimed Indian writer Vikram Seth.

Once again, some Hindu activists protested because it depicted a Hindu-Muslim couple's passionate kiss. The activists claimed that the film was "encouraging love jihad" and had "hurt religious sentiments." Accordingly, they demanded that it be forthrightly withdrawn.

CHAPTER VII

Why do you want to Pluck the Petal ?

On the morning of September 30, 1981, an alarm was sent at Lahore airport: an aircraft was flying without authorization into Pakistani territory. Within minutes, an Indian passenger jet landed at the Lahore airport; the plane was alleged to have been hijacked by five Sikh men while on a regular Jammu to New Delhi journey, and the hijackers forced the captain to reroute the plane to Lahore with 111 people on board.

This was an act committed by Sikh militants seeking a separate nation, Khalistan. The Sikh hijackers demanded that the Indian authorities free their colleagues who were imprisoned in India. They freed all but 45 people and intended to exchange them for Sikh inmates imprisoned in India on allegations of inciting riots.

The Pakistani government reacted promptly. Inside the plane, a clever group of Special Services Group (SSG) commandos claimed to be aviation cleaners. All five knife-wielding Sikh hijackers were apprehended and the passengers were released in a lightning-quick operation. Tejinder, Satnam, Gajendar Singh, Karan Singh Kini, and Jasmir Singh Jima were identified as the insurgents; they were convicted and condemned to life in jail. The Indian administration praised Pakistan's actions.

When the Khalistan movement became active in India and abroad, the Indian government claimed that "Pakistan armed, trained, and to some extent financed Sikh militants."

However, the author of a research paper titled "The Evolution of Sikh Secessionist Movement in Western Democracies" (September 2012) argues that the Sikh movement had three phases. The first was the Home Rule movement, which started in the 1960s and continued until 1978. Terrorism was added to its campaign from 1978 until 1993, as its demand was transformed to an independent Khalistan state.

Following that, the movement developed grievance politics, which began in 1994 and is still in effect today. In the 1970s, Khalistan leader Dr Chohan announced that he would even establish a rival government in Nankana Sahib, Guru Nanak's birthplace, currently in Pakistan.

Khalistan's origins may be traced back to British colonial efforts in the late 1800s and early 1900s that tried to split Sikhs and Hindus. Sikhs were enlisted in great numbers in the British army to fight against Hindu monarchs who revolted against the British Raj. Following Indian independence in 1947, tensions between the state of Punjab and the central Indian government arose, leading to complaints against the Indian government among many Sikhs.

In 1966, Punjab was trifurcated into the states of Punjab, Haryana, and Himachal Pradesh along linguistic lines (Punjab as a Punjabi speaking state, and Haryana and Himachal Pradesh as Hindi speaking states), causing resentment among many Sikhs that the historic contours of Punjab were being further divided after it had already been divided between India and Pakistan in 1947. Given the largely Hindu populations of Haryana and Himachal Pradesh, it was the subsequent split of Punjab that permitted Sikhs to enjoy a religious majority in the state.

Many Sikhs in Punjab also hated sharing the joint capital of Chandigarh with Haryana, and saw water-sharing arrangements with Haryana as unjust, benefitting Haryana farmers at the expense of Punjab farmers.

Although these types of issues are common in newly independent countries such as India, many Sikhs saw them as religiously motivated policies of discrimination against them, which were exploited by radical leaders who built a narrative that Sikh interests would be safe only in an independent Sikh country of Khalistan. This was exacerbated by an "incendiary mix of unprincipled politics and the exploitation of religious identities and institutions" that propelled radical Sikh groups to the forefront of Punjab politics.

"Militants were responsible for numerous human rights violations during the violent separatist struggle for an independent Khalistan, including the killings of Hindu and Sikh civilians, assassinations of political leaders, and the indiscriminate use of bombs, resulting in a large number of civilian deaths in Punjab and other parts of India," Human Rights Watch says. Criminals began to blackmail businesspeople and landowners under the guise of militancy,

demanding protection money."

According to Hamish Telford, "the Khalistan movement deteriorated into thuggery over time." Robbery, extortion, rape, indiscriminate executions, and terrorist assaults on innocent bystanders have become increasingly common among extremists. By 1991, Sikh militants were widely regarded as unethical criminal gangs."

But, amidst the drama of violence and allegations, I feel there are a lot of similarities between Kashmir and Khalisatn's conceptualisation as there have been a lot of misunderstandings regarding the movement of freedom from '21st century colonisation forces'. It seems as if there exists an irony between Indian past to present transition in terms of decolonisation. India spent years struggling against colonialism but India seems to have taken up a new reverse role of 'the coloniser' from the 'the colonised' as seen in the cases of dealing with Kashmir, Khalistan and the minorities.

Is the ideology of Kashmir and Khalistan two sides of the same coin? Lately, Kashmir has seen practically daily clashes, with many lives lost. Despite the fact that it seems practically impossible right now to withdraw Indian soldiers from Kashmir because of the current grasp of the centre,, the desire among ordinary people also remains unabated.

The Khalistan and Kashmir movements shared many parallels, including the fact that both were founded on ethno-religious assertions of difference and injustice with a long history.

According to many studies, Kashmiris were self-governing and members of the Mughal empire during the Kashmiri Sultanate (1346-1586). Before being controlled by the Dogra dynasty following the Treaty of Amritsar in 1846, there were Afghan and Sikh empires.

The region's status as a remote enclave physically isolated from the Dogra court aided the formation of a unique Kashmiri identity. While Punjabi Sikhs have a similar origin to Kashmiris, they have become more absorbed into mainstream Indian society.

This is due to geography, with Punjab being an extension of the Gangetic plains and Kashmir being separated by sometimes impassable mountain ranges. Then there's the social link: Sikhism started in India, and ethnic and sociological ties persist with mainstream Indian society, whereas Kashmiris are more closely related to Turks and Persians. Their cultural, religious, and social practices are unmistakably of Central Asian (Persian) heritage.

According to secondary research by EurAsian Times and a paper published by the Petroleum Institute, "Kashmiri society was controlled by a minority Hindu administrative class of Pandits, while the numerically much larger, religiously-defined Hindu population served a similarly unifying function for Sikhs."

Another striking parallel is the 1921 Montagu-Chelmsford reforms, which established separate electorates for Sikhs in the Punjab assembly; this was duplicated in Jammu and Kashmir, where agitation culminated in political reforms supported by several religious organisations.

Other parallels may be seen in both faiths, which have a strong heritage of martyrdom and a mingling of religion and politics that clashes with Indian secular nationalism. There is the often misunderstood Islamic idea of Jihad, as well as the Sikh concept of miri-piri, which connects the temporal and spiritual realms to authorise religiously controlled political activity.

Furthermore, the central government, led by Congress and now, aggravated by BJP, cynically manipulates politics in both states, frightened of being perceived as soft on minority interests, tried to bolster their credentials in India's Hindu heartland by acting strongly on Sikh and Kashmiri separatists. This fueled anti-India feeling and prompted political factions to take increasingly extremist stances in order to distance themselves from the central government and acquire the mantle of guardian of Sikh and Kashmiri identity.

The most obvious distinction is that Kashmir's political status has been a contentious issue since partition, whereas Punjab's political status, despite a long tradition of anti-centre political activism, only became so after independence, when the Punjab state finally came into being, giving birth to new states Haryana and some parts merged into Himachal Pradesh. In sharp contrast, J&K's borders have stayed unchanged since 1947, despite the fact that the state has a Muslim population of around 65%.

While the Khalistan movement is essentially dead, the Kashmir cause lives on. Over time, government policies such as depriving rebels of local support, amnesties, and growing public readiness to compromise and accept concessions diminished separatism's rhetorical appeal, isolated hardliners, and contributed to a drastic decrease in bloodshed.

However, there have been surges in violence this year. For Kashmiri Muslims, separatist politics and independence from Indian authority remain emotive subjects. In stark contrast, the restoration of peace and order in Punjab has essentially relegated the Khalistan cause to the past as a mistaken phase in Sikh history.

CHAPTER VIII

Your Mind can change Today, But Mine may take time

Luke 3:1–6.

We're tempted to imagine the ancient world of the Bible as far more foreign than familiar. In phrases like, "In the fifteenth year of the reign of Tiberius Caesar" (Luke 3:1), we hear the yammering of our high school history teacher. But Luke's gospel introduces us to a recognizable world. A world where lust for power, celebrity, and wealth reigned supreme. In this world, politics might be made right. In AD 19, for example, Tiberius Caesar exiled the Jewish community from Rome—because he felt like it. In this world, religious loyalties were corrupted by political compromise. Archaeologists believe they may have found Caiaphas's house—its multiple stories, water installations, and mosaic floors all bearing witness to the high priest's cosiness with the ruling party. Much like ours, this world was waiting for rescue.

John the Baptist may have been a member of one of the small holiness communities that fled Jerusalem because of the corruption. From the wilderness, John preached his "baptism of repentance for the forgiveness of sins" (v. 3) and announced a loud cry of salvation (v. 6). As the forerunner of Jesus, John was making a way for people to see what Rome, despite its promises, could never provide.

In the Jewish imagination, repentance was a means for restoring the blessing of God. Although repentance reminded people of their sin, it was nevertheless emphatically good news. We see this clearly in the book of Deuteronomy. As Moses reprised the terms of the covenant God made with Israel, he reminded God's people that sin would always be their ruin. To their own peril, he said, they "invoke a blessing on themselves, thinking, 'I will be safe, even though I persist in going my own way'" (29:19). But despite the pleasure people may think sin affords, it is always cause for eventual catastrophe—as Israel learned the hard way.

Repentance is a call to turn from our sin and turn toward God. To say it differently, repentance is a call to turn from self-harm and turn toward self-preservation. Repentance is a lifesaving measure.

But as the message of John reminds us, this turning is only made possible because God sent a "word ... to John son of Zechariah in the wilderness" (Luke 3:2). The good news announcement is that God himself has prepared the way for God's people to return to him. During Advent, we remember that repentance is made possible because God enfleshed a Word—and sends him to speak, to serve, to save.

Repentance is basically a change of attitude, not a turning away from sin. The Greek term for "repentance" is metanoia, and it simply means "a change of attitude." However, in ordinary parlance, we typically refer to repentance as "a turning away from sin." There's a reason behind this.

In the Bible, repentance is frequently related with salvation. What occurs when the Holy Spirit starts working to lead someone to salvation? The Spirit gives the sinner a personal awareness and unshakeable conviction that the facts about his spiritual situation are correct. These truths include his personal guilt, the everlasting punishment for his sin, the substitutionary character of Jesus' suffering for his sin, and the requirement for trust in Jesus to rescue him from his sin. The sinner repents (changes his mind) concerning sin, the Saviour, and redemption as a result of the Holy Spirit's convicting activity (John 16:8).

When a repentant person changes his perspective about sin, he will naturally turn away from sin. Sin is no longer acceptable or enjoyable since it leads to condemnation.

Repentance as a word often is taken up to mean differently and it is often misunderstood.

Stopping is what repentance entails - It doesn't, in fact. Of course, there is some halting involved, but repentance entails turning. Turning is not the same as stopping. It's more than just not stopping. You may come to a complete halt while remaining facing the same direction and sitting stationary. But repentance is more than just ceasing. It is not enough to just cease. Repentance entails turning, selecting something better than the current action. It is a choice between life with Christ and life with anything else. So repentance doesn't mean quitting what you're doing; it means valuing Jesus more than what you're doing.

The Pen is Mightier depending on who uses it

India remains colonised even today. As much as the statement is controversial, it is true. During the British colonisation, the colonists were aliens on the Indian soil who tried to rape India of all its' glory, and just like that, they succeeded. Power. Power is what assisted their win. Even today, the wielders of power write the story and they create the narrative. In fact, they provide the thesis that the entire country blindly follows. A story can never be the truth when just told by one voice. But, even if a group raises a voice, does it mean that it is the truth ? Well, if it is correct, then why do women still remain empty-handed after screaming for safety on Indian roads ?

It is not the voice or the number of people raising a concern, but it is all about power. Who raises a concern, is all that brings attention.

This takes me to a TED talk, "The danger of a single story," by Chimamanda Ngozi Adichie. In that marvellous collection of emotions voiced through words, she asserts that Single stories often develop from a hostile desire to conquer other communities through misunderstanding, ignorance of others, or prejudice. She explains the dangers of knowing only one-sided stories about the group. A single story creates a stereotype. The problem with stereotypes is that they are wrong and misleading. They make the story the only one that can be heard or taught to others. Using some examples, she describes her own experience of being a victim of false narratives.

> *Stereotypes fall in the face of humanity. We human beings are best understood one at a time.*

Cielo

I was exposed to a staggering amount of diversity while growing up in India. Colours and cows, parks and dumps, traffic and crops, the rich and the poor, and parks and dumps all intrigued me. When I was four years old and taking an arts and crafts class, I was supposed to draw my neighbourhood. In addition to the roads and trees, I also drew the "happy" people with big houses, lawns, cars, and big smiles on their stick figures. The "sad" people were also drawn by me. I drew the trash, the worn-out clothes, the tiny, flimsy houses, and mostly a sad-faced stick figure around them. Although I was only four years old at the time, I was still able to perceive the difference between the rich and the poor, and what's interesting is that I naturally associated the concepts of happiness and sadness with them. No one told me to draw this, nor did anyone hint at it. The single narrative began here. However, this perception was not just my own; it was bolstered by a variety of factors, such as the gentry of my school and playgrounds, where the "poor" children were never seen. Additionally, my parents advised me not to play in certain areas (slums). Sad places where all the poor lived in filth and unhappiness were known as slums. This was fixed in my mind until I was in my teens and saw how unhappy the "rich" homes were as well.I used to play hide and seek with a 14-year-old boy who committed suicide in his bedroom. I realised that the rich had problems as well.

At the same time, Holi, India's festival of colours, seemed to be much more enjoyed by the poor kids than by us, who danced around and shared their treats. I realised that the kinds of issues we faced were what set them apart from me. I now know that material wealth and material possessions should not be the sole sources of happiness.

There are 60,000 buildings in the Dharavi slum, many of which are shanties, and up to one million people living and working on a triangle of land that is only two-thirds the size of Central Park in Manhattan. Dharavi is one of the most well-known slums in the world and a common representation of Indian misery. It is home to more than a million people. Many of the residents are second-generation ones whose parents moved here years ago. I also knew this about Dharavi as a layperson. However, what I found there was unlike anything I had ever imagined. I was speechless and somewhat embarrassed by my preconceived notions of the location.

In Indian planning discourses, the term "slum" refers to a situation rather than a location. I learned that Dharavi did not have a formal water supply, sewerage, electricity, or a solid waste collection and management system. The overall state of hygiene was appalling.The overcrowding was another observation. There was typically just one person who was the breadwinner in a household of eight people on average. Regarding the location's crime rates, I had an assumption. They weren't as high as I thought, but I was mistaken. As a result, I arrived at an unexpected conclusion after conducting a SWOT (strength, weakness, opportunity, and threat) analysis of Dharavi and investigating the current circumstance. Yes, it was a slum with all the conditions, but there were huge advantages and opportunities in the informalities.

Stereotypes are created by a single story, and the issue with stereotypes is not that they are false but rather that they are incomplete.(Chimamanda Adichie) They make one story the only story. As a result, I want to present other perspectives to avoid this. The following is a list of some of Dharavi's issues, starting with the typical one, which is a misconception about any slum. It has no sewage or drainage systems, and it also has noise, water, and air pollution problems. Large, black clouds are released into the air each day by potters' brick kilns, which pollute the air and make the clouds black.

Doctors treat 4,000 diphtheria and typhoid cases per day while children play in sewage waste. Water pipes can break and take in sewage next to the open sewers. This water pipe, constructed on an old trash tip, serves as the hub of the slum.

The land is not owned by the people who live there. A walk through Dharavi is a journey through a dank maze of ever-narrowing passages until the shanties press together so tightly that daylight barely reaches the footpaths below, as if the slum were a great urban rain forest covered in a canopy of smoke and sheet metal. There are also toxic wastes in the slum, including highly dangerous heavy metals. People who list a Dharavi address complain that they are frequently turned down for credit cards. In Dharavi, private banks are reluctant to lend to businesspeople or open branches. The single story, in a nutshell, is as much about the social structure as it is about living in the slum.

However, Dharavi also has another side. I realised that holding presumptions about a location is extremely risky for me as a planner. With an annual turnover of approximately $665 million, Dharavi is a hub of industrial activity. The majority of the area is cleaner than many other parts of Mumbai, and the crime rate is lower there. Many rags-to-riches tales of millionaires living in its narrow streets are central to Dharavi, their land of opportunity. By recycling the garbage of Mumbai's 21 million residents as well as that of the entire nation and the world, Dharavi's recycling facilities generate revenue. Dharavi is home to 20,000 mini-factories. The majority of these goods are produced in tiny factories scattered throughout the slum and sold in domestic and international markets. The residents of Dharavi's slum make leather, textiles, and pottery products. In the 27 temples, 11 mosques, and 6 churches, more than 80 distinct communities practise more than six religions and speak more than 30 languages.

Even though Dharavi as a whole exemplifies the gloomy course that capitalism can take, the people who live there show tenacity, inventiveness, and optimism in the face of the enormous obstacles it faces.

It has been the subject of research by urban planners for a long time and may hold the key to controlling urbanisation over the next 50 years—by 2050, 70% of the world's population will reside in cities. Dharavi is much more than just a crowded industrial area or a slum;It is a community that reveals the unfair system of which we are all a part and sheds light on the essential components of happiness.

Dharavi is a combination of Dickens, Horatio Alger, and Upton Sinclair. It is deeply ingrained in the Indian imagination and can be seen in Bollywood films, books, and the Oscar-winning hit "Slumdog Millionaire. "Urban planners from Europe to Japan have dissected Dharavi in a Harvard Business School case study. However, the attempt to simply define Dharavi is contested. According to Gautam Chatterjee, the principal secretary in charge of the housing ministry in the state of Maharashtra, "Dharavi is a slum, a huge slum. "However, I have also considered Dharavi as an informal city within a city." The architect and urban planner Matias Echanove has argued for a long time that Dharavi should not be considered merely a slum because it functions as a contained residential and commercial city. He asserted that razing Dharavi or even completely redeveloping it would only lead residents to move into additional slums. He stated, "They are going to create actual, real slums. "Dharavi is not a paradise, according to anyone. However, we must comprehend the dynamics to ensure that government intervention does not destroy the existing situation."

It is time to make an effort to free ourselves from the preponderance of oversimplified, one-dimensional perspectives that the media or literature feeds us day after day, year after year. It is time to realise the risks associated with a single story.

Dharavi is a colony made up of communities with limited space sharing, when one passes through

you feel like a space of activity and Work. Daily life there, in the street, show, experience and observe. This represents its own complexity, the informal settlements of cities and the situation in other parts of the world. Differences in local culture and society are reinventing settlements inhabited by multifaceted groups: religion, caste, language, province and ethnicity. Entrepreneurial innovation is prominent and revealed within the city limits. Dharavi is often considered the largest slum in Asia, extremely dense. The area is located in the heart of the megalopolis, heart-shaped, with two main railway lines and the middle-income suburbs around it. Dharavi has long been considered an illegal, criminal and chaotic area by people from the rural areas of India. India. However, Dharavi is a very diverse region with occupations and income groups. It is a diverse agglomeration of communities for culturally and socially diverse regions. Dharavi has both global and local relationships.

CHAPTER X

"Our histories cling to us. We are shaped by where we come from."

We do not just risk repeating history if we sweep it under the carpet, we also risk being myopic about our present.

For centuries, Dalit minorities in South Asia have faced discrimination, exclusion, stigma and violence. Veena Palikal is Executive Director of the National Campaign for Dalit Human Rights in India. She has devoted her life's work to fighting for Dalit rights.

As a member of India's ethnic Dalit minority, Veena Parikal understands the importance of racial discrimination.

Dalits, commonly known as 'untouchables' in India and other South Asian countries, are born into a life of marginalisation, exclusion and human rights violations. They are at the bottom of the social hierarchy, as they are strictly "sorted" based on their ancestry.

In some countries, ethnic discrimination not only permeates institutions, social structures, and daily life, but is enshrined in law.

Parikal herself came from a family that met her needs, including access to her education, but many of her "brothers and sisters in the community" weren't so lucky, she says.

Injustice to Dalits causes deep trauma and suffering for generations. Stigma follows her from birth to death and affects every aspect of her life, including education, housing, employment, access to justice, and political participation. Women and girls are often victims of sexual violence and trafficking, and are particularly vulnerable to early or forced marriage, debt bondage, and harmful cultural practices.

According to the International Dalit Solidarity Network, there are an estimated 260 million Dalits in the world. Dalits live in South Asia (India, Nepal, Bangladesh, Pakistan, Sri Lanka) and in communities that have migrated from South Asia around the world.

"It starts in childhood," says Parikal. "We are not allowed to sit in front of the class, eat with other caste children, or play with other caste children. Creeks form very quickly and exclude Dalits. They don't know the difference and their

adult lives are severely affected by it. "

To bring issues to the international stage, she has also worked closely with UN human rights, other UN agencies, and co-organized side events for the United Nations.

High-Level Political Forum, the United Nations' main forum for sustainable development. She recently spoke at the United Nations Forum on Minority Affairs.

"I can't do anything else in my life right now," she said. "It gives me a lot of satisfaction, but at the same time makes me very angry. How can people talk about peace, happiness and religion when they see a young woman taken from the field where she worked, then raped and killed? We have to be angry, or we're not going to get anywhere - we're not going to stop this.

Violence against Dalits is a tragedy and happens every day. According to India's National Crime Records Bureau, about 45,935 cases of violence are recorded every year.

"In India, dozens of Dalit women are raped every day," says Pallical. "The perpetrators enjoy full retribution and enjoy broad political support. For this reason, we cannot break the chain of violence and oppression.

The National Dalit Human Rights Campaign works with victims of violence to seek justice and compensation from the government, and provides economic and psychological services to families. Hate speech and discrimination against the Dalit minority is another issue that Pallical is very concerned about, and one that she and her organization are fighting against.

While she acknowledges that the online space has allowed marginalised communities to voice their opinions, she says that at the same time it has created an unsafe environment for them where they are vulnerable. abuse from irresponsible people. Many young Dalit women have had to stop using social media because of fear and because the abuse has reached intolerable levels.

"Those who commit these abuses do so without conscience, not taking any responsibility for their actions," she said.

Pallical and the National Dalit Human Rights Campaign have partnered with Twitter India to address this increase in hate speech. They document various abuses and insults against the Dalits, as well as other minorities, to potentially recognize them and immediately stop the perpetrators.

For Pallikal, if children have the same chance, they have every chance to grow and develop. She envisions a day when all children can be equal and become free citizens, deserving of dignity and respect.

She has a list of dreams for a better future for Dalits.

"My dream is that every Dalit child has the same opportunity as any other, so that they can become equal citizens in this country. It is my dream that every Dalit woman is respected for the work she does and not beaten and raped just because she is Dalit. My dream is that if I say that I am Dalit and I am on the table, I will be respected like everyone else.

Another voice about fighting against a single story narrative about dalits among the lakhs of other voices, is also about the war against stereotypes and generalisations.

Although Yashica Dutt's Coming Out as a Dalit was released in 2019, her selection as the 2021 Sahitya Akademi Yuva Puraskar winner is a reminder of her timeless appeal. It captures your attention from beginning to end, as she tells her life story through the horrors of the Indian caste, especially the caste as it is practised against the Dalits.

Dutt's family history reflects the family histories of India's most mobile Dalits - their reticence in higher education and government jobs is absolutely central to their success. Dutt is the third generation in a family whose father and two grandfathers have been successful in public service, having secured his job through Ambedkar's constitutionally mandated policy of affirmative action.

The reserve was undoubtedly the most important political instrument through which the well-trained Dalits could untie their shackles. On top of that, stymied by poverty, and locked into scornful and poorly paid manual jobs, the Dalits have purposefully immobilised in these ghastly jobs, in which cleaning sewers are the deadliest. Dalit men are dying almost daily somewhere in India, doing this work, without the mandatory safety equipment provided to them. No one else wanted to do these jobs - so the poor Dalits were forced to do them, because of their poverty, to do them.

Notably, members of Dutt's family in Rajasthan belonged to the "lower" class of manual scavengers, but they were still able to climb the social ladder. But the price to pay for that success lies in young Yashica herself. Her persistent and remarkable mother realises that her daughter needs to attend good private schools to learn to speak English fluently. And that is what young Yashica and her faithful mother have truly accomplished, at great financial expense. But there is another, much higher price: the young schoolgirl must hide her Dalit identity. She constantly had to pretend to be "upper class" - and she did.

So, while working as a fashion reporter in Delhi, she "passed" a young Brahmin woman and was accepted as such. People seek to "pass over" in many societies, but this phenomenon has been discussed the most in the United States, especially when "white"-looking African-Americans seek to "pass" as "skin." white". "Skin colour," as Ari Sitas noted, has no true ontological state—it is another fabrication of the human mind.

All of these things Dutt weave neatly into her story, taking us through her school days to the almost magical vacation she finally got, which brought her to Columbia University's Master of Journalism program on a full scholarship. And - as was often the case - in another social setting, surrounded by people who didn't think along the lines of racism/classism, Dutt began to realise that she didn't need to be ashamed of her origins. his parents. Instead, the shame belongs to the "elite" of India, who have repeatedly humiliated and denigrated the Dalits in order to control their affairs and thus enrich themselves. Now, she sees herself differently, saying, "My story is one of oppression, not shame."

Reading Ambedkar, Dutt delightfully discovered - like many of us - that he had a truly amazing intellect and a surprising breadth of compassion. She was surprised that he never tried to stray from his roots, but instead used his vast knowledge and immense energy to liberate his people. But, as she revealed, the moment of great judgement came to her when young Rohith Vemula took her own life at her Hyderabad university dormitory on January 17, 2016, after despairing over her actions. action - including the rejection of his scholarship - from university governing bodies. To his horror, Dutt realised that this young PhD student, who had taken his own life, was the same young man who had "reached out" to him two weeks earlier, asking to befriend him. On Facebook.

Dutt said that in that moment of truth, she realized she could easily be Rohith Vemula - a Dalit college student who was "murdered in a research institute". This greatly shocked her, because Rohith had done the exact opposite of her: he had never concealed his Dalit origins, but devoted himself entirely to liberating the Dalits.

Within days of this profound realization, Yashica Dutt "came out", revealing her Dalit identity to the world, even though she was aware it would cost her friendship and the esteem of almost all familiar "upper class" people and colleagues. His compelling book offers, in these dark and terrifying times, a bright and beautiful hope - that young Dalit people will be empowered and be able to claim the right to life as equal citizens. in India. However, this is still a distant dream - Dutt himself sees his future in America. This is hardly surprising - as long as racism poisons our political system, the best educated young Dalits will want to leave their blind society. in search of a better life abroad. Who can blame them? Even Babasaheb will understand.

The risk of the single story, the one perspective, is that it can lead us to default assumptions, conclusions and decisions that may be incomplete, and may lead to misunderstanding. Operating from the context of a single story can prevent us from a more complex, nuanced view of a situation.

Well, stories matter, but that all too often in our lives we operate from the perspective of hearing and knowing a single story — about a person, a situation, or perhaps a conflict. And that we operate from the perspective of the single story unconsciously. In any situation, who tells the story, how and when, can impact situations greatly. The way we make sense of situations leads to narratives that may be harmful if left unexamined. Power enables some to define individuals and situations from a particular lens.

In India, in the case of Dalits, I believe that it is the power of caste that rules the narrative and the victors in the realm of caste, have managed to write the story of Dalits as a community and have successfully prevented the emergence of any other story. But, Dalit literature has proudly taken up the course of mingling with this power and to take up the risky task of being their own voice, which was much needed. After all, an upper caste Hindu sitting in a furnished air-conditioned apartment with a cup of coffee cannot actually narrate the story of a dalit.

Dalit literature is rather a revolutionary form of assertion, a part of the movement aiming to annihilate caste; it is a celebration of dignity of the hitherto marginalised. The usage of the term 'Dalit literature' was first noticed in the

Bombay Maharashtra Dalit Sahitya Sangha conference in 1958. With the establishment of the organisation called Dalit panthers in 1972, the term rose to prominence.

In words of Arjun Dangle, "Dalit is not a caste but a realisation and is related to the experiences, joys and sorrows and struggles of those in the lowest strata of society. It matures with a sociological point of view and is related to the principles of negativity, rebellion and loyalty to science, thus finally ending as revolutionary."

Dalit term is synonymous with oppressed, broken, downtrodden or untouchables and indicate that this discrimination is not self imposing but is imposed by others, historically the upper castes. The term untouchables finds its genesis in the Purusha Sukta of RigVeda which designates them the status of an outcaste community.

Dalit writing is the expounding on and of Dalits or abused. This writing reverberates the pain of the experiences of untouchables. It portrays the humiliation and segregations caused by the upper caste people. It imparts the political awareness that is focused on the fight for self-respect and regard for the community. "Dalit" writing has a recuperating ability to fix the injuries of the past.

Limbale (2004) in his one of the seminal essays entitled as "Dalit Literature: Form and Purpose" suggests certain pivotal traits to discern the form of Dalit literature and has also assayed to explain some of the basic reasons behind this paradigm shift in the literary sphere of Indian literature. He says, "Rejection and revolt in Dalit literature have been birthed from the womb of Dalits pain. They are directed against an inhuman system that was imposed on them. Just as the anguish expressed in Dalit literature is in the nature of collective social voice, similarly, the rejection and revolt are social and collective... The Dalit consciousness in Dalit literature is the revolutionary mentality connected with struggle. It is a belief in rebellion against the caste system, recognizing the human being as its focus. Dalit consciousness is an important seed for Dalit literature; it is separate and distinct from the consciousness of other writers. Dalit literature is demarcated as unique because of this consciousness."

This consciousness for possibilities for their emancipation in modern democratic cultures activates them to protest and the ideological, organisational set up of the movement along with the course of action was provided by Dr B R Ambedkar in the 1920s. He realised that the only way of creating a separate socio-cultural identity for them would be by moving away from the Hindu-fold and he went to convert to Buddhism and so did the Mahar community as a way of protest against the Hindu tradition and to establish their social position. The Dalit Sahitya Movement was a by-product of the endeavour of protest and to create literary and intellectual traditions as components of the socio-cultural ethos of their group. It is a social movement for liberation.

'The Dalit Sahitya (literature of the oppressed) movement in Maharashtra seems to be unique — not in the phenomenon of former Untouchables writing literature, but in the quality of writing, its variety, its aesthetic considerations, its sense of being a movement, its tie to social action, and in the serious attention it receives as a school within me Marathi literary traditions.'

This movement calls the Dalits the 'social proletariate' and the writers identify their interests with the Dalit masses. The writers focus on accelerating the emancipation of the community and universal humanism. They use history as a tool to glorify their past by giving evidence of being the original ruling inhabitants of the land. Dalit literature depict the dalit man and his hard life as the centre of their writings and intellectual deliberations in form of protest in their essays, poetry, drama, stories, autobiographies etc. The literature with 'Dalit sensitivity' regards the hindu intellectual tradition as the main source of their sufferings as it betrays human dignity.

The ideas that Dalit writers create are manifestations of their social consciousness determined by the real factors of their social existence. The literature tries to evolve a communication system and a dialogue among Dalits to foster awareness and propagation of their ideology and commitments. Dalit Sahitya Movement is an extension of the liberation movement of the Dalits and is also a protest literature to stir conscience and a sense of guilt in minds of the oppressors.

The philosophical, scholarly and hypothetical sources of Dalit writing are chiefly acquired from AfricanAmerican writing, Harlem Renaissance, Dalit Panthers Development, the battle for laying out or demonstrating identity as an individual, marxist social struggles, class battles, the battle against untouchability, looking for education and ideological and philosophical attributes chiefly of Buddha, Charvaka, Jyotirao Phule, Lord Shahu, Dr. B.R. Ambedkar and the subaltern view of identity. Dalit writing is a democratic literary movement arisen to eradicate untouchability, caste and gender segregation and to request equivalent opportunities in each field of life. Dalit Panthers and a few other Dalit associations are the models for the perpetrators of change. Dalit writing that initiated as a dissent writing has mellowed to join humankind and justice. It has developed a new personality over the years. Dalitness in the writing is not anymore a monotype.

Dalit caste organizations like 'Dalit Panthers of India' in Maharashtra, 'Dalit Mahasabha' in Andhra Pradesh, 'Dalit Sangharsha Samiti' in Karnataka, and 'Arundhatiyar' in Tamil Nadu were formed in response to the discrimination faced by the community. They primarily ask for equitable shares in opportunities and reservation.

Dalit literature stands for humanitarianism, linguistic directness and plurality; it is a literary movement for social change. Dalit literature stands against the rigidity of caste system which snatches the opportunities of equality in every field of life and thus becomes an instrument of exploitation and an integral part of the Dalit culture.

Dalit literature is also distinct in terms that the writer and the text cannot be separated. A reader's interpretation may be varied on the basis of either he or she belongs to Dalit community or elite caste. Focussing on Dalit liberation in particular and liberation of the oppressed in general, the literature has become a cultural activity coming under the broad movements of Dalit political liberation. It is cultural politics which takes the form of protest. The language of the Dalits becomes the most crucial constituent of Dalit literature and they have a different vocabulary and speech. Writing and reading, as a Dalit, are political practices. The language of Dalits is decent for Dalits and the 'decency' of the oppressors is 'indecent' for Dalits. It is full of texts which talk about the plight of Dalits and one of the most acclaimed poems is 'Habit' written by F M Shinde. I would like to present an analysis of the poem to substantiate the paper's main theme of Dalit literature.

'Once you are used to it you never afterwards feel anything;

your blood nevermore congeals

nor flows

for wet mud has been slapped all over your bones.

Once you are used to it

even the sorrow

that visits you

sometimes, in dreams,

melts away, embarrassed.

Habit isn't used to breaking out in feelings.'

Dalit poetry focusses on the central theme of 'protest' and tries to bring the subdued anger and agony of the Dalit community to the fore. The poem is all about the idea that Dalits would have become so habituated of the injustice and oppression faced by them and they continue to face it even today. It illuminates how the Dalits might have become so adjusted to their oppression that they cease to feel embarrassed and keep on enduring the embarrassment and harassment without even a hint of dissent. The artist compares the Dalit to a clay sculpture, inert and quiet, unequipped for dissent or obstruction.

The study of Dalit literature is significant in the era of 21ˢᵗ century because it has distorted the canon of literature and literary critical theory in India and abroad. The voices of the subsidiary and deprived communities from all over the world and their their appearance through writing should be given space since writing is all about 'individual' and it is the job of writing to offer human culture an equivalent stage and destroy the stains of brutality on the premise of caste, ideology, religion, race, identity, etc.

"Dalit literature is marked by revolt and negativism, since it is closely associated with the hopes for freedom by a group of people, who as untouchables, are victims of social, economic and cultural inequality"

As a literary movement, it continues to grow as new individual keep on adding their voices to the collective outrage of resistance against caste based discrimination and humiliation suffered for ages. A new generation of writers are transforming Dalit literature from merely a narrative of humiliation and exploitation to include issues such as feminism, literary self-consciousness, individual introspection, while tackling with the question of how mainstream this literature may become without losing its authentic Dalit identity. Dalit literature is an outcry of those who were left on the margins: the outcaste, the oppressed, landless, indigenous groups.

Raj Kumar in 'Dalit Literature and Criticism' criticises the upper-caste Hindu writers of the twentieth century who in their novels have tried to portray the lives of 'untouchables' with the aim of bringing about social reform or by sentimental compassion. He argues that these novels belong to genre of 'emotional' literature rather than Dalit literature because these characters are presented from the perspective of upper caste writers. Dalit literature upholds equality, freedom and justice; it emphasises the centrality of the human being and society and therefore it is revolutionary. Suffering and revolutionary awakening are the basis of Dalit literature.

The cultural significance of literature emerges, among other things, from its virtue of being a free platform for any member of society to express himself. However, as hegemonic oppression manifests deep within our caste system, it is not surprising that the term "Dalit literature" was first officially used in 1958, at the meeting first meeting of Maharashtra Dalit Sahitya Sangh. This does not mean that until then, the portrait of Dalit character was completely absent from the literary forum. Rabindranath Tagore's 'Geetanjali' and Premchand's 'Sadgati' are two of the most striking examples, among others, of how Dalit managed to imbue the artists of the time. However, the experiences and observations written by upper caste writers can be largely distinguished from those coming from Dalit writers. The debate over whether there is a difference between paintings depicting Dalit when written by a Dalit and when written by a non-Dalit writer has raged for centuries.

Neha Arora and Arjun Dhangle are among many who support the claim that you don't have to be Dalit to write literature based on their lives and experiences. Arundhati Roy, Amitav Ghosh and Vikram Seth are among those who hail from non-Dalit actors and have written award-winning Dalit literature, thus proving the foregoing position. However, the real distinction comes about whether reality and the characters portrayed in these stories accurately reflect reality on the ground. It should be noted that the source from which non-Dalit writers get their stories and character inspiration is very different from how Dalit writers find theirs. The issue simply stems from a debate over whether the depiction of Dalit's character and the way of life that comes from the source of empathy or empathy can be more authentic than Dalit's own accounts are not.

"Only the ash tree knows the experience of burning" is a famous saying by Ramnika Gupta that helps us understand that while being aware of caste issues can help an individual write much about it, it must have. in the said situation to be able to perfectly describe what the experience was like. This is basically where Dalit literature is written by a Dalit writer and a non-Dalit writer separately. Non-Dalit writers have a penchant for painting a dark and hopeless picture of the Dalit way of life and showing how the Dalits have become victims of their situation. For example, in Premchand's "Godan", the central character dies at the last minute because he can't fight upper-class moneylenders. These biassed descriptions are mostly stereotyped and therefore do not give a genuine impression to the reader. So Dalit writers' claim that non-Dalit writers often portray them in a negative or sympathetic light is true, although we now somewhat understand why.

On the other hand, Dalit writers portrayed Dalit characters as rebels while painting a hopeful picture for the future. By overcoming these difficult circumstances on her own, Dalits realised that literature that did not envision an optimistic future for its community members would not nurture in them the will to fight back. in the face of oppression. Dalit writers often argue that 'Dalit Chetna', the perception that comes with being a Dalit, is essential when writing about difficulties, thoughts, ways of life, etc. by Dalit.

Therefore, they argue that the allure of passion can be portrayed by a Dalit writer not only more believably but also more authentically. Alok Mukherjee's 2004 translation of 'Towards the Aesthetic of Dalit Literature' by Sharankumar Limbale defines Dalit Chetna as 'the revolutionary soul associated with struggle'. This also explains to some extent why Dalit writers try to portray Dalit characters with assertive and rebellious attributes instead of portraying them as victims.

Newer and more comprehensive arguments can be made available to both sides of this debate, but the fact remains that a non-Dalit writer will always be blind to some of the secret ways Dalits deal with. humiliation in their daily lives because the naked eye can only observe so much. This is not to say that Dalit literature should only be for Dalits or anything like that. What we must admit, however, is that the confirmation that a Dalit writer attaches to a Dalit literary work is something a non-Dalit writer can only strive for while rarely succeeding.

"You can't use master's tools to demolish a master's house."

Dalit literature was a postcolonial leap against hegemonic oppression. It depicts the bitter truth of independent India's class-based social structure and the invincible challenges faced by the Dalits. Its main goal is to raise the voice of protest and make the oppressors hear the new voice of justice and equality. But when the oppressed tried to express their long-dead anguish and pain through literature, it was ignored. Their work was not considered as worthy of reading as literature because it did not conform to their standard aesthetic. Audre Lorde rightly said "one cannot dismantle a master's house with his master's tools".

Dalit writers argue that literary standards change with the change of culture. Also, refute the hypothesis that someone's writing will only be called literature when "us"'s literary standards approve it, which is a sign of a literary dictatorship. In addition, Dalit critics propose to include and recognize 'revolt' as the tenth, 'scream' should be accepted as the eleventh 'rasa', to complete the 'rasa' theory. Because Dalit's literature is not about beauty or pleasure, it's about Dalit's sufferings and revolts. Therefore, his aesthetic cannot be based on the principles of a standard aesthetic of literature, where privilege derives from pleasure. It was therefore imperative to develop a distinct aesthetic for evaluating Dalit literature.

Indian literature in English always has stories about Dalit. But much of the "Dalit literature" was retold by Brahmin or Savarna writers with a savior complex. The first-person story of a Dalit man written by a Brahmin or a Savarna scholar, meticulously told as a helpless, preoccupied and self-victimized man. while waiting for a Savarna saviour or tragically dying is a fairly common sight.

This limits the dimensions of the caste story in the early Indian English text. Indian writing is often an exploration of rural India, rural and urban families, the flashy birth of industrialization, urbanisation, and globalisation. These accounts never mention caste other than mentioning support/sympathy or saving the Untouchables or Harijan. The postmodern era, globally, has given voice to all the unprecedented anguish, sighs and tears of the oppressed throughout literature. In India, the dominant literatures in the region and fringe movements were also influenced by the new literary movement. As a result, a multicolored art scene was created and among them Dalit literature played an important role, which obviously means Dalit literature, It clearly depicts the voice of anguish, oppression or of the Dalits.

Today, Dalit literature includes not only works written about persecuted Indians, but also other groups around the world, who are brought down to the ground by the privileged classes. Dalit literature may include articles on the exploitation of nature and the environment, the racism of African Americans in America, the dependence of women, the abandonment of the elderly. The word Dalit has a huge periphery and it says it all the kind of domination that any group must face. It has the power to heal past hurts.

The postmodern era, globally, has given voice to all the unprecedented anguish, sighs and tears of the oppressed throughout literature. The dominant and marginal trends of literature in the region are also influenced by the new literary movement. Therefore a polychromatic art was created and among which Dalit literature played a major role, Dalit literature was an important line of Indian script in English and other Indian languages. Dalit literature emerged in the 1960s, beginning with Marathi and soon appeared in Hindi, Kannada, Telugu and Tamil, through stories such as poetry, short stories and, most of the autobiography, stand out for their austere depiction of Dalit reality and politics.

When caste society became prominent in 500 BC - 500 AD, conflicts between upper and lower classes became prominent in our society. Both the ancient Dharma Shastra and the Rig Veda prioritised the caste system and there are only two castles one is the upper Hindu class called Bharamana and the other is the lower caste called Dasa. According to the ancient Hindu Shastra Dharma, there were a series of restrictions such as economic, social, political and religious restrictions on the lower classes. This caste has different names like Dasa, Rakasa, Asura, Avarna, Panchama, Chandala etc. The British called them the "depressed class", and after independence they were called the "Scheduled Class" and this class belonged to the Dalit communities officially. Dalits are called by various names in different parts of India, coined by people of caste and all related to insults and contempt.

Classified, included or incorporated into a larger category or general rule: Dalits are depicted as labourers and their oppression is clearly depicted. Dalit's life is the source of Dalit literature, therefore, Dalit writers prefer to describe Dalit's dreary life; Dalit writers from all states of India have enriched Dalit literature. The Dalit writers have faithfully presented the Dalit symbolism of their region in its current state.

Today, Dalit literature includes not only writings about oppressed Indians, but also other groups around the world, who are brought down to the ground by the privileged classes. Dalit literature can include writings about exploitation of nature and the environment, racism by African Americans in America, subordination of women, oppression. And since my article is about oppression in dalit literature I have to explain what oppression means, it means that someone or people who are oppressed are usually under the control or rule of others. and they are exploited and treated roughly or cruelly and so this is seen as exercising power or authority over others or others and using them for their own ends painfully, cruelly and unjustly. And the theme of oppression plays an important role in Dalit literature.

The experience of Mahatma Gandhi, is a prime example of the oppression that was a big problem for Dalits. Mahatma Gandhi, then working in Durban, South Africa, was insulted and humiliated under the Racist regime. It was from Durban station that Mahatma began his fateful journey. Gandhi embarked on a train on June 7, 1893 to Pretoria, where he met with legitimate clients. A first class seat was reserved for him and when the train arrived at Pietermaritzburg station at 9:00 PM. A white passenger entering the cabin couldn't contain his anger for travelling with Gandhi because he was a person of colour. So he went out and came back with two officials, who ordered Gandhi to move to the truck compartment. When Gandhi resisted because he had a valid ticket to travel In this compartment, a white policeman grabbed Gandhiji's hand and pushed him off the train. His luggage was also thrown away outside, and the train continued its journey without him.

This experience of Gandhi was shared by A.P.J. Abdul Kalam in an essay "A Changeable Personal Crisis Story". But after this humiliation, Gandhi vowed to stay and fight the so-called disease of racial prejudice. Gandhiji even said "......my nonviolent activity began that day."

Critics have argued that Dalit literature is not the literature of anyone who wrote about Dalit, but only about the Dalits at birth. Anyone else who is not born in Dalit, even if he writes about people oppressed by society sympathetic or empathetic cannot be considered a dalit writer or his literature cannot be considered dalit literature. In this sense, the greatest work of Rabindranath Tagore "Gitanjali" (1913) shows the status of a Dalit, as a non-Dalit writer he shows what is untouchable, how is he humiliated and oppressed in his own country.

Shashi Bhushan Upadhayay pointed out that "Dalit literature is not a movement in the usual sense of the term.

Just like Black Literature, Literature was not written by anyone above dalits. Anyone else who is not born Dalit, even if they write about the oppressed by society with sympathy or empathy, cannot be considered a Dalit writer and his literature will not be considered Dalit literature".

Dalit's rise in assertiveness is supported by increasing levels of education and employment. There has been an overall increase of 51% in literacy in Scheduled Actors, IndiaSpend reported on December 13, 2013. In urban areas, literacy among SCs increased by 62 %. The labour participation rate in CS is 40% higher than the national average rate (39.8%). According to an analysis by IndiaSpend of 2011 census data,

Dalits who converted to Buddhism - also known as neo-Buddhists - enjoyed better literacy rates, higher labor and sex participation rates. than the Hindu castes expected, the group from which most converts emerged. Some Dalits always vote for BJP, in UP or anywhere else for all kinds of reasons:

Firstly, protest effect (can be called Sanskritization, to use MN Srinivas expression) refers to the 19th and 20th century Shuddhi movement when the Hindu Rulers of Mahasabha agreed to dine with Dalits.

Second, clientelism, a process where some Dalits favour BJP celebrities who help them economically or otherwise.

Third, the combination of class rivalry and sectarianism: if one jati supports one Dalit party, the other party will turn to the other. In UP, the Valmikis (renamed in a process of Sanskritization by the Vishva Hindu Parishad) voted for the BJP in response to the Jatav's association with the BSP. In Maharashtra, the Maharas supported RPI and Mangs as well as other Chambhar parties including Shiv Sena and BJP.

That being said, the Dalits were not attracted to BJP in large numbers. Only a fifth of them supported BJP in 2014 and among them did not respect the rule that applies to other constituents, which is "the richer I am, the more I lean towards BJP ".

This opens up the route to another complication in the focus on power which circulates a single story about a community that leads to narratives. Power sharing arrangements also rise up between the power holders and the affluent with accumulation of wealth. As wealth opens up the route for even the oppressed to climb up the ladder, power is then shared as per convenience. The ones who were on the other side of the fence, subsequently shifted their allegiances.

CHAPTER XI

We are born as who we are. What is, then, Gender ?

Gender socialisation begins as soon as a child is born and is assigned a socially defined 'male' or 'female' status (i.e. male or female) depending on its gender. Sexism starts here too. As a place where men are preferred over women, there are numerous cases of female fetuses and infanticide in India. From an early age, girls are encouraged to play with dolls and kitchen sets, while boys are given action figures and are not allowed to play with toys (usually pink) marked "for girls". No. Educational opportunities for girls and boys are also different, with boys having more formal education than girls (Chandra, 2019).

Women are viewed as a burden by families who prepare to marry once a woman reaches a certain age. Both educational and economic opportunities for women are hampered after marriage. Because in India there is an unspoken belief that private rooms in the house are the "female realm" and that men should occupy public spaces. Men are rarely expected to do household chores such as cooking, cleaning, and washing. Women, whether they work or not, must maintain the home and provide for the men of the family.

Certain 'masculine' traits attributed only to men, such as logic and reasoning, and stoicism. It is considered superior to the "feminine" traits attributed to women, such as emotions and sensitivity. Women's participation in important positions is often restricted because of these differences (women are said to be unsuitable for these jobs).

Language and gender

Cielo

Simone de Beauvoir said "one is not born, one becomes a woman". Gender is not something we are born with, but something we run after. Gender, as opposed to gender, is a social construct and it is constructed by different cultural practices or social customs. Language is a communicative practice that influences and is influenced by cultures. A speaker's linguistic competence is his knowledge/ability to create or realise meaning. However, language competence is not enough to make sense. You have to know the social conventions of a particular culture to make sense. Since language is highly dependent on the culture around it, it is also, in many ways, an act of performance. Therefore, gender is influenced by the language they speak.

I want to analyse the correlation between gender and language and how the two influence each other. Robin Lakoff was the first linguist to begin to discuss the relationship between gender and language in his paper entitled "The Place of Language and Women" (1972). He argues that women often use lower/subordinate language forms than men with the use of tag questions (Isn't it? It shows the need to be acknowledged or that they can be wrong.

After Lackoff's assertion, a debate began as to why women's language has such a secondary form, there are two answers, difference and dominance. The different approach suggests that women and men are brought up differently and therefore implicitly differ in their linguistic form. The dominant method asserts that this difference in speaking style is the result of structured discrimination between men and women. This led to male supremacy, and also to male domination of language. Women never had a "room of their own" to form their own language and therefore it was seen as inferior, and men's language was always the norm.

So, in this sense, the question of difference has been integrated into the framework of dominance. However, many critics have opposed both of these approaches. Deborah Cameron, a feminist linguist, argues that most languages are generally male-centred and that feminine words often deviate from words designed "originally" for women. male. For example, words like author and manager are often feminine by adding the suffix -ess. This absence of vocabulary suggests that female languages are generally compared to masculine languages and are still defined by power dynamics.

Women's language is also said to be more polite and empathetic, often accompanied by a smile or minimal replies. An example of this can be seen in children's cartoons, where female cartoon characters often laugh a lot, apologise more for their actions, and often take on a very passive role. They use a lot of questions when talking, almost doubt themselves, and often need confirmation from the opposite sex.

Men and women also talk differently. Bruce Dorval, in his research on same-sex interactions, suggests that men tend to change topics of conversation more quickly than women. On top of that, women tend to expand/build on things that have been talked about before. Also, when men talk, women often listen and agree using terms like "mm" and "yeah" to develop a sense of connection. This agreement can be read as a sign of submission, but it is only a reflective practice. Another observation about the difference is how men tend to come up with sensible solutions if and when someone tells them their problems, while women tend to give more empathetic responses. .However, these observations tend to run the risk of essentializing gender norms. But one could argue that the behaviour is portrayed because gender is generally conditioned and therefore expected to react in a particular way.

In an article titled "Gender in Twitter: Style, Position, and Social Networking," several linguists observed how people of different genders interact differently on social networks. and leave different gender cues while chatting. For example, women tend to be more expressive with their writing, use more emojis and more exclamation points, often lengthening their words (Hiii, nooooo). The difference in how genres interact shows how different genres fit together.

Differences in women's language can also be seen in women-led protests. Because women present differently than men, their protest methods are less violent and more empathetic, with strong collective and community significance. They often use their bodies to express themselves, mainly because sometimes the language offered to them (mostly men), is not enough to articulate their message. For example, the Chipko movement (1973) saw a group of peasant women hugging trees and protests against the armed forces led by naked Manipuri women against the incarcerated rape of Manorama (2004). Women's methods of protest are heavily influenced by language organs or lack of language organs.

Charlotte Gilman's short story, Yellow Wallpaper, gives new discourse to the debate about gender and language. The unnamed heroine repeatedly begins the conversation with a similar phrase, "John said this", suggesting that she has no way of making her mind clear. The dialogue between men and women in the story is aggressive, overbearing and sometimes dangerous, while the dialogue between women and men is gentle, understanding and always in harmony with the male lead's point of view.

The female character is denied a language (she's not allowed to write, talk, or even think) to the point of driving her crazy to discover another form of language. This form of alternate language is represented through patterns on a yellow background that only the heroine can understand.

Women are often rejected by the language authority and their language is always perceived as deficient compared to men. This is reflected in many social customs and practices. Thus, it can be concluded that language has a great impact on gender construction. On top of that, because language is dynamic, it can also reform many gender practices. It has been supported in Indian Ancient history texts.

While describing the respective duties of a mother and a father, in one of Sangam's poems it is said that a mother's duty ends after the birth of a child and it is the father who is truly wise. In another poem, it is said that the (ideal) husband is devoted to his work and to his obligations as dear as his life, while for the wife, who is bound in home, her only life is his. Life husband.

Tolkaappiyam, an ancient Tamil grammar, written 2000 years ago, imposes restrictions on women's speech. A man can say anything to show his knowledge while a woman can only express herself on a limited number of topics within her family. It is also clear from this grammar that learning (education), possessing and displaying bravery, fame, and charity are the sole privilege and goal of a man (and no other privilege reserved for man). for women). Another famous Tamil work Tirukkural (thirukkuraL) also asserts that learning (education) is only for the male group (Kural 67, 69 and 70). On the other hand, he recounts the duties of a housewife as follows: the wife must be responsible, loyal, wholeheartedly devoted to her husband, take care of the housework, take care of her husband (the owner) and give birth to good children (Mural painting 51). According to Tirukkural, an ideal woman is one who does not worship God but is increasingly worshipping her husband. (Mural painting 55). In this way, ancient literature clearly depicts the power structure or social position of men and women in society. Classical literatures in other Indian languages, both sacred and secular, are no exception to this general rule. There's definitely a masculine approach to all of these profiles.

Language is the road map of a culture. It tells you where its people come from and where they are going.

Language is the most powerful mode of representation. Cora Kaplan is able to express the essence of this statement in her words where she says;

Our individual speech does not.... free us in any simple way from the ideological constraints of our culture since it is through forms that articulate those constraints that we speak in the first place. [Kaplan 56]

Language contains meaning and is shared by a given group of individuals which also governs our society. Language serves as a powerful weapon and can be used by a dominant group to establish their superiority and hierarchy on the other one. Feminists around the world focus on the patriarchal agenda behind the language discourses by asserting that language has always been used and continues to be a weapon or a tool by men to establish their identity and perpetuate patriarchy.

Feminists in the west appeared as a result of female subordination and prominence of male society. Feminist theorists have repeatedly struggled for equality of women since ages. A 'female' was understood as a social or cultural construct and language was gendered for the first time when the terms such 'masculine', 'feminine' and 'neutral' were brought into light by the linguists. 'Sex' came to define biological difference whereas 'gender' referred to a linguist category. Sex meant a biological difference which the individual naturally has but gender became not something which a person has but what something a man or a woman acquires, do or perform.

Language also came to define cultural norms as the distinction between 'males' and 'females' became prominent. An example of linguistic expression of gender can be 'the child is a boy'. This not only is just a statement but also contains a hidden prescription which calls for how the child should be brought up and how the child should behave as a boy.

The difference in language of men and women not only lies in the grammatical difference but also social difference. Deborah Tannen in her book 'You just don't understand' talks about the different types of differences in male and female language.

First is all about status which explains how men have an upper hand and dominate in a world where they try to always gain a higher status. Women, on the other hand, seek support for their ideas and see the world as 'a network of connections seeking support and consensus'.

Second focuses on how men concerned about attaining a higher status tend to be more independent but women constantly struggle to preserve their intimacy which results in different views of the same issues or situations.

Third is the difference in how men and women perceive the idea of understanding. Men often see a complaint as a challenge to find a solution. This is exemplified by Deborah Tannen through a situation where her parents themselves had a different way of understanding it. 'When my mother tells my father she doesn't feel well, he invariably offers to take her to the doctor. Invariably, she is disappointed with his reaction. Like Many men are focussed on what he can do, whereas she wants sympathy.

Fourthly, she enhances how through ages men's concerns and ideas were always thought to be important as compared to those of women.

Fifthly, she tells us how women often claim through indirect ways - 'let's', 'why don't we' or 'wouldn't it be good if we..?'. Men, however, prefer a direct way.

Sixthly, women often tend to compromise and complain subsequently and accede whereas men tend to resist vocally. These apply to most men and women but there are always exceptions.

In 1975, Robin Lakoff published a book titled 'language and woman's place' which focussed on women's language. She rules out some basic assumptions which govern the language of women in her other article.

In this article she claims that women often keep these things in mind which governs their language:

• Hedge: use of phrases like 'sort of', 'kind of' and so on

• Use of polite forms: 'would you mind if', 'I would appreciate if' or 'if you mind if'

• Use tag questions: 'you're going to dinner, aren't you?' • Use empty adjectives: divine, lovely, adorable etc.

• Use direct quotation: men often tend to paraphrase

• Apologise more: 'I am sorry but I feel that...'

• Lack a sense of humour: women do not often tell jokes • Overuse qualifiers: for example, 'I think that'

• Avoid coarse language

• *Use hypercorrect grammar and pronunciation*

In much of the written literature, we find much evidence of oppression of women and dominance of men. In European, Middle Eastern and African cultures, women did not have equal political and social rights as men and were often under the control of their fathers and husbands in almost all societies. In Greece too women did not have basic rights which is

often held up as the originator of democracy. Political theorists like Aristotle and Socrates considered women to be incapable of practical thought and not true citizens. Even in India, women have been witnessing the history of subjugation. During the ancient period, although women were seen as contributing equally as men were hunted and women gathered, gradually this notion faded.

Women were often ousted from social life by denying them property rights, social and political rights and also education rights. Women although were considered goddesses, their situation remained unimproved. Instruments of suppression were the practice of Sati and child marriage which prevailed for a very long time. In Mahabharata which is considered to be the great epic and is held proudly, subjugation of women is evident.

Patriarchy prevailed at that time too and women were oppressed which is evident by the example of Draupadi who was shared as a wife by five men and was also lost as a bet by one of her husbands. Women at that point could not claim share of her father's property and could not succeed as a royal heir. Even in the Vedic times, women were not considered as equal and were not even allowed to hear or study the Vedas by the dominant class of men in the society. This was continued even in the Mughal period where women were oppressed by men of the household. Although women slowly started acquiring important status and gaining rights all over the world, true freedom from oppression was never attained. Even today in some parts of the country, women's reproductive functions and sexual capabilities are seen as disgusting to the extent that menstruating women were till recently not allowed to even visit some temples which adorned female goddesses. Some religions and cultures also preach subjugation of women where women are taught to dress, speak and behave in a certain way which is expected to be appropriate.

Some countries support patriarchy through certain rules like in some countries the punishment of rape is that the rapist's wife is given over to the rape victim's husband or father to rape if he wishes, as a revenge. In some extreme cases, rape, the victim is married off to the rapist. There have been many writings on these things by feminists which are ignored. Marxists believe that oppression of women began with the rise of a class society, about 6000 years ago and oppression of women is a creation of culture. Male dominance throughout ages has resulted in erosion of female identity and status as individuals.

Another form of patriarchy called Neopatriarchy coined by Hisham Sharabi in 1988 evolved to suppress women at the household level. It involves control and exercise of power guided by the elder women in the family but supervised by men. In this system, women are responsible for perpetuation of patriarchy by subjugating younger women in the family, especially the bride.

'The second sex' by Simone Beauvoir [1949] is an historical account of women's disadvantaged position in a society. 'One is not born, but rather becomes a woman'. It is one of the earliest feminist works and is used by many contemporary feminists to draw on to women's oppressed position. '...her wings are cut and then she is blamed for not knowing how to fly'

'Still I rise' by Maya Angelou [1978] also draws upon how women had been victims of patriarchy.

You may write me down in history With your bitter, twisted lies,

You may trod me in the very dirt But still, like dust, I'll rise.

You may shoot me with your words, You may cut me with your eyes, You may kill me with your hatefulness, But still, like air, I'll rise.

'Pride and prejudice' by Jane Austen [1813] focusses on marriage and women. Marriage is used as a social validation by the dominant male group. As women had no right to material property, the only way to attain a respectful status in society was through entering into a matrimonial alliance with a man of higher status. Social status was assigned to women based on the reputation of their fathers and husbands. Married women had no possessions due to a law in Britain which stated that husbands could take care of their wives. Women were often seen as wives, mothers or daughters. Women were expected to choose men who could financially support them which also added a survival aspect to the institution of marriage.

All the above examples express female concerns and their voices against the then existing social order which in their own way added to the plight of women and suppressed them. These writings have been used by many feminists as their works impressively analyzed the oppression of women. Feminists believe that patriarchal discourses, both oral and written, subjugate women. Language should be free of male bias for an honest depiction of female experience. Patriarchal norms have been displayed as natural which needs to be reshaped. Language has been used for centuries by men in order to weaken women. But powerful and strong voices have emerged to support the ones who still are caught up in the shackles of oppression today. Thus, I believe that language can empower or weaken groups. Gender differences can be made negligible by wiping out the language distinction between males and females. Gone are the days when literature was restricted to men and inspiration must be drawn from the women in Shobha De's novels who revive their lost fortunes, look glamourous, act different, break the norms, are sexually liberated and free thinkers. As Simone De Beauvoir says 'All oppression creates a state of war. And this is no exception'[Beauvoir 156].

The question of how a woman should be elected president in Hindi first arose when Pratibha Patil became the first woman to hold India's top constitutional office in 2007.

There have been debates over whether she should be called "Rashtrapati" or "Rashtrapati", but this debate has not sparked the outcry that was recently sparked when Adhir Ranjan Choudhary, leader of the opposition in the House of Representatives, spoke before President Draupadi. Murmu as "Rashtrapati".

Launching a scathing attack on Choudhary, the ruling Bharatiya Janata Party (BJP) demanded an apology from the Parliament for insulting Murmu, which led to a huge drama inside and outside parliament. Although Choudhary apologised for his comment citing his poor Hindi, the question sparked a much-needed debate regarding the gendered nature of our language.

The controversy that has raged around Chaudhary's comment can only be understood if we consider what the two words 'pati' and 'patni' mean and what meanings are assigned when these two words are attached to Rashtra. (nation).

The Hindi word Rashtrapati is used as a translation of the English word "president", commonly used to refer to the president of a group and is a sexist term, but its Hindi translation is "Rashtrapati" not due to the suffix 'pati'.

Etymologically, the Hindi word "pati" is part of the Indo-European language family, where it usually means "lord" or "master". When used as a suffix, it usually means "lord of...". For example. The Sanskrit word for a married head of household is "grihapati", which means lord of the family. Similarly, "senapati" means a warlord who commands an army; Ganapati means lord of the tribe; Chhatrapati means lord of kings. Such examples can only be multiplied to show the power relationship that the word 'pati' denotes. In our everyday usage the word 'pati' usually means husband, but again the inherent patriarchal power relationship is reflected in compound words like 'pati-dev' or 'pati-parmeshwar', which refers to the husband who is the lord or god for the wife.

Unlike pati, the word 'patni', used for 'wife', has no such meaning. It is a relational term unlike "pati" which is a stand-alone term and is used only for a married woman. It is simply a feminine derivative of patina and therefore it has inherent sexual connotations and connotations attached to it. Furthermore, there is no equivalent of Hindi words like "pati-dev" or "pati-parmeshwar" in any of the Indian vernacular for married women, which only represents the right difference. between pati and patni in Indian society. And therein lies the root of Rasthrapatni's recent feud.

The word "Rashtrapati" is a combination of two Hindi words, "Rashtra" and "Pati". When used as a translation of the English word President, it is usually understood to mean "head of the republic" and not "husband of the nation". And this meaning is completely synonymous with other words with the suffix pati. But when the word "patni" is combined with the word "Rashtra" to create the compound word "Rasthrapatni", the connotation is sexual to mean "wife of the nation", this still only reflects the way of this word. 'patni' is nested in the Indian spiritual context, i.e. 'sexual creature' and 'wife'.

The problem here is how our language is structured. Since language is a product of society, it reflects and perpetuates the prejudices and power relations that exist in a particular society. As Michela Menegatti and Monica Rubini have argued, "language is one of the most powerful means through which sexism and sexism are perpetuated and reproduced".

According to a study by Francesca Di Garbo, Bruno Olsson and Bernhard Wälchli titled 'Gender and Grammatical Complexity' (2011), about 75% of the world's languages propagate sexism. when using a lot of masculine pronouns, and Hindi is no exception. . In everyday life, we often overlook the use of "strong" gender phrases in our conversations. When we use English words like "police", "firefighter", "president" and "salesman", we ignore the fact of gender deviance. For any individual, these terms refer to jobs that are primarily performed only by men. When these words are used in Hindi for women in these roles, they are almost always referred to by the prefix "mahila" attached to the role/position, so we have "police mahila" , "doctor mahila", etc.

To see why this sexism is pervasive in our everyday language, we need to look at the sources that form our vocabulary such as dictionaries, newspapers or magazines that people use. Editors are mostly men around the world, who probably don't understand rather infer the use of a particular language in a particular way. Therefore, we can say that the existence of the gender language is managed by the global structure itself.

In 2007, when asked about how to address former President Pratibha Patil in Hindi, the late Shiv Sena leader, Bal Thackery, wrote an article for his party spokesman, Samna, in which he begged. the replacement of the word "Rashtrapati" with "Rashtra". -adhyaksh`, a more consistent and gender-neutral Hindi translation of the word president. In fact, all political parties commonly use the word 'adhyaksh' when referring to their national and state presidents.

Therefore, there is no reason why the word "Rashtrapati" should not be replaced by "Rashtriya-adhyaksh" or another term "pradhan" which is used to refer to the president in the draft Indian constitution in Hindi, makes the nomenclature of the highest constitutional position gender neutral. The 'Rashtrapati' dispute, although the result of cold political rationality, has given us the opportunity to reflect on the patriarchal origins of some common Hindi terms such as udyogpati (used for industrialists), sabhapati (used for president/man), lakhpati (used for millionaires) and crorepati (used for billionaires) etc. to create gender-neutral terms for them.

The world always defaults to male gender, a structure reinforced by language. As humans, our collective identity is understood as masculine - we use 'man' to describe our species and 'humanity' as a way to unify us.

In the book Invisible Women: Data Bias in a World Designed for Men, Caroline Criado Perez writes that: "The view of men as a human flaw is fundamental in the structure of the structure. of human society. Our culture and language follow a general framework of masculinity, where, she explains, "masculine prejudice is so ingrained in our psyche that even real words neutrality [like a doctor or an actor] is also interpreted as masculinity."

In some cases, the male form speaks for all genders: for example, in the Indian legal system, documents written in male, are considered to include female unless otherwise stated. . In many ways, language both reflects and creates gender inequalities that exist in society. The way we speak affects the way we think and the way we interpret the world around us. So as we try to recreate our default gender values and build a more inclusive and socially responsible culture, we must also consider language.

Global languages fall into three gender-related categories: gendered languages like Spanish (where nouns and pronouns have gender), genderless languages like Mandarin Chinese (where nouns and pronouns have gender), and genderless languages like Mandarin. genderless words and pronouns) and gendered languages like English. (with gendered pronouns and genderless nouns). The gender structure of the language we speak will have the effect of making us more or less aware of gender. With gender language we have to think about gender when conjugating verbs or using nouns, so is it possible that gender stereotypes and gender power structures are more likely to affect our thoughts and views on gender more?

By learning Hindi, a gender language, I realised that I was expected to respect men, sometimes more than women. I'm not allowed to say the same thing to my male and female classmates: with my boys, I'm taught to use honorific plurals (Aap kya kar rahe hain? on Tu kya kar raha hai? to ask "What are you doing?" "), but respect for women can only be shown by using feminine endings (Aap kya kar rahi hain? on Tu kya kar rahi hai?). Although we can respect both genders, we can't use the same language constructs, which draw attention to the gender of the person we're talking to.

Depending on where we come from and how we learn the language, we may be taught to show equal respect to men and women, or to treat them differently. While formal language can involve respect, formal language can also be used to show intimacy or affection. In Hindi, some wives use aap, the respectful way of saying "you", to refer to their husbands, while husbands use tum, the informal "you" for their wives, and other couples. use the same pronoun l for each other.

The four most spoken gender languages in the world are Hindi, Spanish, French and Arabic. They share many of the same gender patterns: masculine is the default grammatical gender, mixed groups use masculine endings, and feminine nouns are derived from masculine versions. By their structure, they underscore Criado Perez's observation of male defects. For example, Spanish follows a generic masculine word when it is unclear whether a subject is masculine or feminine; one male friend is an amigo and one female friend is an amiga, but a group of friends are amigos. The masculine default also applies to mixed groups, such as amigos, that use masculine endings. Similar to adjectives: a good group of friends is buenas amigos, but as soon as there is a man in the group, it will be buenos amigos. It is also clear that masculine is the standard gender in Spanish, as it is the default form used in dictionaries.

The languages we speak influence the way we build society and can even set a precedent for gender equality in our social systems. In a 2011 study, Jennifer Prewitt-Freilino, an associate professor at the Rhode Island School of Design, along with colleagues, found that countries with languages by gender have higher average gender inequality. Research also shows that gendered languages like English have the most equality, although genderless languages can be expected to have the most equality.

"Historically, genderless language can cause the mind to turn to masculinity, without calling it specifically [as suppose the term 'congressman' refers to men]".

Cielo

That's why we find that natural gender language seems to be better because when they make reformed language they create new genderless words in gendered language, this draws attention to modifying the gender system [and facilitating the recognition of prejudices].

Language is not something that always has to remain the same

Not everyone fits in the rigid definitions of the 'constructed' gender today. Or, better still, we fail to accept ourselves as being clung onto the myopic view of addressing gender through language. What pronouns do you use to define yourself? He? She? Surname? Something completely different? This is a question asked with increasing frequency as acceptance of multiple genders and sexual identities increases.

Some languages, such as Chinese and Persian, do not assign gender to nouns or already have a form of sexism for everyone. But in languages whose traditional grammar is based on male or female-specific options, the answer to this question may still need some explanation. So how do you talk about being weird or non-binary or gender-nonconforming in grammatically gendered languages? How do you address your language fluidly ?

In recent years, LGBTQ activists and linguists around the world have advocated for a more inclusive language, by creating entirely new non-binary terms and by improving and existing grammatical structures. It's not always easy. For some people, continuing to explain why they need more inclusive language can be difficult, intimidating, or simply tedious. And it can be dangerous: In the United States alone, hate crimes against the LGBTQ community have increased over the past three years, according to the FBI.

Given the rise in realisation of the existence of a 'third gender' or 'fluidity in gender', a lot of changes have been witnessed in the languages themselves as they strive to be more inclusive.

English grammar does not discriminate except for assigning a masculine or feminine singular pronoun. In 2019, the Merriam-Webster Dictionary added "they" as a pronoun to use for "a single person whose gender identity is not binary". Two years ago, in 2017, "them" as a form of sexism was added to the Associated Press Stylebook, the gold standard of journalistic categories. Meanwhile, the Washington Post changed its style guide in 2015.

Critics of the change have argued that the singular and plural "them" can confuse and obscure the syntax of sentences. Shakespeare and Jane Austen, among many other famous English writers, do not think so. They used "they" and "their" in the singular, as was customary in English until Victorian grammarians changed direction and imposed "he" above all.

Spanish has feminine and masculine cases added to all nouns. Even the word for "the" is different whether the noun is masculine (el) or feminine (ella). However, some Spanish speakers say it doesn't have to be. In the United States, it is now common to use "x" or "@" to create sexist names: that's why you may see "Latinx" or "Latin @" instead of the Latino binary (male) and Latina (female). However, the widespread use of this form angered some Spanish speakers, who saw it as a figurative term imposed on Spanish by English-speaking Americans rather than an inclusive move from within.

A new movement is underway globally for a gender neutral language, ignited by the teenagers in Argentina who, as The Post reported, are leading the charge to remove gender from their languages.

"In classrooms and everyday conversations, young people are changing the way they speak and write - replacing the male or female 'o' 'a' with the gender-neutral 'e' in a number of words - to change what they see as gender profoundly. Their efforts are at the heart of a global debate about gender, amid the growing possibilities of non-identifying identities. binary around the world". The movement caused a stir in Argentina last year after a young activist, Natalia Mira, used inclusive language in an interview and was attacked by a reporter during a live broadcast.

Spanish is a widely spoken language around the world, so there's also no set standard, as different dialects and communities have their own preferences. Another form to know is "she" as a gender-neutral pronoun along with ella (she) and él (he).

Arabic is a grammatically different gender language, with every verb, noun and adjective always conjugated with a masculine or feminine case. Male is the default plural, even if it's just a single male in another group of girls. Modern Standard Arabic, based on Classical Quranic Arabic, also has a dual option for nouns and verbs that are not related to a particular gender. As a result, some people use the dual of them and you - "huma" (هما) and "intuma" (انتما) as a sexist substitute. The colloquial Arabic spoken today has largely eliminated duality, so this form may seem very formal to those who do not know it.

Others play with the language in different ways, such as swapping masculine and feminine pronouns or one speaker choosing to reverse the paternal dominance of the male case and default to the female form. Arabic has many dialects, each with its own distinct grammatical and word structure, so different communities have developed their own colloquial codes.

For example, in some dialects of Tunisia, the use of feminine pronouns is common to all. For gay and feminist communities in the Middle East, the struggle for social *acceptance has come to another conversation: how to define words like gay, bisexual and transgender in Arabic. Some people transcribe English words in LGBTQ by default, others prefer the phrase "mujtama`a al meem" (مجتمع الميم) - or community meem - a reference to the Arabic letter with the m sound that begins the words. This term after being translated into Arabic. After years of efforts by activists in Lebanon, the words "mithly" (لي) and "mithila" (مثلية) have now become the norm in many media (replacing the previous term). here, translated as "deviant") or "perverse").*

Community awareness and acceptance of this inclusive language is still very low in Arabic-speaking countries. To change this, Arabic speakers describe their efforts as part of a larger movement to de-Westernize and reorient the discussion of gender and sexuality. Instead of simply copying English words, they try to hone and standardize the language needed to talk about these topics from the rich vocabulary and history of Arabic, such as taking Inspired by poetry describing same-sex relationships in the Middle Ages. The work is also supported by feminist groups, such as Wiki Gender, a collaborative platform that creates a gender-neutral Arabic dictionary.

Hebrew, like Arabic, assigns genders to verbs, nouns, and adjectives based on nouns. Jewish LGBTQ activists and feminists have also advocated reversing gender segregation, such as choosing to default to the plural as female or using a "mixed" gender, sometimes masculine. and sometimes feminine for the same person.

Among Hebrew speakers in Israel and other Jewish communities, there are also ways to eliminate the grammatical binary and express verbs or nouns in a gender-neutral way.

For example, the Non-binary Hebrew Project has systematically constructed a third gender in Hebrew, based in part on non-binary and exotic references in Hebrew texts such as the Talmud and Torah. As the group argues: The male rabbis who wrote the Mishnah, a third-century book of Jewish commentaries, recognized some sort of gender classification, so certainly do Jews today.

In Israel, a related approach is to put both masculine and feminine cases in nouns and verbs, sometimes with a period in between them, so that it all comes in smoothly. For example, "I write" - "kotev" (כותב) in masculine and "kotevet" (כותבת) in female - alternatively it could be כותב.ת in this form.

A Jewish summer camp in the United States designed another build that included transgender or non-binary campers: with "chanich" (חניך), male campers, and "chanichah" (חניכה) , female campers, now they have "chanichol". (חניכול), an unidentified camper. In addition to this new singular ending "ol", they created a new plural ending: "imot", which combines "im" at the end of masculine plural nouns and "ot" at the end of the noun. female. Despite the many alternatives floating around, the Hebrew Language

Academy refuses to consider them.

The famously complex German syntax includes masculine, feminine, and exotic grammatical genders. Neutrality doesn't generally apply to everyone, with a few notable exceptions. It changes. In January 2019, Hannover became the first German city to require all official communications, such as emails, flyers and forms, to use a neutral name. For example, instead of using the words male (wähler) and female (wählerin) voters, municipalities will instead use words that do not convey one gender or another, such as voter (wählende). This is in line with previous rulings by other German agencies, such as the Federal Ministry of Justice, which in 2014 required all state agencies to use gender-neutral language in their documents, the Guardian reported.

The languages are rich and vibrant, so of course there are other options around. As Germany's DW explained, "Traditionally, gender segregation in German is indicated by the suffixes 'r' or 'rn' for male (singular and plural), and 'in'. or 'innen' for females (singular and plural)... Currently efforts to shorten the space for acceptable forms of distinction have included the introduction of a capital "I" in compound nouns used in compound nouns to refer to both men and women "

French also assigns masculine or feminine gender to all personal nouns; references to a group of people are identified by default by masculine pronouns unless the group is purely female. France's legendary guardian of the language, the

French Academy, is fine with this. Others are not. For many years, a campaign mainly led by French feminists has sought to democratize this more subtle Romance language by pushing back against gender norms that have been confusing for English-speaking students from England for centuries. According to critics, certain linguistic constructs keep women from being recognized for their personal and professional competencies. different professions.

Instead, the idea is to use an asterisk to combine upper-case endings and create a more inclusive, gender-neutral plural - like "friends" for friends - the first step does not privilege male as a standard nor excludes male and a gender spectrum from the syntax. However, every action has a reaction, and in 2017 the French government banned the use of inclusive and sexist language in official documents.

In 2015, Sweden added the word "hen" to the country's official dictionary - a sexist pronoun that linguists have proposed as an alternative to the male pronoun "han" and the female pronoun. "hon".

Five years ago, almost nobody in Sweden knew that word. According to experts, the "chicken" revolution in Sweden has two main origins: LGBT groups promote pronouns as a way to raise awareness of their cause. Support for the idea, however, also comes from a more unexpected side: daycares, kindergartens and preschools like Egalia increasingly argue that the use of pronouns allows children to grow up without feeling the impact of gender stereotypes.

In Argentina, Mira's use of gender-neutral language in a television interview helped her spread across the country. Now, the new grammar form is being officially accepted.

The faculties of at least five universities across Argentina have announced that they will accept this "inclusive" use of Spanish in academic work. Gender-neutral words were splattered on campaign banners, flyers and graffiti across the capital. After a judge caused controversy using the form in a recent court ruling, a panel of judges overseeing judges said judges are now allowed to use sexist words . Books have been translated into sexist Spanish, including a version of "The Little Prince". This form has reached Hispanic speakers in the United States, sparking discussions in university language programs.

Just weeks before becoming the president-elect of Argentina, Alberto Fernández used it publicly in a speech to high school students. And the new form has appeared in WhatsApp messages and Instagram posts as thousands of people, including Mira, prepare to join the largest annual gathering of women in Argentine history over the weekend in early October.

But removing gender in Spanish, the language spoken by more than 577 million people worldwide, is not as simple as using a sexist pronoun. The Royal Spanish Academy, the preeminent authority on secular languages, said such grammatical changes were "unnecessary and contrived". For many Spanish speakers, this form of sexism is a misnomer. The linguistic form has divided the feminist movement from which it emerged. While some in the movement insisted on speaking in a way that included non-binary people, others resisted, preferring to emphasize women's voices by using female words. count. Others wonder if it's worth the effort to change the language - will it make a difference?

But when Mira and her friends sang at their protest, sexism was everywhere - in the songs they had memorised, on the banners hanging from the marble building behind them.

Cognitive scientist Lera Boroditsky says the way we speak can shape the way we think. For example, the word "bridge" is feminine in German but masculine in Spanish. In experiments, Boroditsky found that German speakers described the bridge with feminine-related adjectives, such as beautiful or elegant, while Spanish speakers were more likely to describe the tree. is stereotypically masculine — tall, stout, or strong.

"If you can do it even with tables and chairs and watering cans, it becomes a lot easier and more persuasive for humans," says Boroditsky.

Sometimes these gender differences can have real effects in society. World Bank researchers found evidence that "grammatical gender" has a negative causal effect on women's labour force participation. And a recent study of speakers in Sweden, where the gender-neutral pronoun "hen" was added to the official Swedish dictionary in 2015, shows that the application of the non-binary pronoun is associated with more favorable attitudes towards women and the LGBTQ community.

In France, activists introduced a mixed style known as inclusive writing, adding both gendered endings to a word to make it genderless (ami e s). Organisations are also showing their support, with the European Union setting up an autonomous body called the European Institute for Gender Equality, which works to uphold gender equality on the basis of policies. and even funded research on language reform.

"Language is a constantly evolving process, but people feel there is a good side and a bad side. The problem is that not everyone agrees on that wording. There has been an important interplay between conversations about gender and identity, and how they are expressed in language. For years, the Latino community in the United States has discussed different identification terms - first pushing back the word "Hispanic" which was seen as a colonial word promoting Hispanic heritage, then using uses "Latino /a as a way to bring together different ethnicities in a meaningful way. and is currently working on reforming terms by gender through the label "Latinx." But despite "Latinx" used by some young

people in the United States, many Latinos in other countries do not identify with it.

Even if it's not fully endorsed, it's now part of the conversation. It's exciting to see this unfold as a social scientist. You can talk about whether you don't like the word or not, but once you use it, it really affects the way you think about politics.

People may reject a gender-neutral language as unnecessary or purely ideological, but Pérez's research shows it does have an impact on public opinion. Her 2019 study with Margit Tavits found that the use of gender-neutral pronouns increases positive attitudes towards women and LGBTQ+ people, reduces the prominence of male identities, and thus causes less gender bias.

Pérez explains: "Our language essentially directs our attention to certain aspects of reality and away from other aspects of reality. If I speak English, I can hardly speak English. more male/female distinction than if I spoke Spanish". You can't change the culture, but as some of these gender-neutral terms reveal themselves, you can adjust the terms you use. Maybe we can't change the entire vocabulary, but once you introduce some sexist options to the extent that people use them or subscribe to them, it's very important.

People have also found ways to create sexist choices in existing language constructs. Shweta Vaidya, a transgender writer living in Mumbai, uses the Hindi plural form hum (we) as a sexist substitute. Hindi, as people speak Hindi in places like Kanpur, Chhattisgarh and Madhya Pradesh in central India.

Gender identity and expression are unique in each culture, but the language around them is still limited. Western definitions of gender differences tend to overshadow how we view gender identity, even in other parts of the world. "Transgender in the Western vocabulary is a system that we follow right now, there are certain limits to what people consider the norm. Gender has been colonized – gender minorities like the Fa'afafine community in Samoa are portrayed as gays, despite their own understanding of gender identity," adds Vaidya. "We knew there was a language bleaching where cultural nuances around gender were lost in translation, but we didn't correct our mistakes. Translation is not easy, especially when trying to translate cultural experiences into identities.

But even if cultures have languages for gender differences, that doesn't guarantee understanding or acceptance. The Hijras, a sociocultural group of transgender women and transgender people known as the "third sex", has a long history in South Asian culture. But for centuries, hijra and "transgender" have been used interchangeably, leading to misunderstanding and underappreciation of India's transgender community. When the Transgender Bill was passed last year, the Hindi translation used the term ubhaylingi (bisexual) to represent transgender people, so the law does not protect or recognize the community as a whole. Vaidya explains: "Many transgender people have repeatedly asked, 'If we were the third gender, who would be the first? In this way, language has an undeniable impact on those who can't access equal rights.

Language reform is possible, but it takes time. This does not necessarily mean dismantling existing systems, but making space for more comprehensive options. Instead of letting language shape our view of the world, we can push in the other direction, asking ourselves how we can reflect our world through our language choices.

"It's hard to think about language systems without thinking about the more globalised context in which we live," says Prewitt-Freilino. "I think it's about give and take - what terms are made; how language changes and is used in different ways. What really interests me is the interplay between language and culture. .

In a landmark decision, the Rajya Sabha Secretariat ordered various ministries to use gender-neutral provisions from the next session of Parliament. The decision was made in response to a letter written by MP Shiv Sena Priyanka Chaturvedi to Parliamentary Affairs Minister Prahlad Joshi seeking to change the usage of phrases like "no sir" which are commonly used in responses to the House of Commons.

In a letter dated September 8, MP Maharashtra said they were "concerned about following the gender mainstreaming institution" of Parliament, which is the "temple of democracy".

To this letter, the Rajya Sabha Secretariat replied that "in accordance with the conventions and rules of business conduct and procedure in Rajya Sabha, all proceedings of the House of Commons are settled for the Speaker and Answers to parliamentary questions that are part of the discussion are also addressed to the President only, however, Ministries will be advised to give gender-neutral responses to the questions. of Parliament from the next session of Rajya Sabha.

That is your space, This is my territory

Gender is a social relationship that flows throughout life, historically and geographically dependent, and created by what we do rather than by who we are. For example, we know how the roles of women and men were defined in our families at the time. The early 1900s were very different from how they are defined today. Social relations between women and men change a lot as we move geographically from the northern matriarchal communities in Eastern India to Haryana villages under strong patriarchy. Notice how the meanings attached to being a son or daughter changes as you "establish" social relationships with your friends and loved ones throughout your life as you grow up.

Judith Butler (1990) argues that gender identity is realised and there's nothing "natural" about it. She claims that male and female bodies don't necessarily mean male and female identity - and that gender identity is nothing more than the effect of a performance.

In Butler's words: .....

gender is repeated stylisation of the body, a set of repeated acts within a highly rigid regulatory framework that congeal over time to produce the appearance of substance, of a natural sort of being....The effect of gender, hence, must be understood as the mundane way in which bodily gestures, movements, and all styles of various kinds constitute the illusion of an abiding gendered self. (Butler, 1990: 33)

Understood in this way, gender relations are socially constructed and context-dependent - they are different in time and space. Although we have argued that gender identity is flexible, we also know that most people don't attribute intentionality to their performance according to their gender - gender do not feel fluent or open to choice. In fact, it often appears as a fixed identity which authorises and binds them in different ways. Think of the little girls getting scolded for being loud and not showing their feminine characteristics, are not shy and serve the elders. Think of the embarrassed boys crying. Not that girls' bodies are innately accustomed to good and shyness or that boys do not have tear glands. However, by continually reinforcing certain behaviours over others, we strengthen this category. These repeated love relationships also materialise as spatial relationships - as in the concepts of public and private spaces.

Space is not a neutral context to explain gender identity, but an active ingredient that helps

also structure gender-dynamic enactments. Therefore, we can say that gender and space

constituting each other, that is, they constituting each other. Every action happens somewhere at some time. She needs space and she needs time. Society's subsequent processes are also spatial and temporal processes. Our daily actions and our society manifests itself in certain spatial configurations and thus "production space" (Lefebvre 1991).

These places, in turn, help shape our identity and allow certain social processes while inhibiting others. If space were an integral part of our social nature relationships, it is imperative that we understand our space to try to understand ourselves as social creatures. The transformation of economic and social life with the birth of Industrialization or colonialism necessarily played a role in how spatial relationships are shaped.

The commodity industry has caused a great change in the way economic and social activities operate. Factories are set up in urban areas and surrounded by crowded buildings for male immigrant workers. In pre-industrial societies, men, women, and children all participated in economic activity that often takes place within families. The spatial division of social activities have resulted in somewhat fixed gender roles and domains. Suitable places for women are considered her home and her work is mainly related to reproduction. While the men had to venture out and work in factories. They are considered manufacturers. If seen in public spaces, especially without men, women will be suspected of promiscuity. The roles of men and women and their place in space have been studied through places that were strictly scripted in the early 20th century, especially for the middle and upper classes of women in the cities of the industrialised world (Rothman, 1978). Cities in these parts of the world also have special shapes. Chicago Urban School Sociologists, analysing urban mutations, discussed the emerging spatial separation in the American cities in the early 20th century.

Their concentric city pattern marked the space population density based on race and ethnicity and a core description of the activity of suburban residential areas. Although they do not explicitly discuss gender, their plans show the domestic central and periphery production core clearly demarcates the positions of men and women in town.

Feminist scholars see these segregated landscapes as a material expression of our patriarchal heritage and capitalist societies. In Chicago too, in the late 19th and early 20th centuries, the distinction of spheres and definite roles went unnoticed. When women started using it openly as means of transport such as the tramway to get into the city centre and meet In canteens and theatres, they began organising political and social action efforts. They fought for women's suffrage and, after World War II, "equal pay for equal work" movement started in the urban context. Using the term "city sanitation", many classes of women are fighting for better services in the city and reorganising garbage collection, clean milk and care for mothers and children. They campaign for women's political rights arguing that care of the city is a natural extension of their role as caretakers of the home.

Gender, like any other type of difference, does not work in isolation. Other aspects of the identities such as class, race, ethnicity, age, etc., combine to influence opportunities and

position in life. This concept is called intersectionality (Crenshaw, 1989).

In the context of the city, we find that middle- and upper-class women experience the city very differently than their working-class sisters. Working-class women, in addition to working in factories, also work in indoor spaces of upper and middle class women. Thus, while their work is made invisible, middle-class women can go out and participate in public life. Working class on the other hand, especially those from immigrant groups, struggle with poverty and distinguish in order to maintain a certain respect for themselves, who emphasised

strongly against notions of working-class solidarity and hegemonic ideals of masculinity. Urban slums have emerged as a result of economic and social transformations in the lives of immigrant populations and they also become areas of the city, where these notions of masculinity translate into territories and gangs.

Some researchers have also shown that women are more afraid of public spaces than men

town. Valentine (1989) describes this fear as a "spatial expression of patriarchy" and as limiting women's choices in sticking to urban spaces. Women are most afraid of rape and

of aggression when encroaching upon unfamiliar territory in urban areas. Strict land use patterns that separate residential areas from work areas, effectively emptying large urban areas into evening hours, creating a secluded space where women (and men) are afraid to take risks. Therefore, there is a paradox that even when women are afraid to go out in public, they are vulnerable to sexual violence in their home. It is now widely recognized that most cases of violence against women; the perpetrators are family members or friends - partners, co-workers, relatives and acquaintances (Hanson and Pratt, 1988). However, it is the fear of public spaces today that are even more common and limited to women's movements in the city (Pain, 2001; Miethe, 1995).

There is also another view that a city is hindering women's access to city space. In his book "The Sphinx in the City", Wilson (1991) asserts that the city provides strength to Unleash the potential of women. Its wide open space and the anonymity provided to them by the city

freedom. Women can escape the narrow confines of cramped neighbourhoods where their mobility is monitored and experience more freedom of movement in the city space. Moreover, the spaces of the city. create opportunities for celebrations and public gatherings that allow women to participate in urban life Activities. However, this participation is usually temporary. The researchers argue that such a performance only gives 'negative freedom' leading to invisibility and the "extinction of society". (Garber, 2000).

Women fear the public space, rightly given the fear of security hanging between a guillotine. When the public space is hostile, women have no choice but to accept the misogynistic definition of a woman's rightful place in society.

A 'Save the Children' 2018 report on public space safety for Indian girls found that one in three girls was scared to cross narrow local alleys, as well as the way to the school or local market. Nearly three in five girls said they felt unsafe in crowded public spaces. More than a quarter of adolescent girls perceive an increased risk of physical assault, including rape, when venturing into a public space, while a third of girls are expected to be touched. inappropriate entry or even harassment.

"Khadar ki Ladkiyan " is part of a larger project called "Gender the Smart City" funded by the Arts and Humanities Research Council, UK, and led by Ayona Datta, Professor of Geography Humanities at University College London. The project aims to understand how women use technology and its impact on how they negotiate about homes and towns on a daily basis. The participants were from Madanpur Khadar, a resettlement colony in Delhi. Jagori, a feminist NGO in Delhi, and Safetipin, a well-known ICT social enterprise, have collaborated with Datta on this project.

Datta describes the Khadar girls as "urban millennials living in the paradox of India's digital revolution in the urban age.... They are mobile phone users and active on social networks, through which they create relationships of solidarity, friendship and support networks... in these paradoxes, they stand out. rising as young millennial citizens, with gender, living in "new" and "old" India, eager for their song, she continued, "lighting up on opportunities and challenges in navigating the city as these women leave home to pursue paid work and education, and constrained by the limitations of traditional gender roles. `

A very important aspect of the daily lives of Khadar girls is violence, not only sexually, but also structurally. They repeat that the state knows "we need better roads, they know we need public transport". They knew we needed water and toilets. They know we need safe roads. The problem is not lack of knowledge but lack of interest.

In 2012, a young student, Jyoti Singh, was raped inside a moving bus by six men, then thrown onto the street to die. Her parents had migrated to New Delhi from a small village in Uttar Pradesh in search of a better life for their children. His father worked as a porter at the Delhi airport and sold his ancestral land to pay for his education. The tragedy that befell her highlights the struggles of this new generation of disadvantaged women and girls, empowered by education, forced to work to earn an income for their families. Her gruesome rape and murder underscored the impending need to make public spaces safer for women.

"When we talk about security, we are not just talking about violence," said Kalpana Vishwanath, sociologist and urban safety and women's rights activist. It's about eliminating fear." 2015. Citing the example of Delhi, "there is a large amount of fear, which may be higher than the actual manifestation of violence.

Vishwanath, co-founder and CEO of Safetipin, a social enterprise that uses data and technology to build safer and more inclusive smart cities, argues that safety is more than just an experience. experiences of violence, but rather a fear of violence that makes women more dependent on men for protection, or forces them to limit their mobility. She also rightly pointed out that when women are seen as victims, the story becomes one of protections rather than one of rights. "And we say that safety is a right, not fear of violence."

"Cities are not well planned; they are not gender specific. Should we ask ourselves, are we planning cities to be gender inclusive? Are we planning for more transportation? Are the places well lit? We need to address many stakeholders, not just the police. We need to talk to city planners, municipalities and local governments to build safer cities," she said. `` Instead of a top-down model that planners decide on. We need to build cities that locals want, women want. A safe city where you can live without fear.

The death sentence for rapist Nirbhaya has attracted a lot of attention lately - but how life has really changed for young women like her, who study, work, Watching movies and travelling, who bravely overcome the hostile world for a more fulfilling life? Justice for the 2012 gang rape, and the crimes since, can only come when our public spaces are fully open, when women feel welcome and at ease in the city.

Sustainable Development Goals (SDGs) 5 and 11, as well as the New Urban Agenda, emphasising gender equity and safe, resilient and inclusive cities. That means Women can enjoy urban life in all its aspects as much as men. In other words, women have as many rights to the city as men. Although the "right to the city" mediates existing social inequalities in terms of class, religion, race, ethnicity and caste in the Indian context (Kabeer, 1994),

Above all these actions is a layer of gender inequality. Although violence against women is legally prohibited in many countries, centuries-old veils of superstition and cultural and religious practices continue to be violate women's rights. Women's frequent contact with forms of violence in their daily lives reinforce gender inequalities and restrictions on their mobility in cities and metropolitan areas white spaces. This "everyday" and "normal" violent nature or fear often limits or weakens their interactions with the city. It also violates their 'right to a public space' and thus their "right to the city", understood as a state in which all citizens have equal rights and access to the city and its public spaces (UNHABITAT, Department of Women and Child Development, Government of the Elderly Delhi, Jagori and UN Women, 2010).

As a result, women are often reluctant to be in public spaces without a 'good' reason, as they are still seen as 'illegal' users of public spaces. Women feel the need to prove their "purpose" to stay in public spaces and rarely tend to sit in parks or standing on the street corner, smoking, or just watching the world go by like a man. Many activists, Scholars and feminists believe that true women's empowerment is allowing women to "roam" the city, as noted above (Phadke et al., 2009). In an effort to create a safe space for women, barriers to entry have been installed. People in a hierarchical society like India, tend to exclude "non-priority" people, i.e. men of low income and caste, from other social segments. Thus, women activists in India also point out that Public spaces cannot be made safe for women at the cost of others being (the "unwanted" parts of society such as lower class men) free. Public spaces must be real "public"; they must be accessible to everyone everywhere day. Translated by public space, this means the rights of all citizens - regardless of class, caste, gender, religion, sexual orientation - must be protected. A city can only belong to a woman, when it belongs for everyone (Phadke, 2007)

A study of public spaces in Kolkata shows that in pre-colonial times, although public spaces experienced gender segregation, the concept of participation or competition remained absent. In colonial Calcutta, the controversy revolved mainly around the exclusion of those who were not considered culturally and socially sophisticated rather than spatial (Choudhury, 2017). For women, there is no access to neighbourhood public spaces or umbrellas. They are not allowed to participate in organised activities in public spaces (Sen & Sengupta, 2016; Sengupta, 2018).

In pre-colonial times, women, regardless of class and class, had restrictions on the use of public places. Upper class women are required to maintain 'power' and lower class women due to the rules of the right not to touch are not allowed in all public places. The struggle for independence, social movements and reforms aimed at empowering the lower classes, improved educational facilities broke down many of the barriers that prevented Bengali women from accessing public spaces and public life. Over time, community festivals such as Durga Puja have provided the canvas for women to renegotiate their access to public spaces (De Matteis, 2018).

In present-day Kolkata, contested spaces such as the Burrabazar wholesale market, parks, paan shops, teahouses, populated mainly by men restrict the participation of women, while some spaces Cultural gatherings and literary works such as Nandan, Dakshinapan are relatively less controversial. but provides access to more educated and middle-class women (Choudhury, 2017; Paul, 2011). Tea stalls, strategically located to maximise participation, are the focal point for discussions and debates among young and old, playing an important role in social, economic and politics and seem to be male-dominated (Bandyopadhyay et al., 2012; Paul, 2011).

Public spaces in Kolkata are controversial, preventing women from fully participating (Bandyopadhyay et al., 2012; Bhattacharyya, 2016; Choudhury, 2017; Roy, 2003). Kolkata women mostly use avoidance and protection strategies and rarely find the courage to speak out. Women's limited access to public spaces in Kolkata is indicative of a social fear shaped by the way space is perceived (Paul, 2011; Sen and Sengupta, 2016).

Most of the streets, especially in the commercial and business areas of Kolkata, are busy and active throughout the day. Almost 65% of trips in Kolkata daily are made on foot (IDFC & Superior Global, 2008). Kolkata's congested streets are also home to nearly 70,000 homeless people, of which about 78% are men and 80% work in the informal sector (Roy & Siddique, 2018). Men are more present in public spaces throughout the day, moving around, sitting, chatting, waiting; while women are considered to be just moving, too limited by purpose and time of day (Fairchild, 2007; Paul, 2011).

In December 2012, a large number of men and women in Delhi took to the streets to protest the government's lack of interest in making Delhi a safe space for women. The protests were sparked by the brutal gang rape of a middle-class young student home after watching a movie with her friend. The incident changed the discourse involved rape and brought a previously taboo subject into the public arena. A special commission headed by Judge Verma solicited public opinion on violence against women laws and received a large number of answers. The recommendations of this committee are with great urgency translated into law. While the protests and subsequent actions both played an important role in initiating a discussion about women's safety, we still have a long way to go.

What is your experience?

Are cities safer for women today than they were in 2012?

What more do you need to achieve the same ?

Some scholars have argued that the historical cores of many present-day cities such as Jodhpur, Benares and Ujjain are places where women feel safer and more comfortable than we sayn emerging urban centres such as Gurgaon or Noida. They claim that this difference is

human scale, pedestrian distance and dense urban environment of collective life. According to this argument, cities are safer when city streets are more than traffic and functional areas instead of expanding homes, shops and community spaces (Desai, 2007).

However, modern cities are designed for private cars that most women don't own. Furthermore, the interior confront and alienate the built cultures of these cities that do not allow free interaction with the spaces from the city. Most of the public spaces designed like city parks, shared office spaces and the like are single-use spaces and largely occupied by men. On the other hand, if women are seen "hanging out" in public spaces for no apparent reason (such as grocery shopping or accompanying their children to park) is considered a cowardly act. Indian law also reinforces the same understanding of appropriate and inappropriate behaviour in particular spaces. Although prostitution itself is not Illegal. The Prevention of Unscrupulous Traffic Act (1986) regulates solicitation of prostitution in public space. Therefore, any woman who does not conform to the traditional notions of "appropriate" or "Proper" body movements are very suspicious and likely to be detected by the police.

There is a lot of public debate about women's clothing, movements, and activism. It often happens that even when a woman is raped or sexually harassed, she is still blamed for being in the wrong place, at the wrong time, in the wrong clothes, or in the wrong style or images. Such an attitude raises questions about women's rights to be alone in public spaces. On the one hand, women in India find more freedom and mobility in urban areas because they

away from class and rigid gender hierarchy in their home communities. On the other hand, the same patriarchal structures take on a different form in the urban context. For example, researchers have pointed to the lack of public toilets for women in urban (and rural) areas.

white spaces.

By not making urban spaces well-lit, safe, accessible (via public transport) and having basic amenities (such as public restrooms), planners made sure that women's access to public spaces will remain restricted. Even in places where there are public restrooms for women, there is a large disparity in the number of women's and men's toilets. Suppose, I think at any given time, a quarter of women get their period, and women have to

use the toilet longer, which is a blatant denial of women's rights because citizens don't have enough infrastructure for their needs in public spaces. It's also a common sight in urban areas when seeing men urinating along a wall.

Women interviewed in a study in Mumbai expressed their feelings of being embarrassed and annoyed when walking past a man urinating in public. Distinctive urban space commitments and expectations for men and women create unequal access and comfort levels for both sexes.

Why can't women and men participate equitably in urban activities?

Watch the movement of men and women walking around your city. In all likelihood, you will see women walking with shopping bags, college backpacks or surrounded by children. So walking alone, women will often talk (or pretend to talk) on their cell phones, to create barriers between them and those around them. Most men will be seen slightly bowing their heads and crossing the arms in front of his chest. You can also notice groups of men playing

cards on the ground or standing next to panwala without much of a clear purpose. A part of

Their group might be sitting on a park bench with their legs spread wide looking at women and men as they pass.

Such bodily gestures reveal deep connections between gendered ways of being and unspoken things like behavioural expectations in urban public spaces. As we can see, much of the discourse about women and cities revolves around women's safety depicting women as people in need of protection and therefore public figures in public space is inappropriate, especially if it is purposeless. Women's engagement as citizens with legal rights to inhabit and occupy public spaces are often not well understood. Women Movements in India have traditionally also been more vocal on issues such as domestic violence, rape and dowry but was largely silent about women's rights to public spaces.

In their writings that is from the Gender and Space project called 'Why have a lover?' Shilpa Phadke, Shilpa Ranade and Sameera Khan (2011) argues that the desire for pleasure, enjoyment and the fight against violence is interconnected. According to them, the quest to find a space free of violence lies in the fact to exclude and separate "us" from "them", often punishing "them" with violence to Protect us.' Such conceptualization is restrictive and inherently violent. On the other hand, the quest for pleasure can be framed in more inclusive terms and is necessarily related to the right to a life free from violence in public space. They then argued that loitering as a policy would provide an opportunity for Comprehensive, safe and fun city.

Loitering refers to being in a public space without a clear purpose - also known as hanging out. It is a radical idea that challenges not only social norms but also the desired goals of the left and the right to make cities safe for women. The concept of women as people in need

protection and discourse about women's safety is inherently limited. If such a goal is achieved

through the exclusion, monitoring and control of women's participation in urban spaces, then

Women's rights to the city will never be established. The right to walk has the potential to change the terms of negotiations in the city's public spaces and create possibilities. The city has completely changed, not only for women, but for everyone" (Phadke, Khan and Ranade, 2011:178).

It's not that safety is not a desired outcome, but rather by empowering trespassers, we conceptualise the relationship between gender and urban space much more broadly. Moving on from safety politics to pleasure politics, the authors urge us to question the ideas around respect and sexuality of women, and question surveillance practices and exclusion. Going for a walk not only challenges patriarchal notions, but the act of pleasure also bothers the capitalist urban order. A walk after that is a civil right, a right to the city that doesn't rely upon owning private property. Gay, lesbian and transgender people have very different experiences in the city when compared to people of the opposite sex (and even when compared with each other). Simple gestures like using Public restrooms, shopping for clothes, taking the train, all of which can be uncomfortable for the unfit perfect in masculine-feminine binary.

Transgender people and transgender people also face discrimination when looking for housing or other structured work ideal of a nuclear family (Valentine, 1993). Also in the Indian context, the gay and lesbian populations are subjected to discrimination and harassment, socially and legally and are therefore not visible actors in public spaces. However it's fast changing with the gay community in India claiming their space through gay parades and active pride. Most of India's metropolitan cities, especially Delhi, Mumbai and Kolkata, have hosted the event of these walks. On the other hand, transgender people (Hijra, Kothi, Khusre) identity was recognized by the supreme court in 2014. Even before that, the cities of India always had Transgender people as seen conspicuously at weddings, births and festivals. However, they are often feared or reverent in a way that prevents them from engaging with urban life that is not specified by their sexual identity.

For cities to be truly inclusive and for the diversity of urban life to flourish, we will need to meet the different needs of all men, women, transgender and transgender people of different ages, classes, classes and religions. For the "right to the city" to become a reality for everyone, we have a long way to go indeed.

Wherever you go becomes a part of you somehow

Gender plays an important role in every aspect of our lives. It carries and imposes certain established beliefs and regulations on people, to which most people consciously or unwittingly follow. It seems inevitable. It is learned, accepted and seldom questioned. The commandments and beliefs that apply to each gender are instilled in childhood. This is when the child begins to observe the behaviours and appearances exhibited by elders of the opposite sex and follow them as an indication that the part is of that gender. beyond acceptable. These beliefs and regulations are observed and learned by children and are instilled throughout life through a variety of sources, including the media, politics, social networks, families, and other social institutions.

It turns into a stereotype in your own society. It affects all genders through the development of power struggles, individual performance in society, independence and the need to form identities at their own will. Trying to find a purpose helps us understand their existence, thereby preventing us from seeing the world and all that we are exposed to through our perception of gender.

Gender stereotypes relevant to LGBT communities and their representation in the context of India are discussed below using various visual text examples, mainly composed of films, advertisements and textual materials.

In The Namesake, the conflict between traditional stereotypical women and Jumpa Lahiri's modern-minded women is caused by Ashima's character. The contrast between her wife and mother and the character of Moshmi, who is portrayed as a rebel who is tired of following traditional female standards. Ashima cannot be fully understood as the stereotypical traditional wife and her mother, she is comfortable with her position as a wife and mother. She is not oppressed or oppressed. Instead, she finds happiness in her position, especially in her relationship with her husband Ashok. However, her character has been labelled as a stereotype because of the Westernised understatement of female empowerment that is at odds with what Ashima's character portrays which encourages her to have power and independence within her own family. Transnational feminism opposes Liberal feminist thinking, which promotes the idea that women should be educated and independent. For them, anything that is far from traditional, stereotypical women is considered oppression. They have established their own definitions of independence and freedom, rejecting outright the idea that women can be energetic and independent in their roles within the home. We naturally assumed that women faced similar situations and lived in similar social structures. Throughout the book, Ashima can be experienced as a quiet, peaceful empowerment.

The movie "Lunchbox" shows the neglected wife Ira. At the beginning of the film, she is shown as a dependent wife desperate for her husband's attention. A good cook, Ira relies on food to sustain her marriage. Food has no symbolic meaning to her husband, but Ira is a means of bringing her distant husband closer to herself. She is financially dependent, lonely, neglected and desperate. She conforms to society's norms of being a loyal, loyal, hardworking and completely devoted wife. Her outsiders may scramble for her husband's attention, but she believes that only her husband can make her happy.

Her situation, her role as a married woman in society that leads her to believe that it is her wife's job to keep her husband happy, can be explained by the following quote from her The Second Sex: .

She is defined and differentiated in her relationship with her man, but not in her relationship with him. It is contingent, not essential, as opposed to essential. He is the subject, he is the absolute, she is the other." (Simone, 15)

By assuming that she cannot live without his approval, she becomes a victim of social norms. She becomes a neglected, helpless and isolated subbaltern. By being a subbaltern, she loses her dignity, loses her purpose, is robbed of her emotional autonomy, and despises her existence. She becomes inferior. But in the end, she realised her own mistake was choosing how to get out of her marriage, she made her decision on her own, understood the futility of their relationship and Therefore I decided to leave. Her decision to leave her husband symbolises a change in her previous belief that only her husband can save her.She finally understands that she is her saviour. Thus, throughout the film, we see her character evolve from dependent to independent and from lonely to self-sufficient woman.

In the past, the LGBT community in India did not receive widespread media coverage, but that is now changing. There have been many films depicting the difficulties of being part of the LGBT community. facing and facing social pressures to conform to their gender-assigned roles, conflicts over choosing to be honest with society, and the consequences of criticism and rejection. accept. The movie 'Welcome to Sajjanpur' shows various problems prevailing in India. In one case, a widow's remarriage was thwarted by villagers who killed the couple because they were of different castes. The character Munni is a eunuch who aspires to become the village's sarpanch, but is threatened by his landlord. Ultimately he was murdered, but this was largely based on his sexual orientation and not his decision to vote in the election.

Ardhanaari is a Malayalam film based on the lives of transgender people living in Kerala. It focuses on the difficulties they face in society, society's perceptions and actions towards them. Viewers get a glimpse into the daily life of being discouraged and humiliated by people despite being human.Vinayan tells us that she is a woman trapped in a man's body. is the main character who finally notices. Because of his sexual orientation, he faces a lot of ridicule and disrespect. However, he is eventually accepted into a group of transgender people.The film is riddled with ridicule as it sometimes includes transgender characters to add comical effect to the plot.

Thus, the representation of non-genders in the media and other texts teaches people how they are being attacked by gendered ideas that we unconsciously accept. And Indian democracy guarantees equality through universal suffrage. Therefore, regardless of sexual orientation, a person has the right to be treated with respect and dignity. However, the media has portrayed both stereotypes and exceptions regarding all genders in India, and these have certainly influenced audience perceptions of gender norms in some way.

What do we mean when we use the word 'gender' in the context of history?

We often use statements such as 'rewriting history' through the lens of gender, but what does it mean? Is it just a study of women's history? This course explores India's socio-economic and political relations from the 1800s to the present day, and uses gender relations as a tool of historical analysis to answer such questions. Postcolonial space explores Indian society and conveys a differentiated understanding of historically specific politics.

Gender was central to the Indian experience of colonialism. From battles over widow remarriage to age of consent for ties to caste, labour and nationalism, the status of women in India has attracted the attention of missionaries, colonial legislators and metropolitan liberals. For Indian conservatives, reformers, and later nationalists, women and families became powerful symbols that conveyed the identities of different classes, communities, and nations.

Colonialism has created some thorny problems for men and masculinity. The colonial experience, often in the face of troubling claims about women's rights and freedoms, produced new moral visions for men and gender in families, communities, and nations. The increase was not as pronounced as in times of division. At this time, violence against women on both sides emphasized the role of women as symbols of community, class, and nation. A longer history continues to resonate, but an independent India has also taken its own distinct path on gender issues.

Women are active at all levels of politics, women's organizations are thriving, and the emerging urban middle class across the region is redefining sexual norms and expectations for both men and women. At the same time, many communities are experiencing a bitter backlash against expanded freedom for young women, while increasingly distorted gender relations place more value on sons than on daughters. It reflects that it is getting taller. The rise of Hindu nationalism is also creating space for female ideologues, with RSS and Shiv Sena women themselves reinforcing narratives of militant Hindu patriarchy.

In India, where religious myths and traditional attitudes define (in terms of interpretation) virtues and vices, these influence the public imagination for shaping socio-culture, and women's ideal and acceptable cultural role becomes a huge problem in unified terminology. .

However, careful observation confirms the fact that patriarchy is prevalent in most traditional norms across the country,with its distinctive patchwork of regionally distinct cultures, serving as a template for a special kind of sexism. This discrimination is often an unchallenged commonality of women because of selective "biblical" justifications for maintaining community order, bringing together diverse oppressive practices from various traditional communities. This form of discrimination has, over time, acquired normative status that permeates across cultural approaches that define women's rights on multiple levels, and production rights are already global. It is constrained by the forces of transformation. Under the guise of wealth underpinned by steady growth in economic indicators, gender discrimination can therefore adversely affect the human development of a significant segment of the population, making them vulnerable to poverty and related security challenges.

Families invest more in boys' careers and more in girls' future marriages. To develop this further, the child learns that, 99% of the time, a woman was born to marry and go to her in-laws' house. This comes with the idea of properties and inheritance. Women are always supposed to marry according to social norms, so families naturally place more emphasis on sons than daughters as heirs. Of course, this tends to make the girl believe she's responsible, but the boy runs the house in the long run, so she believes he has the right to stand up for her own claims. While laws have been enacted to ensure that women get their fair share, the reality is that few women recognize the need to stand up for their rights to that law and safety. Marriage and its aftermath pose a different kind of security problem for women in India.For the most part, especially in rural and semi-urban areas, marriage is a social ritual and sometimes a kind of economic affair between families. It's a contract and the bride and groom have very little say in all matters. It's not about them, it's about what their parents want.

In some cases, the bride and groom met for the first time on the day of the wedding! After her marriage, a woman is not allowed to have her own bank account, so she often has to leave all her jewellery and her assets with her in-laws. A woman may have to obtain permission to see a doctor.

For young girls, safety is once again becoming the main reason for dropping out of school. The idea that women represent family honour, makes school away from home a 'threatening' factor to honour, making girls more likely and desirable to interact with a wider range of men without supervision. It leads to opportunities for relationships that are not (that is, not regulated by family).

Since the family unit is a fundamental aspect of every Indian life, all members of Indian households of various ages have learned from the long-standing legacy of women being 'socially' treated as second-class citizens. To get out of the quagmire, you have to go through a journey of consciousness in a country that promises them legal authority on paper.

CHAPTER XV

The Politics of Space – Redefined Identity in an Online Space

Rhetoric is more than merely the right of citizens to communicate or enjoy communicative situations. It refers to the right to use our senses - to touch and feel, to socialise, to share, to eat, and to be with others - in the context of groups that are central to public interaction. In this sense, there are clear links between free expression and the right to public space, as one cannot exist without the other. While governments across the world are wary of the right to free expression, they have gradually eroded public space, which is essential to enable freedom of opinion.

We are witnessing the politicisation of public communications and public space in countries such as India. Although it is completely acceptable to participate in public forms of religious information exchange that involve millions of people, such as at the Kumbh Mela, an important gathering of Hindu sects and devotees, it is not natural for cooperative societies to gather in a public space and/ or share interactions or communicate the need for social transformation and change in the current dispensation. So, it appears that the fundamental concept of what defines a public is being rebuilt, remade, and reviewed in unique ways.

In Delhi, public demonstrations are held in Jantar Mantar. It has been the location of various notable protests, including the Right to Information, anti-corruption, Nirbhaya and Hathras rape cases, anti-CAA (Citizen Amendment Act) rallies against disputed citizenship rules, and the Farmer's protest, among many others. Despite efforts by the National Green Tribunal, the police, and right-wing parties to limit and disrupt protests. A variety of National Security statutes, including a colonial-era Sedition legislation, have been utilised to imprison journalists, students, social activists, and demonstrators - a threat that, in the context of Covid-19, can lead to the death penalty. Spaces like Jantar Mantar, it may be said, are where the meanings of democracy are debated, articulated, and listened to, where truth is held up to power, where causes and concerns become 'public,' and where people become conscious of the strength of collective power. Democracy, on the other hand, is anathema to the present hyper-nationalist administration in power and its proto-Fascist leadership, which follows in the footsteps of Bolsonaro in Brazil, Trump in the United States, and Erdogan in Turkey.

Within this frame of reference, the interconnected public sphere simply has to contend with a centrally supported misinformation regime - often referred to as the BJP's infamous IT Cell and its support for troll farms and counter-publicity initiatives aimed at spinning the story of the government's successes even in the context of its tragic, even criminal mismanagement of India's second Covid wave. While this propaganda machine is in full swing, we are witnessing the unrelenting annihilation of the public's right to talk, criticise, and present alternative stories. It is remarkable that people who speak out against the government's lack of readiness, hospital beds, and oxygen in Delhi and neighbouring Uttar Pradesh have been imprisoned.

Another example of public space destruction is the ambitious ambition of constructing a new Parliament building - The Central Vista (which sounds like a hotel complex in Singapore!) presumably because the old one, which spans 2,800 hectares and includes 3,000 government-owned homes and 600 private bungalows, is a reminder of India's colonial past. It does not sit well with the strong men and women of Hindutva, who would rather include cows and peacocks in their vanity projects than regular Indians. In India, there is an assault on public space, and common lands are rapidly vanishing under the twin assaults of the State and the Market. Indeed, Lutyens' Delhi is for sale. Gods and gurus have also had a part in appropriating public space. Sadhguru, the South Indian godman, constructed his huge Isha Foundation on tribal grounds that were also vital elephant migration lanes. It would be such a beautiful gesture if the government took over the land and purposefully allowed it to deteriorate and revert to forest, elephants, and tribals.

One of the possible implications of Covid-19 has been a retreat into private space, with few opportunities to "encounter," to meet, by coincidence or design, the Other. In that sense, Covid-19 lockdowns have resulted in the dying of public space and the unmaking of cities designed for crowds and minglings. Simultaneously, individuals in lockdowns have utilised their balconies to communicate - to sing, perform music, exchange and engage in a variety of social and cultural activities - emphasising the importance of public spaces that we often take for granted. There are distinctions to be made here as well, between the forced symbolic publicness imposed by the political class to celebrate the contributions made by poorly paid nurses in the UK and India, or the clanging of pots and pans and the lighting of lamps to ward off the spirits of Covid-19, and spontaneous manifestations of publicness and celebrations of public space by neighbours in Covid-affected neighbourhoods around the world. Perhaps such spontaneous displays of publicness could be preserved in a repository of pandemic convivialities, from which ideas for enriching and enabling public spaces in a post-pandemic world could be taken.

What about online public space? Is it truly possible to participate in what is sometimes described as endless space? In the framework of Web 2.0, governments, the commercial sector, and civil society have all put their faith in the digital revolution as a means of increasing economic productivity, citizen involvement, and improving access to products and services. While there are certainly efficiencies in the platform economy, grandiose, ostensibly public programmes like Digital India have been revealed for what they are - exclusive, market-driven in a climate where chances for both market and state monitoring have grown enormously.

Covid's experience has ruthlessly revealed the digital gap. While online education was beneficial to the privileged who had access to laptops, smart phones, and the Internet, students from lower caste and class backgrounds in prestigious institutions such as the Indian Institutes of Technology (IIT) on one end of the spectrum and children in rural schools on the other suffered from a lack of access to basic technologies such as a connected laptop. There have been some incredible examples about a single smartphone being used by numerous youngsters in a rural location because lessons and learning resources are given over Whatsapp. There are heartbreaking examples of rural residents who had to accompany their sick loved ones to a hospital on foot or by autorickshaw because they did not have a smartphone or access to social media to find out if an oxygen cylinder was available at poorly equipped neighbourhood health facilities.

The shift to online registration for most, if not all, social security programmes has left unconnected informal workers high and dry. Even Covid-19 registrations through the government initiative CoWIN necessitate the use of smart phones, which are not as widely available as media coverage has regularly stated. This epidemic has highlighted the dismal status of rural health services in India, including a lack of primary health care, basic health facilities, and a shortage of doctors and health workers. It's upsetting to consider that billions of dollars have been wasted on vanity projects while regular Indians have been left to fend for themselves.

Covid-19 may have exposed the very real limitations of the digital revolution. The fact that people with smartphones can access services but are also susceptible to misinformation and deception says little about the quality of the online environments they occupy. The heinous distribution of Covid treatments on social media in India, ranging from the innocuous to the absurd and downright dangerous, reveals the current gaps in digital knowledge.

Anything goes in a largely uncontrolled society, and all manner of religious charlatans and self-made physicians offer all manner of treatments. Baba Ramdev, the business guru and yoga specialist, mocked individuals desperately hunting for air, claiming that there is enough oxygen in the atmosphere that can be acquired via the use of efficient, yogic breathing methods! These are the parallel worlds that people in India live in today.

So, where can one find instances of people in India safeguarding, preserving, and developing public space? There are several instances of women running decentralised public services in the Southern Indian state of Kerala, with the Kudumbashree project, which focuses on financial inclusion for women through micro-initiatives, being one of the most advanced in the country. This initiative, which began in 1998, has been a success due to the important role played by women in neighbourhood groups who have assisted one another in empowering activities.

The People's Archive of Rural India (PARI), founded by well-known Indian journalist P. Sainath, may be the finest source of material about people and public space. This archive contains a wealth of stories from rural India about the incredible challenges faced by India's forgotten people, whose public spaces have been steadily eroded but who still have incredible resources of hope that are public in nature - from music, art, and performance to sharing traditions that keep these communities and public spaces alive. The section Things We Make contains several instances of creativity as well as the skills and traditions that continue to supply musical and artistic goods and services that are necessary for public performances.

Sangamam is a government-sponsored effort that introduced various types of music to certain parks, including Carnatic/Classical and traditional styles. It was free and open to everyone, rich and poor, low and high caste. The paraiattam, Dalit drummers, and Brahmin Carnatic vocalists and instrumentalists shared the same platform and appeared to be of equal merit and rank for a brief while. The urban Chennai audience was treated to a plethora of performing customs from their home state, ranging from the joyful to the staid.

Political will governs public places. In India, where rampant and predatory forms of neoliberalism have dictated public space and the parameters for public interactions, public spaces have been steadily securitised, leading to the formation of gated and privileged publics. In other words, publics are divided along caste, religious, and social lines. This establishes a hazardous precedent. To counter this trend, there is a need for cultural and political literacy and movements that support the public, as well as online and offline environments that enable celebrations of commonality, minglings and understandings, and the unity in diversity that the framers of India's Constitution believed in - all of which are threatened by Hindutva forces.

The new era vulgate of digital India is bombarding us. The neoliberal Indian lexicon now includes premises relating to the overarching concepts of 'digitally empowered society' and 'knowledge economy.' The future of India is being envisioned via indigenous talent and information technology. Critical minds are sceptical about 'the digital' as distinct from 'India.' In other words, everything generated in the digital world should resemble the physical world. To hide the digital field's inactivity from the actual world, it is also stated that geeks are not "anti-social," but rather "anti-unintelligence." Access to basic quality education, instructors, schools, infrastructure, and so on are important concerns for India's impoverished.

Cyber commentators and cyber libertarian social scientists applaud the role of ICT in the abolition of rural poverty. On the contrary, a lack of education, a complicated social structure, and a lack of access to Information and Communication Technologies (ICTs) have widened the digital gap (DN, 2001) 1. 35% of the population has an internet connection; the social composition of individuals having access to ICTs is dominated by Indian castes, and they are separated from reality for the bulk of Indian society. As a result, it increases the access and social mobility gap. Adivasi-Dalit-Bahujan students are taking advantage of the blogosphere's capabilities. They are use YouTube to reach the majority of people with initiatives such as Dalit Camera. They have also begun to use Twitter, and the advent of Dalit Twitterati thereby undermines the socially/politically privileged Twitterati's dominance. The development of Dalit-Bahujan girls/women and their new modes of digital articulation is one of the important transformations.

Round Table India is another online endeavour that has received significant recognition from India's social movements. It is critical to examine the nature of the form and substance of this particular online resistance strategy. Surprisingly, Round Table India connects us to a social and political realm that has been overlooked by the prevailing value-free, peer-reviewed, elitist academic sphere. Through this anti-caste/religion scholarly-online arena, the dominant's meritocracy and epistemic hierarchy associated with knowledge are therefore questioned. It also confronts the Brahmanic-homophobia that underpins power dynamics including caste, gender, and patriarchy.

According to a report by The Bachchao Project, a techno-feminist research and advocacy group, the rights of women from India's marginalised communities are being disproportionately limited and undermined in digital civic spaces. According to the research, these places are dwindling for such women because they are excluded from and underrepresented in mainstream feminist civic groups. The project covers the online experiences of 12 marginalised women organisers, including confrontations with the State, unending abuse and hatred from non-State actors, and apathy from platforms. The findings indicate a never-ending cycle of online harassment, self-censorship, and persistent fear of State persecution as they attempt to develop online groups and networks.

The survey determined that this online abuse is exacerbated by women's existing marginalised socioeconomic status. Vocal women from oppressed groups who speak out about politics or religion experience sexualized insults on a regular basis. Over the last two years, online auction applications such as Sulli Deals and Bulli Bai have been used to silence Muslim women activists, students, and journalists through hypersexualization and objectification. According to an Amnesty International investigation, up to 95 female politicians in India received over 10,000 problematic or abusive tweets every day between March and May 2019. It discovered that Muslim women politicians were subjected to 94% more racial or religious insults than women politicians of other faiths.

The 2014 general elections, dubbed the "First Social Media Election" in Indian political history, marked the beginning of a social media revolution in Indian politics. Shashi Tharoor, a Congress MP who had previously served as UN Under-Secretary-General, was the sole Indian politician having a Twitter account prior to the 2009 general elections. Prior to the 2014 elections, all major political parties considerably increased their social media footprints.

The success of the Bharatiya Janata Party (BJP) in organising India's digital generation through social media platforms has compelled other parties to rethink their social media participation. As a result, millions of politically charged communications are now flooding India's digital domain, putting elections vulnerable to social media manipulation. According to reports, the BJP controls 18,000 bogus Twitter identities and 200,000 to 300,000 WhatsApp groups. Hindutva has emerged as the key unifying point of the BJP's misinformation campaign as it has taken advantage of the social media domain. According to 2018, misinformation in India focuses on four themes related to Hindu nationalist ideology: "Hindu Power and Superiority, Preservation and Revival (Hindu Culture), Progress and National Pride, and Narendra Modi's Personality and Prowess."

The BJP has utilised "anti-national" rhetoric to delegitimize the recent farmers' protest, revealing its exploitation of internet channels to silence dissenting voices. As part of this, the BJP sought to depict farmers demonstrating as "Khalistan supporters." In November 2020, BJP Information Technology Director Amit Malaviya posted a video on Twitter in response to claims of police violence against protesting farmers. When bogus news contradicts current ideas, people are more inclined to trust it. The more intimate the information, the bigger its influence on voter thinking. The capacity of the BJP's social media approach to spread messages that are more personal and hence have a higher potential to affect a wide spectrum of individuals' political perceptions has been a crucial component of its success. To enhance the impression on voters' minds, the BJP generates digital material in local languages and employs memes from popular shows and movies with the help of professional firms. For example, it used trolls and campaign advertising based on Game of Thrones memes.

The advent of new technologies and the acceleration of life's pace significantly influence the creation of narratives in digital space, which is based on a count of influences, such as: the possibility of a "second life," i.e. a different presentation of oneself (of life) at the virtual level, an increase in social favorability, changing one's impression of oneself and access to new acquaintances and experiences, data and information, and personal data. Abuse and repercussions are possible with digital identity. These include the circumstances of insufficient privacy protection, the discovery and illegal use of permanently memorised data in meta-media society and digital space, particularly on social networks, and the possibility of manipulating and controlling the identity of another, as well as the placement of multiple identities, which calls into question the legitimacy of data. Aside from the fact that digital space has opened up opportunities for changing the way of life in many areas, it appears that the most pronounced influence (both in terms of quality and quantity) is particularly apparent on changes in the design of the individual's personal identity.

When a person enters digital space, his or her identity is formed, and the individual begins talking. It is precisely at this time that the question of with whom/with what the individual is speaking is raised. Another person, or another person's virtual identity? Using digital content, we get to the chatterbot - the human principle vs the digitally recorded one, which opens up a new field of inquiry, namely at the level of digital identity formation.

Freedom from any type of bondage is one of the most basic human wants, and many people have spent their whole lives pursuing it. This is due to the fact that freedom and identity are inextricably linked; an individual cannot have a sense of self without the ability to make decisions about their lives. Today's emerging identities in the global arena exemplify this type of contradiction. The idea of home as a fixed location where we feel rootedness is antiquated. Identities are not just rapidly growing and flexible; we cannot identify home other than as a place where we concentrate our intellectual efforts. If we've climbed Maslow's ladder of needs to a secure position where our lives are engaged in education, technology, politics, and personal growth, we've discovered global connectivity in ways that don't need us to define home and identity. We would find home in our different experiences, belonging with the people we encounter in an ever-changing terrain, and yet preserve the ability to go ahead and away from it all, seeking only the freedom to build our brains as best we could. Identity in digital domains is flexible and dynamic; it is no longer created by physical borders, nor is it based in a relationship to the past.

Teenage girls in the late 2010s and early 2020s have been able to relate with others who do not conform to the normal expectations of a teenage American girl, what Heather Mooney might call the "can-do girl," or, as Angela McRobbie coined, the "post-feminist masquerade," through the use of platforms like Tumblr. Instead, these girls utilise shared musical preferences and individual clothing styles to distance themselves from mainstream American adolescent society and show their dissatisfaction with current culture, as well as their opposition to hegemonic femininity and obligatory heterosexuality. Dick Hebdige wrote Subculture: The Meaning of Style in 1979, the first book to critically and analytically examine young subcultures. Hebdige investigated how subcultures were a form of resistance to mainstream culture, politics, and ideals, illustrating how members of these groups (primarily teenagers and young adults) defined themselves against the mainstream culture, primarily through clothing style and musical taste, but also through political beliefs and attitudes. A common thread running through the many subcultures Hebdige examines in the book is that they all come from a specific area.

As a result, the subculture existed in contrast to and outside of the dominant culture; yet, to be a part of a subculture, one had to not only reside in a certain area but also participate in specific alternative activities, such as dressing unconventionally and listening to specific bands. Subcultures, however, have grown less distinct from mainstream culture since "old forms of culture and politics are being revived, collapsed into, and merged with wholly new cultural and political modes in a global media culture." 1 As the internet and social networks grew and changed, they became venues for young people to "test out numerous roles, identities, and ways of acting. A person does not need to reside in a certain region or era to be a part of a subculture in modern American society. On the internet, several subcultures may coexist, frequently mixing with one another and with the mainstream cultural awareness. However, they continue to provide channels for young people to establish a sense of identification and attachment to a group that exists outside of the cultural norms of their homes and hometowns.

The internet and social media may give kids with a wide range of outlets and opinions that can help them create their own identities early in their lives and communicate with people who are similar to them or have similar interests. Tumblr and TikTok, in example, have exposed kids to fresh viewpoints since they are not networks that require users to engage with people they know in real life in order to get the experience the app was created to deliver. Unlike Facebook or Instagram, which require users to communicate primarily with their real-world friends and acquaintances, Tumblr and TikTok's algorithms allow users to identify others with similar interests or experiences to them who they may not know in real life. When a person initially joins TikTok, the algorithm will offer them random movies from various regions of the platform; if the user watches the entire video, they will be rewarded.

TikTok will presume they enjoy the material and will display them similar videos based on the video's subtitles and tags. The algorithms of TikTok and Tumblr provide especially exciting digital places for young subcultures to originate and thrive. Despite their differences in form and aim, youth have utilised both to create and portray the self as a distinct identity and feeling of individuality rather than presenting the self as having an ideal look or perfect existence. Part of this is probably because it is simpler to communicate with strangers and have meaningful conversations with them on these sites than on Instagram. As a result, Tumblr in the 2010s and Tik tok now have distinct internet subcultures, such as Sad Girl and Lolita on Tumblr in the early-to-mid 2010s and E-girls on Tiktok in the late 2010s.

Teen females have excelled in building and engaging in separate subcultures on these social media sites. I use the term "subculture" because it is via these social networks that young females may develop a unique identity through style and music while also demonstrating "major kinds of resistance to dominant gendered discourses." Online subcultures such as Sad Girls on Tumblr and E-girls on TikTok frequently utilise clothes to oppose conventional gendered discourses by not always dressing appropriately feminine.

This is particularly visible in E-girls, who frequently wear layers and loose garments in dark, grungy colours and patterns. Furthermore, as Heather Mooney explains in "Sad

Girls and Carefree Black Girls," the subcultural online identity of "sad girls" can "address the effects of sexism and patriarchy" in a way that the mainstream "can-do girl" cannot because "sad girls" conform to the expectations that American society has for them as teenage girls. 4 Unlike the 'can-do' girls, who are happy, easygoing, and often involved in a variety of activities at their high schools, 'Sadd Girls' are moodier, usually detached from their high school lives, but commemorate online with others who share their cynical beliefs about society, listen to Lana Del Rey.

A common thread running across the online subcultures in which young females participate is an endeavour to embody hegemonic femininity through a distinct fashion sense. Through their musical interests and likes, females' critical attitudes toward popular society and defiance of societal norms are frequently revealed. Subcultures are finding it more difficult to operate in the internet arena since "old forms of culture and politics are being revived, imploded into, and mixed with wholly new cultural and political modes in a global media culture."

In an increasingly connected society, determining a person's value or how that person compares to others has become a daily struggle. As a result of maintaining several social media personas at all hours of the day, we must think about what we have chosen to represent ourselves digitally. If there are no checks and balances for the identity we display to the public, the planned image will drift away from reality over time. "Aim low and miss low." Aim for a button, and you'll strike a shirt; aim for a shirt, and you'll miss by feet," is an adage that may be applied to digital identities.

The internet has created a new channel of expression in which the faithfulness of an individual's distinctiveness may connect with others who share similar beliefs. According to the tiny world phenomenon, any one individual can be related to another by a maximum of six steps. Frigyes Karinthy proposed six degrees of separation in the 1920s as a post-World War I idea investigating the connectivity of individuals all across the world. In the 1960s, social scientist Stanley Milgram became interested in the hypothesis. Technological advancements have altered how humans engage with visuals and information today. Technology offers the door to exploration and grows till new technology is born.

The growth of technology has an impact on self-perception, since social media users freely allow digital profiles to track interactions they conduct over time. The user will continue to share information with the all-seeing internet until this information is exploited against the profile creator. In many respects, the digital self is the finest aspect of our identity. Moments or highlights from one's physical existence are *used as building blocks for the digital character. This identity is nurtured and protected in order to approach people who are, by nature, the most likely. Magazine subscriptions have been supplanted with YouTube subscriptions, but the function remains the same: content consumption.*

We have been totally enmeshed in a digital existence faster than anyone could have predicted. We'd rather leave the house without our wallets than without our phones. TiVo has revolutionised the way we watch television. iTunes and similar services have drastically changed our music purchasing and listening habits. E-mail reaches us regardless of where we are. More and more households are furnished with wireless networks in addition to internet connections. We have evolved into people who are constantly on and always connected.

However, as users of this technology, we are being swept up in a wave of change. Companies in the business technology sector, such as Dell and HP, are expanding into consumer electronics. Sony and other consumer technology businesses have firmly established themselves in the PC market. New firms like Akimbo, Sonos, and Roku have entered the fray. As existing brands reinvent themselves to compete in the converging consumer electronics and computing sectors, and new brands strive to establish themselves as innovators, nothing is guaranteed as this new market strives to define itself. Will the goods be programmable computer platforms? Will computational power and electronics be concealed under elegant designs and simple user interfaces, or will they be exposed? Will outdated corporate structures trump customer choice and flexibility, or will technology address knotty digital rights issues?

Digital life is life itself, and technology has now become an important component of being human. More people in the world have access to a smartphone than flowing water, which is an incredible truth. Whether or whether you own a mobile device, mobile technology has become ubiquitous. Digitisation drives global healthcare services and research facilities, utilities infrastructure, education systems, revolutionises how we operate businesses, and, more fundamentally, enables the human race to connect across boundaries.

The great benefits that technology has delivered to the globe in such a short period of time are remarkable. Never before have we seen such unilateral development sweep the planet and effect such transformation. That is why, for many years, Telefónica has advocated for making technological potential available to everyone. Our goal is to assist breakdown adoption barriers and encourage individuals to seize the opportunity and enrich their lives using digital technology in a safe, responsible, and transparent manner. There is also a more basic economic impact that digital technology has achieved that we just cannot ignore. In the world's more technologically developed countries, the use of digital technology currently accounts for up to 10% of total GDP.

CHAPTER XVI

Fashion is the armour to survive the reality of everyday life.

Gender, as we currently understand it, is a social construct. According to a 2016 market research report by the Innovation Group, more and more people, particularly members of Generation Z, are discovering this. According to to the study's findings, 56% of 13- to 20-year-olds knew someone who used gender-neutral pronouns like they, them, or ze, and more than 30% of Gen Z respondents strongly felt that gender did not define a person as much as it used to.

What happens to conventionally gendered apparel as the gender binary disintegrates?

Is a shirt bought in the men's category but worn by a woman still considered a men's shirt?

It's only a shirt, after all. In this, too, Gen Zers are breaking the mould: in the same Innovation Group poll, only 44% said they always bought items intended for their own gender, compared to 54% of millennials. Gucci to Target are listening as younger shoppers seek a disruption of the fashion dichotomy. In 2015, Ken Downing, Neiman Marcus' fashion director, told The New York Times that he feels there is a "seismic change in design, a broader embrace of a style with no bounds — one that mimics the way young people dress." This, combined with the fact that The Council of Fashion Designers of America, a trade group comprised of approximately 500 leading American designers, added the first unisex and nonbinary category to the New York Fashion Week calendar in 2018, suggests that lines are being blurred and binaries are being transcended. Consumers and fashion businesses alike are disrupting gendered apparel, yet mandated expectations for women's and men's clothes did not emerge from thin air.

Sports is one of the most prominent frames of gendered fashion. We've all seen it: females in short black spandex on the volleyball court, or in flouncy skirts sprinting along lacrosse fields or working on their tennis serves. On the softball pitch, women with full faces of makeup and pigtail ribbons, their mascara stained by perspiration. All while men's basketball shorts swish pleasantly about their knees and football padding bulks up already strong guys, providing them a Hulk-like machismo. Athletes are expected to appear certain ways by society, and their uniforms assist them reach that aim. Male athletes, like female athletes, should seem fit.

However, female athletes are typically conditioned to seem seductive and conventionally feminine when they slide across the grass or fling their bodies on the ground to keep the ball in play. In the 1970s, homosexual men used the handkerchief code to indicate their sexual availability and preferences. Men carried hankies in their back pockets, which indicated different fetishes or positions based on the positioning and colour of the hanky. The code, which is still in effect today, was critical in the progress and maintenance of LGBTQ+ groups prior to and throughout the Gay Liberation Movement. This isn't to imply that everything you've heard about coded clothing and sexuality is correct — no, not every bisexual person cuffs their pants — but to say that clothes are more than just fabric stitched together.

I've always believed that clothes are our second skin. We live in it every day of our lives. It allows us to express ourselves, exhibit ourselves, and represent ourselves. Given the attire I choose to wear, I stand, move, and even speak differently. Is it all black? Maybe I'm in a punk mood. Shades of nakedness? I awoke feeling lighter that morning. Of course, clothing is not a one-size-fits-all mood ring, but it relates to the greater issue of how important clothes are to our sense of ourselves.

Clothes enable us to transform into chameleons, shifting to suit our moods.

Ariel from The Little Mermaid was my style icon since I was a child. And as soon as I could dress myself, I developed my own personal style. I was going to wear what I wanted to wear. Mismatched. Tag-less. Couture. Whatever. I wrapped a crimson towel around my head and I was transported to another universe — all thanks to the magic of fashion.

Gender conceptions, unlike sex, which defines an individual's biological attributes, are flexible social and cultural concepts that vary over time. The way we establish our gender identity via clothes today is not the same as it has been throughout history. Fashion was not always as gender-specific as it is today. Today's gender-scarred fashion statements are the outcome of a protracted evolutionary process that has been influenced by numerous socio-political phenomena over time. Until the 18th century, both men and women enjoyed to dress in long, elaborate garments. Though there were few noticeable variations in men's and women's clothes until the 18th century, it is feasible to study the evolution of clothing as a medium of gender expression and its link to gender specific roles and social position.

Cave paintings, sculptures, and other iconography are used to study the clothes of the oldest civilizations. Though clothing did not differ much by gender in the ancient world, social class identification was created through dress conventions even in the oldest civilizations. In most ancient civilizations, including Egypt, Greece, and the Indus Valley, nudity was a fairly natural idea. In reality, in most areas of the world, gender specific nudity rules labelling breast exposure as obscene were created only after the influence of Christian missionaries and Islamic conquest.

A rectangular fabric was the major source of clothing until the demise of the Romans in late 400AD. A rectangular fabric was draped or embroidered into a tunic with handholes. The length of the hem was one of the first gender-specific clothing norms to be established. Men and women both wore tunics in Egyptian and Greco-Roman cultures, with women's tunics reaching to the ankles and men's reaching to the knees. It was a product of gender norms in which males were expected to go out and work, particularly army men, horseback riders, and travellers who wore shorter tunics for comfort.

However, by the time the length of men's tunics eventually increased to resemble a shirt-like garment, European attire had been sexualized to the point where it was no longer acceptable for women to show a lot of skin. From 321BC to 850AD, India was one of the world's greatest civilizations, rivalling Rome in the west and China in the east. Due to the hot climate, Indians typically wore draped clothes. Both men and women wore antariya, a lower garment wrapped around the waist (as shown in the Yakshini statue), and uttariya, a cloth worn over the back, laying over the shoulders. Prior to Roman influence, it was socially acceptable for women in Indian civilization to not cover their breasts.

The Mauryan empire had direct trading relations with the Roman empire, and the former even married a Greek royal princess. Greco-Roman influence during the Mauryan era may have contributed to the growth of two-piece antariya & uttariya into a modern Indian sari. Even gender-specific modesty standards in India were relaxed, as women now wore stanmasuka or Pratidhi, which is akin to the mammillare worn by Roman ladies. Men continued to wear antariya, which developed into dhoti and is still worn by many Indian men today. As a result, by the time of the Mauryan era, clothing had definitely established itself as a medium of gender expression in India.

By the Medieval era, gender-specific modesty/nudity, hem length, and the advent of pants had clearly distinguished men's attire from women's. However, before the 18ᵗʰ century, apparel mostly reflected variations in class rather than gender. Both men and women gained lavish decoration, a plethora of lace, beautiful velvets, wigs, and embellished shoes. Men, too, wore corsets, but less commonly than women. King Louis XIV donned tights and high heels to draw emphasis to his calves and a high wig to heighten his stature.

Following the great male desertion, the most systematic divergence between men's and women's dress emerged in the mid-late 1800s. Men fighting in the arenas of politics and business were inspired by protestant principles of hard labour and economic advancement, so donating the ornamental portion to women to portray men's social position via clothing and appearances of wives. While women's clothes remained clumsy and ornate, embroidered silks and velvet prepared the way for beautifully designed woollen ensembles in the male arena. Men wore geometric design lines, neutral and muted colour palettes, bifurcated clothing for the lower body, natural but not too tight shapes, robust materials and shoes, and uncomplicated hair and facial maintenance.

Full-length clothing or ornate fabrics impeded the image of masculinity by the nineteenth century, while womenswear grew more decorative and restrained than ever before. Those contrasts in clothing grew to represent the alleged gender differences: Men were serious and functional, like a suit, but women were frivolous and superficial, like a flouncy garment. Women's independence trends began in the late nineteenth century. Women were more involved in outdoor activities in the twentieth century, resulting in the greatest transformation in women's apparel history. In the early twentieth century, Paul Poiret introduced women's pants. Feminist icons such as Coco Chanel took it upon themselves to liberate women from restrictive clothes by wearing soft roomy pants, but few women dared to wear them until the 1940s.

Coco Chanel also produced fitted suits for ladies in the 1920s, which became fashionable after World War II. Women frequently cut their hair into shorter styles to flout gender stereotypes. As women bucked gender conventions associated with femininity and rose to positions of power, fashion designer Yves Saint Lauren adapted the masculine tuxedo to a women's line. When Mary Quant introduced micro skirts for women, she demolished hemline regulations and made low hemlines no longer belong to males. Hippies and ravers were the first to advocate for a gender-neutral approach to dressing. Several pop cultural superstars, like David Bowie and Mick Jagger, fought against the concept of traditional masculinity by dressing as women.

If the twentieth century altered women's social position (therefore radically altering women's clothing), the twenty-first century continues the unfinished work of the 1970s by asking for expanded personal freedom. Popular topics include sex, unisex, nudity, gender, and sexuality. The gay and lesbian, bisexual, and transgender movements have evolved and developed into these concepts of a non-binary conception of gender. Throughout history, many socio-cultural phenomena have limited masculinity to males in male bodies and femininity to women in female bodies, which is not true for all individuals. Our culture is becoming more conscious that gender is not binary, but rather dual. Every person is born with both masculine and feminine characteristics. Fashion responded on time by recognising the need to eliminate genderism in clothing.

Clothing was historically used to defend oneself from natural environmental risks before becoming decorative to display an individual's social position or succumbing to societal constraints of modesty. The gender disparity in clothes is a direct outcome of women's lower social position as compared to men's. We continue to live in a very gendered world. However, fashion's campaign towards gender-neutral apparel is simply the first step toward a world free of gender norms and divisions.

One curious irony of this sector is that designers aiming to move away from labels are met with additional labels defining what their work isn't. In fashion, terms like unisex, genderless, and gender-neutral are not synonymous but are used interchangeably. It's simple to turn to buzzwords to define one's brand and stand out as forward-thinking or nonconformist.

Urvashi Lele (intentionally or unwittingly) addressed this by coining her own terminology. The name of her Indo-British label, Maison Audmi, is a combination of aadmi and aurat. The brand's beautiful hand-block-printed and ikat outfits are classified as womenswear for men.

While witnessing a tall, bearded man in a voluminous dress may be a chance occurrence, it's also not all that revolutionary for many in liberal, queer-friendly communities. At the risk of repeating myself, no discussion about men in dresses today is complete without mentioning Harry Styles. In case you missed it, clothing does not have a gender. So why choose 'womenswear for guys' instead of simply selling gowns to everyone?

"One day, I hope to stroll into a store and see skirts and dresses in both the masculine and womenswear departments." However, I believe that many labels are moving too hastily by labelling their collections as gender-fluid or androgynous.While it is the end goal, there is a lot of unlearning to be done first, particularly in how we see menswear. We must teach our minds to believe that "it is OK for a dress to exist in menswear, and if I want to buy a dress, I can click on menswear, and the drop-down menu will provide me with dresses and skirts as well."

One of the main societal challenges of our day appears to be the altering terrain of gender. There are indicators of rising acceptance and understanding of those claiming a non-binary gender identification in many developed economies, and an increasing number of people indicating that they no longer conform to standard gender notions. Gender conventions are changing, and society is following suit. It is estimated that one million Americans identify as nonbinary. Several prominent celebrities have advocated for their own gender fluidity, which has aided in the adoption of the they/them pronoun in public discourse.

Gender-fluid fashion is ambiguous.

It can signify different things depending on who you ask because there is no single, well-established concept. According to fashion industry experts, fully gender-fluid clothing isn't even an outfit. Fashionably speaking, it's more of a state of mind. "In principle, gender-fluid or gender-inclusive clothing may be any clothes," said Nick Paget, senior analyst at World Worldwide Style Network (WGSN), a global trend forecasting organisation that monitors consumer purchasing behaviour. "The societal construct that has to be dismantled is the concept that clothes as an expression of our personality belongs to one gender or the other."

A little girl of roughly nine years old follows her mother through the clothing aisle of a bargain store. She sweeps her fingers through the gowns' various colours, textures, and sizes as they loom over her on the rack. Her younger brother, who is roughly seven years old, follows her down the aisle, bouncing. Suddenly, the young girl yanks a frock from the rack, racing after her brother and crying, "You should wear this!" "Eww, no way, that's for females!" exclaims the brother. This hilarious interplay between brother and sister is great. At this young age, these two youngsters intuitively recognise their own gender, recognise that these genders differ, and recognise that clothing constitutes one outward manifestation of their young identities, their gender identity.

Clothing is a component of everyday life in the Western culture, and it is undoubtedly a part of the lives of these two youngsters. The implication of the clothing is that by wearing it, the kid will no longer be a boy, and will no longer be what society expects of him. The clothing is a sign that supports the girl's identity as a girl and the boy's identity as a male. Dress, however, reinforces not just gender identification, but also race, class, and sexual orientation. It generates identities, separates them, and shows them. Clothing is a tangible representation of one's individuality. The story's seemingly basic interaction of the children emphasises the necessity to explore questions about clothes, identity, and society.

Dress is a negotiation between identity and the social cultural milieu in which that identity is lived out, not just a personal concern or decision. This negotiation implies individual agency, but it also suggests limits, since attire is a virtual need for participation in the social, cultural environment. Involvement in western civilization and culture, in most situations, entails participation in the occupation of clothing.

One of the most fascinating perspectives for evening wear design was unveiled during the recent Golden Globe Awards. As journalists examine actresses with the standard inquiry, "Who are you wearing?" The gorgeous, couture dresses receive as much attention as the nominations.

Actresses spend months grooming themselves and keeping a close eye on their bodies in the hopes of wearing the right gown that will improve their careers and placing them on a magazine's "best dressed" list. On the big day, stylists labour feverishly to tape, tighten, and tuck their clients into these exquisite and extremely expensive outfits before sending them off to seem as natural as possible. However, one actress opted for a less typical black-tie look this year.

"I'm not trying to protest clothing," said actress Evan Rachel Wood. "I wanted to make sure that young ladies and girls understood that they are not required and that you are not required to wear one if you do not want to." Simply be yourself, since your worth is far greater."

Her decision to wear a pantsuit on the red carpet is a reflection of the present social mood in modern fashion. Fashion reflects the societal zeitgeist and promotes stereotyped sexism and gender norms, which have plagued our country for decades. Fashion has always been used to indicate social position. Individuals who could afford to buy expensive silk dresses and exquisite clothes embellished with needlework flaunted their affluence. The clothing was meant to make movement physically impossible, emphasising that this upper social class did not engage in hard work.

The notorious crinoline was a circular undergarment that physically bound women. A lady would stand confined in this framework while she began to dress, watching as servants placed heavy clothes and petticoats on her, increasing the weight and physical strain on her body. The expensive and aesthetically pleasing clothing sent a message. The goal of a lady was to be beautiful. Her major goal in life should be to change her body to meet whatever beauty standard society imposed at the time, even if it meant suffering or immobility.

Take the cellphone, for example. Everyone has one, but most pockets created for women in their jeans or coats aren't functional. If the garment does have functional pockets, they are too tiny to hold an average-sized smartphone.

A man's jacket, on the other hand, has a number of pockets that allow him to carry his wallet, keys, and phone without being hampered by dragging about a purse, emphasising the gender disparity. In reality, the purse has evolved into a quiet burden that drags women behind their male coworkers.

The lack of pockets in women's clothing has long been an issue that has yet to be remedied. Women had to wear sacks wrapped around their waists and tucked in the 1700s.

Society propagates the impression that a gorgeous heel is the pinnacle of femininity and a definite method to attract males. We see successful women represented in periodicals and films wearing fancy dresses and stiletto heels, reinforcing the heel's association with power and femininity. The product is lovely in terms of style, but the shoe's structure inhibits a lady from moving fast and painlessly. Have you ever trapped your foot in a train vent or broken one while rushing to a meeting?

And what does it imply to be chasing after your male peers who can stroll fast and painlessly to lunch?

Designers are aware of this societal imbalance, and some of their collections address it. Alexander McQueen created inventive and stunning designs that told his story via spectacular visuals. He empowered women by empowering them with haute skills and utilising fashion to depict the traumas they experienced. He once stated that he wanted people to be terrified of the ladies he clothed, and that he used fashion as a type of expressive power to resist the cultural ideals that were imposed on them.

Even today, the bulk of fashion designers contribute to women's oppression by designing clothing that is either visually beautiful and physically confining or utilitarian and basic. Why can't a woman have it both ways?

The fashion business is predominantly about and for women. Nonetheless, its roots are almost totally based on the male gaze and masculine ideas about how women should exhibit themselves. Can women ever completely reclaim their clothing as an expression of their choice, if the very foundations of fashion are steeped in patriarchal control, if clothes are a method for individuals to express themselves? Historically, women's clothing has been designed to restrict free movement and deny function. The female body and its covering have traditionally been patriarchal and capitalist prerogatives, with religion and globalisation complicating matters for women across socioeconomic fault lines in society.

An essay published in the American Quarterly in 1963 describes the roots of women's fashion and the motivations behind it. It contends that women's fashion is a result of greater patriarchal propaganda aimed at subjugating women through the cultivation of a constrained, slave mindset.

"Women's attire was purposefully meant to hinder them from earning an income and/or being successful, save via marriage," claims author Robert Riegel.

Can Katy Perry's "daisy dukes-bikinis-on-top" optimism ever reclaim women's fashion as genuinely theirs, with the foundation of women's design built in sexism and control? According to a 2014 research, over one-third (29%) of female flight attendants were sexually harassed while on duty; this makes sense given the extent to which the business sexualizes air stewardesses to literally make them a part of the service the airline gives to consumers. It has something to do with preserving the pornographic-mile-high-club, tea-or-me dream. The job description itself puts women on display for consumption, helped by tight grooming and fashion requirements such as hair and cosmetics rules, necessary high heels when air hostesses travel through an airport, and the all-too-common no-pants rule. Or the Avianova airline campaign, in which flight hostesses strip from their uniform skirts into bikinis as the male personnel looks on.

Since 9/11, when Islamophobia rose, the burqa, hijab, or veil has been a source of contention in both the West and the rest of the world. It became clear very quickly that there was widespread prejudice and misunderstanding regarding Muslim lifestyles, habits, and rituals. When former British Prime Minister David Cameron portrayed Muslim women as historically subservient, he did not believe he was stereotyping. In the context of the worldwide discussion, the term "burqa" has become over-politicized and is now considered synonymous with a Muslim woman's identity.

"By interacting with this story, I intend to demolish it from inside," Khan writes. Muslim women are more than burqas and hijabs, and they are more than society has permitted.

Muslim women who wear the burqa, according to Boris Johnson, resemble "letter boxes" and "bank robbers." Would it be OK if I suddenly decided I didn't like white women wearing heels or short skirts and characterised them in a way similar to Johnson's Islamophobic remarks about Muslim women? Women who wear burqas are oppressed. They are sluts if they wear skirts. I'm sick of this binary. Johnson's words are not only Islamophobic and demeaning of Muslim women, but they also dehumanise them. Muslim women are objects in his eyes. To say this is demeaning is an understatement. Using his position and power, he willfully legitimised a narrative that physically and verbally abused Muslim women on the streets of Britain.

The Only Real People Are The People Who Never Existed

Humankind is not a pretty picture towards the conclusion of the twentieth century. We, humans, have made millennia of natural-scientific and technological advancements. With this enormous advancement in our ability to comprehend and modify the natural environment, we should be able to live comfortably.

Instead, mankind appears to be under the clutches of an unseen, malicious entity. This uncontrollable devil drives us to rip our reality apart, using our own human creative capacities against ourselves and twisting them into self-destructive forces. When we are pitted against one another, we are reduced to a position of complete impotence, mere observers of our own acts, unable to control or interpret them. This is what makes the world's recent developments look so weird.

We commit a large portion of our energy and intellect to lie and cheating, as well as injuring or murdering each other, for reasons we cannot fully comprehend. Over many decades, a significant portion of scientific and economic work has been devoted to developing tools to murder, torment, and maim humans. They worked quite well: millions perished in world wars and concentration camps. Following the Holocaust

The third quarter of the twentieth century was overshadowed by the potential of nuclear self-destruction, bringing the entire production to a dramatic finish.

Following World War II, a few decades of economic progress brought a new threat to the fore. It began to appear probable that, even in the absence of conflict, the use of modern technology might destroy the natural environment on which all human existence depended. Again, this threat to humanity is both the result of human action and completely beyond of human control.

There has been a worldwide push to grow business and use chemical and biology findings to agriculture and medical. The results, on the other hand, have never been what was planned. They involve the loss of not just natural ecological systems, but also earlier ways of social life.

A homogenous cultural muck now covers almost the whole world. It is mechanised, poor, and fractured, preoccupied with surface, shape, image, and packaging. Appropriately, a high-tech, tabloid, 'entertainment' industry, driven solely by greed, chums out a highly polished and debased product for the people on every continent.

The presenting of 'news' has become an integral component of this 24-hour flood of visuals. Images of war and natural disasters are masterfully blended with titillating gossip and mechanically produced 'comedy.' Parallel to this, and similarly focused with money, cultural goods for a restricted middle-class stratum are increasingly reduced to self-conscious, shallow posturing.

Of course, millions of individuals strive to live good lives in the middle of all this chaos, raising their children as best they can, but such human relics are driven to the margins of social life. Every day, another fragment of community life vanishes, replaced by the impersonal machinery of state bureaucracy and the market. Is it any surprise that drug and alcohol misuse are so prevalent? These self-destructive reactions are only unsuccessful attempts to obscure the current world's meaninglessness and irrationality. At a time when whole national governments are disintegrating, it is not unexpected that more than a quarter of the inhabitants of many nations get some type of mental illness therapy at some point.

For over a century, millions of people organised in a powerful working-class movement attacked the existing system, certain that a radical change was on the horizon. A socialist future would ensure that human ingenuity and resources are used rationally.

This future seemed to many in the years immediately

following the Russian Revolution. The dream, however, vanished. The revolution quickly degraded because it was contained within a devastated, underdeveloped country. A bureaucratic state machine, increasingly dragged into the global market, replicated the worst corrupt and ruthless aspects of the disintegrating international order it purported to supplant. Even when desperation pushed large numbers of people to revolution, they never appeared to think beyond a change in political authority.

So here we are in the final decade of what is commonly referred to as the second millennium. Human beings, although having the ability to manage the natural world, lack the ability to regulate their own life. At the same time, people are enslaved by modes of thought that make the ensuing monstrous ways of life look completely 'normal.' Because their lives are becoming increasingly fragmented, how can they possibly comprehend the actual nature of the problem as a whole?

The Rise Of The Global Society

The idea of international society is based on the assumption of the "social" nature of intergovernmental relations.

This term is commonly interpreted to mean that order in international politics is maintained through the social ties between states. Hedley Bull was the author of the most succinct definition that an international society "exists when a group of States, aware of certain common interests and shared values, form a society in the sense that they conceive of themselves as bound by a common set of rules in their relationships with each other and participate in the functioning of common institutions" Despite this often repeated characterization, international society remains an enigmatic concept.

Although it can appear persuasive and evokes rather positive connotations through its promise of orderly international relations, it has amassed a loyal following as well as passionate critics. Notably, the early discussion of international society developed in the context of the development of international relations as an academic discipline. In its simplest form, international society is one of the ways of characterizing relations between states, both historically and in the present. The idea is largely based on a specific historical narrative used to explain the rise of the European intergovernmental system. Through the process known as "spreading", the institutional structure of international society is said to have spread across the world.

The idea of a society in general - the society in preference to the country - is, we've got visible in bankruptcy 4, a structural absence in worldwide family members principle. Where society is admitted, it's miles withinside the confined feel of a society, wherein it's miles recognized with country and ethnic group, themselves the social concomitants of states. While this absence or narrowness of sociological attitude weakens worldwide principle's information of the breadth and intensity of safety issues, as we argued above, it additionally significantly inhibits its information of world society. It leads worldwide theorists to disclaim the lifestyles or minimise the relevance of world society.

International refers, in truth, both to family members among states or, at a minimum, to family members throughout the country limitations that are appreciably based via way of means of those limitations. The idea of the worldwide is an inherently statist idea, and even though it is hard to keep away from the usage of this terminology that's so embedded in popular, political and educational language, we should usually be privy to its incipient statism. Relations among states can not be assumed to be family members among nations, and social family members throughout the country or country-wide limitations can not be assumed to be worldwide.

International society, as used in this context, is neither worldwide nor a society, however, refers to a selected fashion towards 'society-like' capabilities withinside the country-gadget. In this bankruptcy, we pursue the critique of 'society' in worldwide principle, and the contradictions of a principle of family members among states which neglects their context in worldwide society, via way of means of unravelling the that means and ancient importance of the concept of worldwide society.

The Cold War situation, wherein the global country structure contained the emergence of a worldwide society, is coming to an end. Groups, actions and establishments inside international society are making themselves felt in the global state's institution which politically mediates international social relations. It is the handiest proper and right that they ought to do so, even though it threatens the assumptions of the country's institution and demands situations like norms of global society together with sovereignty and non-intervention. This isn't always to mention that those norms are thoroughly redundant, however, is to insist that they have to be certified through trendy responsibility to the desires and desires of the individuals of worldwide society.

We ought to welcome this process, but embryonic it is able to be, and but many traces it introduces into the state's institution a good way to then spill over into the lives of humans inside international society. What is involved, but modestly and contradictorily, is the start of the improvement of what we might also additionally call international civil society, wherein individuals of worldwide society are beginning to attempt to make the country device responsible - withinside the manner wherein countrywide civil societies have, withinside the past, generated pressures to make sure the responsibility of countrywide states.

At the centre of the improvement of worldwide civil society is the idea of international obligation. Again embryonically, this concept may be visible in paintings in a lot of developments - the tries through international ecological actions to make the country device reply to needs for international environmental management; the tries through stress organizations to make sure that human rights and democracy are judged through an international standard; and the needs, fuelled through media coverage, to make appreciate for human desires and human rights powerful ideas in global conflicts. The stress on Western governments to interfere to shield the Kurds - to just accept obligation for the oblique sufferers in their conflict towards Iraq - and to interfere for only humanitarian motives in Bosnia-Herzogovina are very current manifestations of this precept of worldwide obligation.

Each of those current interventions has implicitly or explicitly challenged the ideas of sovereignty and non-intervention that have been visible as centre assumptions of a global society. The ideas have, of course, been waived or various in reaction to comparable pressures withinside the past, and there's not anything to signify that states are but inclined to subordinate them in large part, but by myself entirely, to ideas of worldwide obligation. Rather there was an actual battle among the instincts of statesmen to keep the ideas of sovereignty and non-intervention, and the stress from international civil society to go beyond them.

The instincts of President Bush and Mr Major had been to abstain, in sensible phrases, from the civil conflicts in Iraq after the Gulf War, even when they had morally and politically incited rebellion towards Saddam Hussein. The Shi'as of southern Iraq had been efficiently deserted to their destiny in March 1991 with US troops a rely of miles on Basra, the principal centre of the rebellion. The Kurds had been likewise deserted till global political and media stress abruptly constructed up in mid-April 1991. Even after the intervention, the allies and the UN maintained the fiction of Iraqi sovereignty in search of Iraqi settlement to the operation of UN remedy agencies (the fiction fee them dearly in legitimate foreign money quotes and different Iraqi rake-offs). Nevertheless, in army phrases, the ceasefire settlement itself breached Iraqi sovereignty by presenting extensive UN surveillance of Iraqi army preparations.

In this episode, it became pretty clear that Western leaders had been running with an ideology of global society, wherein the defeated Iraqi country, but uncovered as morally and politically bankrupt, became nevertheless accorded the rights and prerogatives of a sovereign country. While the allies had been organized to breach those of their very own country interests (the manipulation of guns of mass destruction) they nevertheless upheld the idea of non-intervention which became simply a difficulty of a danger to Iraq's very own citizens. Only beneath intense political stress from an implicit stance of worldwide obligation did they concede intervention.

In the Yugoslav case, the ideology of global society operated towards any concept of intervention while it first have become apparent - withinside the repression of Kosova withinside the later 1980s - that a competitive nationalist regime had come to energy in Serbia which became precipitating the break-up of Yugoslavia. The thought that those had been the home issues of a sovereign country prevailed, as Western states and global bodies endured to understand Yugoslavia lengthy after its death had emerged as inevitable, and without critically trying to interfere to adjust the break-up in phrases of ideas like appreciate for current borders, the rights of minorities and human rights in trendy.

In the very last irony, despite the fact that recognising the brand new Bosnian country and notionally admitting it to global society, the West made no try to assist stable its truth at the floor however in large part deserted it to its destiny. Only while the media made it clear that this probably covered the sluggish hunger of 1/2 of 1,000,000 humans in Sarajevo, the 'ethnic cleansing of over 1,000,000 Muslims and Croats, massacres and awareness camps, did the stress of worldwide civil society push the West to define - on the London convention of August 1992 - the ideas with which it ought to have attempted to adjust the situation, politically, from 1989 or 1990 onwards, a good way to save you conflict. Under this stress, too, West European army intervention extended beneath UN auspices however with no clear political goals. By mid-1993 it became glaring that Western states had been unwilling to significantly shield threatened civilians in this crisis.

The vital issue, then, is to stand as much as the need that implementing those concepts could impose to systematically breach the concepts of sovereignty and non-intervention. An international society angle calls for reputation withinside the establishments and way of life of the nation machine of the needs of society for accountability. This has to consist of the more and more systematic intervention of global society and global establishments in character states which fail to satisfy desirable standards.

This process, moreover, isn't always simply a reliance on disciplining Iraq or Serbia, however, includes problems which include the function of USA, Japan and the European Community states withinside the distribution of worldwide wealth and using electricity resources; it may additionally contain calling the united states to account for unilateral navy interventions like the ones in Grenada and Panama. In this sense, the problems raised are big and the pursuits threatened are to a degree the ones of all states. This means, of course, that we're not going to peer an essential and specific shift withinside the path endorsed here. The problems are probable to stay foci of contestation over a completely lengthy length of time.

The international society angle, therefore, has an ideological importance that is in the end against that of a global society. No decisive end result may be expected, at a political and ideological level, to the war among those positions, for the easy cause that at the same time as the pressures for international duty are growing, the power of the global machine and of the splendid powers inside it are nevertheless formidable. While the worldwide society angle can now not be disregarded, as naive or utopian, it's miles not going to turn out to be vital to international politics withinside the short or medium term.

Globalisation patterns have called into question the exclusive role of nations as participants in international affairs. Globalization connects disparate communities and creates opportunities for new social actors. Public-interest non-governmental players, sometimes known as civil society organisations, are among the non-state entities benefiting from this development. Along with the state, profit-driven corporate players, and international governmental organisations, civil society organisations round out the mosaic of actors on the international arena. Civil society is commonly defined as the realm outside of government, family, and market. A location where individuals and collective organisations promote ostensibly shared interests.

Community groups, non-governmental organisations, social movements, labour unions, indigenous groups, charitable organisations, faith-based organisations, media operators, academia, diaspora groups, lobbying and consultancy groups, think tanks and research centres, professional associations, and foundations are examples of civil society organisations. Political groups and private corporations are other examples of borderline circumstances. The role of civil society organisations in international politics has grown in importance. They have contributed to the development of agendas, international law, and diplomacy. They have also been involved in the implementation and oversight of a number of critical global concerns. Trade, development, and poverty reduction are among them, as are democratic government and human rights, peace and the environment, and security and the information society.

Because of these factors, international relations cannot be properly understood without including the activities of civil society organisations.

To interpret global civil society, several theoretical viewpoints might be applied. Liberals may see it as a bottom-up contributor to the efficacy and legitimacy of the international system as a whole. In essence, it is a democracy since the population holds power accountable. Realists, on the other hand, may see global civil society as a weapon utilised by the world's most powerful governments to further their ultimate goals overseas, frequently through supporting and popularising views critical to national interests. Marxists may regard global civil society as political vanguards capable of disseminating an alternative worldview that challenges the current system.

A variety of special situations have aided global civil society organisations' involvement.

To begin, some international organisations have advocated for the participation of civil society actors in international decision-making. For example, the 1992 United Nations Earth Summit in Rio de Janeiro brought together previously disparate parties to develop shared platforms and networks. The European Union has taken a similar approach, including various forms of civil society organisations within its governing systems.

Second, due to a tendency toward the privatisation of industries, the state's objectives for resource allocation shifted in the 1980s and 1990s. It was typical in that atmosphere for state-owned industries (such as utilities) to be sold to private companies. As a result, the state's overall involvement in public affairs has been curtailed in many Western countries. Civil society organisations were able to outsource various services from the state and take on new responsibilities as service providers in this setting.

Third, the globalisation process has instilled in civil society participants a feeling of shared purpose. This has triggered internal cohesion, enhancing civil society organisations' sense of togetherness. It has also brought together organisations who wish to expose the negative aspects of globalisation. Finally, organisations from all over the world have been able to become acquainted with other political realities thanks to the internet.

Most worldwide regulatory authorities have begun to create deeper relationships with civil society organisations in recent decades, particularly to bridge this legitimacy gap. For example, the UN Food and Agriculture Organization's Committee on World Food Security has reserved seats for various types of organisations, including non-governmental organisations and social movements, research centres, financial institutions, private sector associations, and private philanthropic foundations. While the function of civil society organisations in these circumstances is mostly advisory, they do provide civil society organisations with a place at the table.

Given the need to combine the increased societal effect with more legitimacy, global governance institutions have been pressed to be more inclusive and responsive to political demands from below. As a result of such processes, civil society actors have gained more access to international agenda-setting, decision-making, monitoring, and implementation of global concerns. At the same time, the involvement of civil society actors in global governance systems remains a key problem. New institutional frameworks are always evolving, and the task of integration is therefore perpetually revisited. New institutional filters are being developed, and civil society actors must continually refocus and adapt to changing conditions.

Civil society organisations require financial resources, public recognition, and political backing, all of which the political system may offer or facilitate. At the same time, the political system may take advantage of the fragmentation and multiplication of civil society organisations by picking and choosing the groups most likely to collaborate with the present political agenda based on political convenience.

As a result, there is a risk that some civil society organisations may be utilised as a tool to promote top-down representation of specific interests. However, questions of violence and opposition to political systems are always contentious, depending on political interpretation. To paraphrase an old adage, one person's terrorist is another person's freedom warrior. Those who take a stance against the current quo and advocate for tangible change are frequently criminalised and/or politically marginalised. We must constantly keep in mind that the term "civil" is normatively laden and is often defined in accordance with the dominant ideology.

As a result, history can be ironic: famous political figures such as South African President Nelson Mandela and Palestinian leader Yasser Arafat were long thought to be leaders of criminal gangs, if not terrorists, and yet they were both given the Nobel Peace Prize in due course.

A primary objective of the human rights movement is the abolition of the death penalty. It is a modern illustration of how efforts supported by civil society organisations may have long-term influence. While the death penalty has been discussed for millennia, substantial institutional changes have happened in recent decades, with a number of countries deleting capital punishment from their legal systems. Only via the distinctive international mobilisation of civil society organisations has the anti-death penalty viewpoint gained relevance at the United Nations level. While prior activity helped to create the necessary political environment at the national level, the movement for a moratorium on the death sentence expressly targeted the United Nations. This eventually resulted in a large UN General Assembly resolution in 2007, which was reconfirmed multiple times over the next few years. Even if the death sentence exists in certain jurisdictions, the resolutions and changing attitudes of a number of governments represent notable successes in terms of human rights advancement

Civil society initiatives have made a number of significant contributions in recent decades. While this is far from a major step toward global political democratisation, the gradual developments should not be overlooked. There are at least two types of impact. In the first case, civil society organisations have been able to sway political decision-makers by providing the voiceless a voice and defining new concerns. At the same time, they have succeeded in putting pressure on global governance institutions, such that the general degree of openness, consultation, outside review, and efficiency is now far higher than it was previously. These outcomes cannot be credited completely to civil society, but they have been accomplished in part through civil mobilisation.

With notable exceptions in Latin America and Southeast Asia, most international activity has originated from Western organisations. Other sections of the world remain socially isolated. Russia, China, much of Africa, and the Arab world are islands that have remained largely insulated from the overall expansion of global civil society. And, just as civil society organisations are unevenly distributed in the Global North, the political outcomes they have produced reflect a geopolitical imbalance. However, as agendas emerge from the developing world and worldwide Western power and influence steadily fade, this is unlikely to continue. In such an environment, Western civil society organisations will have to share the stage with developing-world civil society organisations. This, presumably, will make global civil society more 'global'.

Populism is a long-standing phenomenon that emerged in various forms in the mid-nineteenth century. At that time, the notion of "the people" caught the interest and curiosity of intellectuals, first signifying "the honest, self-sacrificing agent of revolution and modernity". In the Cold War period, populism was seen in the West as combining ignorant and authoritarian people, while in the Soviet Union, it symbolised the "empire of people's democracies and popular fronts". Because of the great ethnoreligious variety that characterises the civil society realm and the socio-political context, the Indian situation is a valuable subject of investigation. Politics is affecting minority relations and the exercise of their rights in this setting.

Hindu dominance and purity, as promoted by Hindutva, are important factors in rising violence between minorities and restraining civil society players. Civil society has played a significant part in the development and history of India. A diverse spectrum of players, including NGOs, grassroots organisations, women's groups, labour unions, and mass movements, have made significant gains, particularly in providing basic services and advancing human rights. Ethno-religious minorities are rapidly developing networks, non-governmental organisations (NGOs), and grassroots organisations to advocate and protect their interests. The Indian situation demonstrates how populism may have a tremendous impact on civil society and civil freedoms, such as religious freedom. Populism, in its most extreme manifestations, poses a threat to liberal democracy.

Populism is frequently associated with nationalism, as seen in India, allowing for authoritarian and discriminatory behaviours against persons or opinions deemed anti-national. Indeed, while the democratic Constitution is being upheld in certain ways, ethnic minorities appear to be severely marginalised. The Indian scenario indicates that populism displays anti-elitist and people-centred traits with a definition of "the people" that can be exclusionary. Populism, on the other hand, emphasises a more equitable allocation of resources and is frequently devoted to a more egalitarian society, which attracts support from the lowest levels of society.

Citizens must protect their interests and fundamental rights in order to avoid the growth of radical populism and to preserve a liberal democratic society. In this sense, civil society plays a critical role in solidifying democracy and liberal philosophy, emphasising that no human person has an inherent right to rule over others and that all legal power is justified by a mutual compact. To begin further contemplation, I cite John Locke (1960), one of the most essential thinkers for our understanding of liberalism:

"Men are naturally in a state of perfect freedom [...] a state also of equality, wherein all the power and jurisdiction is reciprocal, no one having more than another: there being nothing more evident than

that Creatures of the same species [...] should be equal one among another without Subordination or Subjection. (p.189). **"**

The idealistic narrative of Locke's remark, as well as a knowledge of the worldwide development of populism and nationalism, help to reconsider liberal democracy. As a result, it is reasonable to believe that this development demonstrates the individualistic nature of human beings, moving away from concepts of universal equality, "absolute freedom," and an ideal political structure. The case study described in this article demonstrates how populism may lead to the delegitimization of particular people's voices, therefore challenging core democratic values.

References For Further Reading

CHAPTER 1

Alavi, Seema. *Sepoys And The Company Tradition and transition in Northern India 1770–1830. Oxford University Press India. 1998. Print.*

Béteille, André. *Caste, Class, and Power: Changing Patterns of Stratification in a Tanjore Village. Berkeley: University of California, 1965. Print.*

Bouglé, Célestin. *Essays on the Caste System. London: Cambridge UP, 1971. Print.*

Corbridge, Stuart, and John Harriss. *Reinventing India: Liberalization, Hindu Nationalism, and Popular Democracy. Cambridge, UK: Polity, 2000. Print.*

Daniel, Aharon. *"Caste System in Modern India." Adaniel's Info Site. Web. 4 Nov. 2010. Ghurye, G. S. Caste and Race in India. Bombay: Popular Prakashan, 1969. Print.*

Hampton, Andrea. "The Untouchables." Home - CSU, Chico.

"Hinduism and Buddhism"a Comparison." *Essortment Articles: Free Online Articles on Health, Science, Education & More.*

Hutton, J. H. *Caste in India: Its Nature, Function and Origins. Bombay: Indian Branch, Oxford UP, 1963. Print.*

"Kshatriya , Indian Caste." *Free Encyclopedia & Web Portal on Indian Culture & Lifestyle. 28 Jan. 2009.*

Lahiri, R. K. "Caste System in Hinduism by Dr. RK Lahiri, PhD." *Boloji.com - A Study in Diversity - News, Views, Analysis, Literature, Poetry, Features - Express Yourself. 20 Nov. 2005.*

Malalasekera, G. P., and K. N. Jayatilleke. "Buddhist Studies: Caste System." BuddhaNet - Worldwide Buddhist Information and Education Network.

Pintane, Andrea. "Brahmans Within the Caste System." Home - CSU, Chico.

Pyakurel, Sourav. "Caste System in India | Articles." Rajput Brotherhood: A Blog Focused on Technology and Web-development.

Sekhon, Joti. Modern India. Boston: McGraw-Hill, 2000. Print.

Smith, Brian K. Classifying the Universe: the Ancient Indian Varna System and the Origins of Caste. New York: Oxford UP, 1994. Print.

Tweet, Jonathan. "JoT Rel Reincarnation." JoT Welcome Page. July 2004.

V, Jayarama. "Hinduism and Caste System." *Hinduism, Buddhism, Jainism, Sikhism, Zoroastrianism and Other Resources "Vaishyas." Gurjari.net.*

Velassery, Sebastian. Casteism and Human Rights: Toward an Ontology of the Social Order. Singapore: Marshall Cavendish Academic, 2005. Print.

Abrams, D., Marques, J. M., Bown, N., and Henson, M. (2000). Pro-norm and anti-norm deviance within and between groups. J. Pers. Soc. Psychol. 78, 906–912. doi: 10.1037/0022-3514.78.5.906

PubMed Abstract | CrossRef Full Text | Google Scholar

Ambedkar, B. R. (1925/1989). "Essays on untouchables and untouchability I," In Writings and Speeches, Vol. 5, ed. V. Moon (Bombay: Education Department, Government of Maharashtra).

Google Scholar

Biernat, M., Vescio, T. K., and Billings, L. S. (1999). Black sheep and expectancy violation: integrating two models of social judgment. Eur. J. Soc. Psychol. 29, 523–542. doi:

10.1002/(SICI)1099-0992(199906)29:4<523::AID-EJSP944>3.0.CO;2-J

CrossRef Full Text | Google Scholar

Branscombe, N. A., Castle, K., Dorsey, A. G., Surbeck, E., and Taylor, J. B. (2000). Early Childhood Education – A Constructivist Approach. Boston: Houghton Mifflin Company.

Google Scholar

Branscombe, N. R., Ellemers, N., Spears, R., and Doosje, B. (1999). "The context and content of social identity threat," in Social Identity: Context, Commitment, Content, eds N. Ellemers, R. Spears, and B. Doosje (Oxford, UK: Blackwell), 35–58.

Google Scholar

Branscombe, N. R., Wann, D. L., Noel, J. G., and Coleman, J. (1993). In-Group or out-group extremity: importance of the threatened social identity. Pers. Soc. Psychol. Bull. 19, 381–388. doi: 10.1177/0146167293194003

CrossRef Full Text | Google Scholar

Brewer, M. B., and Gaertner, S. L. (2008). "Toward reduction of prejudice: intergroup contact and social categorization," in Blackwell Handbook of Social

Psychology: Intergroup Processes, eds R. Brown and S. L. Gaertner (Oxford: Blackwell Publishers Ltd), doi: 10.1002/ 9780470693421.ch22

CrossRef Full Text | Google Scholar

Castano, E., Paladino, M.-P., Coull, A., and Yzerbyt, V. Y. (2002). Protecting the ingroup stereotype: ingroup identification and the management of deviant ingroup members. Br. J. Soc. Psychol. 41, 365–385. doi: 10.1348/ 014466602760344269

PubMed Abstract | CrossRef Full Text | Google Scholar

Cotterill, S., Sidanius, J., Bhardwaj, A., and Kumar, V. (2014). Ideological support for the indian caste system: social dominance orientation, right-wing authoritarianism and karma. J. Soc. Polit. Psychol. 2, 98–116. doi: 10.5964/ jspp.v2i1.171

Deshpande, M. S. (2010). History of the Indian Caste System and Its Impact on India Today. New York, NY: California University Press.

Google Scholar

Dirks, N. B. (1989). The original caste: power, history and hierarchy in south asia. *Contrib. Indian Sociol.* 23, 59–77. doi: 10.1177/006996689023001005

CrossRef Full Text | Google Scholar

Doosje, B., Ellemers, N., and Spears, R. (1995). Perceived intragroup variability as a function of group status and identification. *J. Exp. Soc. Psychol.* 31, 410–436.

Google Scholar

Dreze, J., and Khera, R. (2009). *The Battle for Employment Guarantee.* Available at: http://www.frontline.in/static/html/fl2601/stories/20090116260100400.htm

Google Scholar

Dube, L. (2001). *Anthropological Explorations in Gender: Intersecting Fields.* Thousand Oaks, CA: SAGE.

Google Scholar

Duncan, B. L. (1976). Differential social perception and attribution of intergroup violence: testing the lower limits of stereotyping of Blacks. *J. Pers. Soc. Psychol.* 34, 590–598. doi: 10.1037/0022-3514.34.4.590

CrossRef Full Text | Google Scholar

Fiske, A. P. (1991). Structures of Social Life: The Four Elementary Forms of Human Relations. New York, NY: Free Press.

Google Scholar

Fiske, A. P. (1992). The four elementary forms of sociality: framework for a unified theory of social relations. Psychol. Rev. 99, 689–723. doi: 10.1037/0033-295x.99.4.689

PubMed Abstract | CrossRef Full Text | Google Scholar

Flintoff, C. (2010). India Struggles to Stem Rise in Honor Killings. Available at: http://www.npr.org/templates/story/story.php?storyId=128567642

Gayer, L. (2000). The globalization of identity politics: the Sikh experience. Int. J. Punjab Stud. 7, 223–262.

Google Scholar

Giessner, S. R., and Schubert, T. W. (2007). High in the hierarchy: how vertical location and judgments of leaders' power are interrelated. Organ. Behav. Hum. Decis. Process. 104, 30–44. doi: 10.1016/j.obhdp.2006.10.001

CrossRef Full Text | Google Scholar

Goli, S., Singh, D., and Sekher, T. (2013). Exploring the myth of mixed marriages in India: evidence from a nation-wide survey. J. Comp. Fam. Stud. 44, 193–206.

Google Scholar

Gupta, D. (2005). Caste and politics: identity over system. Annu. Rev. Anthropol. 34, 409–427. doi: 10.1146/annurev.anthro.34.081804.120649

PubMed Abstract | CrossRef Full Text | Google Scholar

Hayes, A. F. (2013). Introduction to Mediation, Moderation, and Conditional Process Analysis: A Regression-Based Approach. New York, NY: The Guilford Press.

Google Scholar

Hoff, K., Kshetramade, M., and Fehr, E. (2009). Caste and Punishment: The Legacy of Caste Culture in Norm Enforcement. Policy Research Working Papers. Washington, DC: World Bank. doi: 10.1596/1813-9450-5040

CrossRef Full Text | Google Scholar

Hogg, M. A., and Turner, J. C. (1987). Intergroup behavior, self-stereotyping and the salience of social categories. Br. J. Soc. Psychol. 26, 325–340. doi: 10.1111/ j.2044-8309.1987.tb00795.x

CrossRef Full Text | Google Scholar

Jaspal, R. (2011). Caste, social stigma and identity processes. Psychol. Dev. Soc. 23, 27–62. doi: 10.1177/ 097133361002300102

CrossRef Full Text | Google Scholar

Jetten, J., and Hornsey, M. J. (2014). Deviance and dissent in groups. Annu. Rev. Psychol. 65, 461–485. doi: 10.1146/ annurev-psych-010213-115151

PubMed Abstract | CrossRef Full Text | Google Scholar

Judge, P. S., and Bal, G. (2008). Understanding the paradox of changes among Dalits in Punjab. Econ. Polit. Wkly. 43, 49–55.

Google Scholar

Kumar, V. (2001). Untouchability in Uttaranchal. Econ. Polit. Wkly. 36, 4536–4537.

Google Scholar

Mahalingam, R. (2003). Essentialism, culture, and power: rethinking social class. J. Soc. Issues 59, 733–749. doi: 10.1046/j.0022-4537.2003.00087.x

CrossRef Full Text

Mahalingam, R. (2007). Beliefs about chastity, machismo, and caste identity: a cultural psychology of gender. Sex Roles 56, 239–249. doi: 10.1007/s11199-006-9168-y

CrossRef Full Text | Google Scholar

Mand, K. (2006). Gender, ethnicity and social relations in the narratives of elderly Sikh men and women. Ethn. Racial Stud. 29, 1057 1071. doi: 10.1080/01419870600960305

CrossRef Full Text | Google Scholar

Marques, J., Abrams, D., Paez, D., and Martinez-Taboada, C. (1998). The role of categorization and in-group norms in judgments of groups and their members. J. Pers. Soc. Psychol. 75, 976–988. doi: 10.1037/0022-3514.75.4.976

CrossRef Full Text | Google Scholar

Marques, J., Abrams, D., and Serôdio, R. G. (2001). Being better by being right: subjective group dynamics and derogation of in-group deviants when generic norms are undermined. J. Pers. Soc. Psychol. 81, 436–447. doi: 10.1037/0022-3514.81.3.436

PubMed Abstract | CrossRef Full Text | Google Scholar

Marques, J., Yzerbyt, V., and Leyens, J. P. (1988). The 'black sheep effect': extremity of judgments toward ingroup members as a function of group identification. Eur. J. Soc. Psychol. 18, 1–16. doi: 10.1002/ejsp.2420180102

CrossRef Full Text | Google Scholar

Marques, J. M., and Paez, D. (1994). "The black sheep effect: social categorisation, rejection of ingroup deviates, and perception of group variability," in European Review of Social Psychology, Vol. 5, eds W. Stroebe and M. Hewstone (New York, NY: Wiley), 38–68.

Google Scholar

Miller, J. G., and Bersoff, D. M. (1992). Culture and moral judgment: how are conflicts between justice and interpersonal responsibilities resolved? J. Pers. Soc. Psychol. 62, 541–554. doi: 10.1037/0022-3514.62.4.541

PubMed Abstract | CrossRef Full Text | Google Scholar

Miller, J. G., Bersoff, D. M., and Harwood, R. L. (1990). Perceptions of social responsibilities in India and in the

United States: moral imperatives or personal decisions? J. Pers. Soc. Psychol. 58, 33–47. doi: 10.1037/ 0022-3514.58.1.33

CrossRef Full Text | Google Scholar

Niedenthal, P. M., Barsalou, L. W., Winkielman, P., Krauth-Gruber, S., and Ric, F. (2005). Embodiment in Attitudes. Soc. Percept. Emot. Pers. Soc. Psychol. Rev. 9, 184–211. doi: 10.1207/s15327957pspr0903_1

PubMed Abstract | CrossRef Full Text | Google Scholar

Otten, S. (2009). "Social categorization, intergroup emotions and aggressive interactions," in Intergroup Relations: The Role of Motivation and Emotion, eds S. Otten, K. Sassenberg, and T. Kessler (New York, NY: Psychology Press), 162–181.

Google Scholar

Pick, D., and Dayaram, K. (2006). Modernity and tradition in a global era: the re-invention of caste in India. Int. J. Sociol. Soc. Policy 26, 284–294. doi: 10.1108/ 01443330610680380

CrossRef Full Text | Google Scholar

Pinto, I. R., Marques, J. M., Levine, J. M., and Abrams, D. (2010). Membership status and subjective group dynamics:

who triggers the black sheep effect? J. Pers. Soc. Psychol. 99, 107–119. doi: 10.1037/a0018187

PubMed Abstract | CrossRef Full Text | Google Scholar

Pratto, F., Liu, J. H., Levin, S., Sidanius, J., Shih, M., Bachrach, H., et al. (2000). Social dominance orientation and the legitimization of inequality across cultures. J. Cross Cult. Psychol. 31, 369–409. doi: 10.1177/0022022100031003005

CrossRef Full Text | Google Scholar

Rai, T. S., and Fiske, A. P. (2011). Moral psychology is relationship regulation: moral motives for unity, hierarchy, equality, and proportionality. Psychol. Rev. 118, 57–75. doi: 10.1037/a0021867

PubMed Abstract | CrossRef Full Text | Google Scholar

Rimal, R. N., and Real, K. (2005). How behaviors are influenced by perceived norms. Commun. Res. 32, 389–414. doi: 10.1177/0093650205275385

CrossRef Full Text | Google Scholar

Sagar, A., and Schofield, J. W. (1980). Racial and behavioral cues in Black and White children's perceptions of ambiguously aggressive acts. J. Pers. Soc. Psychol. 39, 590–598. doi: 10.1037/0022-3514.39.4.590

PubMed Abstract | CrossRef Full Text | Google Scholar

Schubert, T. W. (2005). Your highness: vertical positions as perceptual symbols of power. J. Pers. Soc. Psychol. 89, 1–21. doi: 10.1037/0022-3514.89.1.1

PubMed Abstract | CrossRef Full Text | Google Scholar

Sheth, D. L. (1987). Reservations policy revisited. Econ. Polit. Wkly. 22, 461957–461962.

Google Scholar

Sidanius, J., and Pratto, F. (1999). Social Dominance: An Intergroup Theory of Social Hierarchy and Oppression. New York, NY: Cambridge University Press. doi: 10.1017/ CBO9781139175043

CrossRef Full Text | Google Scholar

Siddique, Z. (2011). Evidence on caste based discrimination. Labour Econ. 18, S146–S159. doi: 10.1016/ j.labeco.2011.07.002

CrossRef Full Text | Google Scholar

Spears, R., Doosje, B., and Ellemers, N. (1997). Self-stereotyping in the face of threats to group status and distinctiveness: the role of group identification. Pers. Soc. Psychol. Bull. 23, 538–553. doi: 10.1177/0146167297235009

CrossRef Full Text | Google Scholar

Stamkou, E., van Kleef, G. A., Homan, A. C., and Galinsky, A. D. (2016). How norm violations shape social hierarchies: those who stand on top block norm violators from rising up. Group Process. Intergroup Relat. 19, 608–629. doi: 10.1177/1368430216641305

CrossRef Full Text | Google Scholar

Tajfel, H., and Turner, J. C. (1986). "The social identity theory of intergroup behavior," in The Social Psychology of Intergroup Relations, eds S. Worchel and W. Austin (Chicago, IL: Nelson–Hall), 7–24.

Google Scholar

von Hecker, U., Klauer, K. C., and Sankaran, S. (2013). Embodiment of social status: verticality effects in multilevel rank-orders. Soc. Cogn. 31, 374–389. doi: 10.1521/soco_2013_1006

CrossRef Full Text | Google Scholar

Wang, L., Zheng, J., Meng, L., Lu, Q., and Ma, Q. (2016). Ingroup favoritism or the black sheep effect: perceived intentions modulate subjective responses to aggressive interactions. Neurosci. Res. 108, 46–54. doi: 10.1016/ j.neures.2016.01.011

PubMed Abstract | CrossRef Full Text | Google Scholar

"What is India's caste system?," (2016). Available at: http://www.bbc.com/news/world-asia-india-35650616

CHAPTER 2

Wiert Wiertsema, The Caste System and the Hindus and Muslims of Kerala Journal Of Kerala Studies, March-December 1984, Vol..XI, Parts 1-4., p-82, Kerala University, Thiruvananthapuram. 1984

A. Sreedhara Menon, Cultural Heritage of Kerala, An Introduction, East-West Publications Pvt. Ltd., Cochin, January 1978, p-208 http://www.ijser.org International Journal of Scientific & Engineering Research The research paper published by IJSER journal is about The Paradigm and Practice of Pollution in Caste System in Malabar, ISSN 2229-5518

C.A. Innes ICS, Malabar (Gazetteer) Vol. I and II. Edited by F.B Evans ICS , 1908 Government of Kerala, Kerala Gazetteers Department , Thiruvananthapuram, 1997

Census of India,1921, VOL. XIII, Part I, Madras,1922, P-57

J.H.Hutton, Caste in India: its Nature, Function and Origins, Oxford University Press, Bombay,1969, pp-79-85

Bibek Debroy and Laveesh Bhandari, District Level Deprivation in the New Millennium(Ed), Konark Publishers Pvt. Ltd, New Delhi,2003

Poonam Arora, Professional Women Dual Role and Conflicts- Manak Publications (p) Ltd. New Delhi, 2003.

T.K.Roy and S.Niranjan, Indicators of Women Empowerment in India, Asia- Pacific Population Journal, Vol. 19, No. 3,September 2004,ISSN 0259-238X, p- 23, United Nations, Thailand

Human Development Report 2000, p-1, Published for the UN Development Programme (UNDP), Oxford University Press, New York, 2000.

Harper, Edward B. "Ritual Pollution as an Integrator of Caste and Religion." The Journal of Asian Studies, vol. 23, 1964, pp. 151–97. JSTOR, https://doi.org/10.2307/2050627. Accessed 17 Dec. 2022.

CHAPTER 3

Agarwal, B. (1994). A field of one's own: Gender and land rights in South Asia. Cambridge University Press.

Google Scholar

Anselin, L., Syabri, I., & Kho, Y. (2006). GeoDa: An introduction to spatial data analysis. Geographical Analysis, 38(1), 5–22. https://doi.org/10.1111/j.0016-7363.2005.00671.x

Article Google Scholar

Arokiasamy, P. (2007). Sex ratio at birth and excess female child mortality in India:trends, differentials and regional patterns. In I. Attane & C. Z. Guilmoto (Eds.), Watering the Neighbour's Garden: The Growing Demographic Female Deficit in India. Paris: Committee for Intern ational

Cooperation in National Research in Demography.

Arokiasamy, P., & Goli, S. (2012). Explaining the skewed child sex ratio in rural India: Revisiting the landholding-patriarchy hypothesis. Economic and Political Weekly, XLVI, I(42), 85–94.

Google Scholar

Bagchi, D. (1981). Women in agrarian transition in India: Impact of development. Geografiska Annaler: Series B, Human Geography, 63(2), 109–117. https://doi.org/ 10.1080/04353684.1981.11879465

Article Google Scholar

Bansal, S. (2017). Indian states and women: where are they empowered, where are they not Hindustan Times. Retrieved from https://www.hindustantimes.com/interactives/ women-empowerment-index/.

Bharadwaj, S. B. (2012). Myth and reality of the khap panchayats: A historical analysis of the panchayat and khap panchayat. Studies in History, 28(1), 43–67. https://doi.org/10.1177/0257643013477250

Article Google Scholar

Bhat, P. N. M., & Zavier, A. J. F. (2003). Fertility decline and gender bias in northern India. Demography, 40(4),

637–657. https://doi.org/10.2307/1515201

Article Google Scholar

Bhatnagar, R. D., Dube, R., & Dube, R. (2005). Female infanticide in India: A feminist cultural history. State University of New York Press.

Google Scholar

Bhutia, Y., & Liarakou, G. (2018). Gender and nature in the matrilineal society of Meghalaya, India: Searching for ecofeminist perspectives. The Journal of Environmental Education, 49(4), 328–335. https://doi.org/10.1080/00958964.2017.1407283

Article Google Scholar

Blumberg, R. L. (1988). Income under female versus male control: Hypotheses from a theory of gender stratification and data from the third world. Journal of Family Issues, 9(1), 51–84. https://doi.org/10.1177/019251388009001004

Article Google Scholar

Bongaarts, J. (2013). The implementation of preferences for male offspring. Population and Development Review, 39(2), 185–208. https://doi.org/10.1111/j.1728-4457.2013.00588.x

Article Google Scholar

Bose, A. (2006). Where women prevail: 2001 census and female heads of households. Economic and Political Weekly, 41(22), 2192–2194.

Google Scholar

Cain, M. T. (1993). Patriarchal structure and development change. In W. Position & D. Change (Eds.), Nora Faderici, Karen Oppenheim Mason & Solvi Sogner (pp. 43–60). Clarendon Press.

Google Scholar

Centre for Development Studies. (2005). Human Development Report 2005. Thiruvananthapuram: Government of Kerala.

Chakraborty, T., & Kim, S. (2010). Kinship institutions and sex ratios in India. Demography, 47(4), 989–1012. https://doi.org/10.1007/BF03213736

Article Google Scholar

Chaudhuri, S. (2012). The desire for sons and excess fertility: A household-level analysis of parity progression in India. International Perspectives on Sexual and Reproductive Health, 38(4), 178–186. https://doi.org/10.1363/3817812

Article Google Scholar

Dalmia, S., & Lawrence, P. G. (2004). The institution of dowry in india: Why it continues to prevail. Journal of Developing Areas, 38(2), 71–93.

Article Google Scholar

Das Gupta, M., Zhenghua, J., Bohua, L., Zhenming, X., Chung, W., & Hwa-Ok, B. (2003). Why is Son preference so persistent in East and South Asia? A cross-country study of China, India and the Republic of Korea. The Journal of Development Studies, 40(2), 153–187. https://doi.org/10.1080/00220380412331293807

Article Google Scholar

Davis, D. R., Jr. (2010). The spirit of hindu law. Cambridge University Press.

Book Google Scholar

Desai, S., & Andrist, L. (2010). Gender scripts and age

at marriage in India. Demography, 47(3), 667–687. https://doi.org/10.1353/dem.0.0118

Article Google Scholar

Durkheim, E. (1933). The division labor in society. The Macmillan Company.

Google Scholar

Dyson, T. (2012). Causes and consequences of skewed sex ratios. Annual Review of Sociology, 38(1), 443–461. https://doi.org/10.1146/annurev-soc-071811-145429

Article Google Scholar

Dyson, T., & Moore, M. (1983). On kinship structure, female autonomy, and demographic behavior in India. Population and Development Review, 9(1), 35–60. https://doi.org/10.2307/1972894

Article Google Scholar

Engelen, T., & Wolf, A. P. (2005). Marriage and the family in eurasia. Perspectives on the Hajnal hypothesis. In T. Engelen & A. P. Wolf (Eds.), Marriage and the family in Eurasia. Perspectives on theHajnal hypothesis (pp. 15–34). Aksant, Amsterdam.

Engels, F. (1884). The origin of the family, private property and the State. Hottingen, Zurich.

Ferrant, G., & Nowacka, K. (2015). Measuring the drivers of gender inequality and their impact on development: The role of discriminatory social institutions. Gender & Development, 23(2), 319–332. https://doi.org/10.1080/ 13552074.2015.1053221

Article Google Scholar

Fuller, C. J. (2003). The renewal of the priesthood: Modernity and traditionalism in a south Indian temple. Princeton University Press.

Google Scholar

George, S. M., & Dahiya, R. S. (1998). Female foeticide in rural Haryana. Economic and Political Weekly, 33(32), 2191–2198.

Google Scholar

Geske Dijkstra, A. (2006). Towards a fresh start in measuring gender equality: A contribution to the debate. Journal of Human Development, 7(2), 275–283. https://doi.org/10.1080/14649880600768660

Article Google Scholar

Gough, E. K. (1956). Brahman kinship in a tamil village 1. American anthropologist, 58(5), 826–853.

Gruber, S., & Szołtysek, M. (2016). The patriarchy index: A comparative study of power relations across historical Europe. The History of the Family, 21(2), 133–174. https://doi.org/10.1080/1081602X.2014.1001769

Article Google Scholar

Halpern, J. M., Kaser, K., & Wagner, R. A. (1996). Patriarchy in the Balkans: Temporal and cross-cultural approaches. The History of the Family, 1(4), 425–442. https://doi.org/10.1016/S1081-602X(96)90011-1

Article Google Scholar

Harris, R. (2007). India: aryan patriarchy and dravidian matriarchy. Retrieved September, 26, 2020, from http://www.integralworld.net/harris32.html.

IIPS. (1995). National Family Health Survey (MCH and Family Planning), India 1992–93. Bombay: IIPS.

IIPS, & ICF. (2017). *National Family Health Survey (NFHS-4), 2015–16: India. Mumbai: IIPS.*

IIPS, & Macro International. (2007). *National family health survey (NFHS-3), 2005–06: India: Volume I. Mumbai: IIPS.*

Plan India. (2017). *Plan for every child gender vulnerability index Report-1: Plan International.*

Jäger, U., & Rohwer, A. (2009). *Women's Empowerment: Gender-related Indices as a Guide for Policy CESifo DICE Report (Vol. 7, pp. 37–50). Munich: ifo Institute Leibniz Institute for Economic Research at the University of Munich.*

Jayachandran, S. (2015). *The roots of gender inequality in developing countries. Annual Review of Economics, 7(1), 63–88.* https://doi.org/10.1146/annurev-economics-080614-115404

Article Google Scholar

Jeffrey, P., Jeffrey, R., & Lyon, A. (1988). *When did you last see your mother? Aspects of female autonomy in rural north India. In J. C. Caldwell, A. G. Hill, & V. J. Hull (Eds.), Micro-approaches to demographic research (pp. 321–333). Kegan Paul International.*

Google Scholar

Jeffrey, R. (1992). Politics, women, and well being: How Kerala became "A Model." Palgrave Macmilan.

Book Google Scholar

Kabeer, N. (2015). Caste system, patriarchy working against India's gender equality. Paper presented at the International Conference on Gender Equality, Thiruvananthapuram, Kerala.

Kakar, S. (1978). The inner world: A psychoanalytic study of hindu childhood and society. Oxford University Press.

Google Scholar

Kapadia, K. M. (1966). Marriage and family in India (Vol. Third). Oxford University.

Google Scholar

Karve, I. (1953). Kinship organisation in India. Poone, India: Deccan College Post-graduate and Research Institute.

Krieger, N. (2011). Epidemiology and the people's health: Theory and context. Oxford University Press.

Book Google Scholar

Kukreja, R. (2017). Caste and cross-region marriages in Haryana, India: Experience of dalit cross-region brides in jat households. Modern Asian Studies, 52(2), 492–531. https://doi.org/10.1017/S0026749X16000391

Article Google Scholar

Larsen, M. (2011). Vulnerable daughters in India culture, development and changing contexts. Routledge.

Google Scholar

Lin, Z., Desai, S., & Chen, F. (2020). The emergence of educational hypogamy in India. Demography, 57(4), 1215–1240. https://doi.org/10.1007/ s13524-020-00888-2

Article Google Scholar

Littrell, R. F., & Bertsch, A. (2013). Traditional and contemporary status of women in the patriarchal belt. Equality, Diversity and Inclusion: An International Journal, 32(3), 310–324.

Article Google Scholar

Malhotra, A., Vanneman, R., & Kishor, S. (1995). Fertility, dimensions of patriarchy, and development in India. *Population and Development Review, 21*(2), 281–305. https://doi.org/10.2307/2137495

Article Google Scholar

Mandelbaum, D. G. (1959). Social uses of funeral rites. In H. Feifel (Ed.), *The meaning of death* (pp. 189–217). McGraw-Hill.

Google Scholar

Mies, M. (1980). Capitalist development and subsistence reproduction; rural women in India. *Bulletin of Concerned Asian Scholars, 12*(1), 2–14. https://doi.org/10.1080/14672715.1980.10405557

Article Google Scholar

Miller, B. D. (1981). *The endangered sex: Neglect of female children in rural north India.* Cornell University Press.

Google Scholar

Moore, M. (1973). Cross-cultural surveys of peasant family structures: Some comments. *American Anthropologist, 75*(3), 911–915.

Article Google Scholar

Moran, P. A. P. (1950). Notes on continuous stochastic phenomena. Biometrika, 37(1/2), 17–23. https://doi.org/10.2307/2332142

Article Google Scholar

Nasir, R., & Kalla, A. K. (2006). Kinship system, fertility and son preference among the muslims: A review. The Anthropologist, 8(4), 275–281. https://doi.org/10.1080/09720073.2006.11890976

Article Google Scholar

Nunnally, J., & Bernstein, I. (1994). Psychometric Theory (3rd ed.). McGraw-Hill.

Google Scholar

OECD. (2019). Measures discrimination against women in social institutions. Social Institutions and Gender Index (SIGI) Retrieved Sept. 28, 2020, from https://stats.oecd.org/Index.aspx?DataSetCode=GIDDB2019

Permanyer, I. (2013). A critical assessment of the UNDP's gender inequality index. Feminist Economics, 19(2), 1–32. https://doi.org/10.1080/13545701.2013.769687

Article Google Scholar

Pillai, M. S. (2016). Ivory hhrone: Chronicles of the house of travancore. Harper Collins.

Google Scholar

Raj, A. (2017). Evidence-based measures of empowerment for research on gender equality (EMERGE). Resources: Global Indices and Indicators on Gender. from http://emerge.ucsd.edu/resources/

Roberts, L. R., & Montgomery, S. B. (2016). India's distorted sex ratio: Dire consequences for girls. Journal of Christian Nursing, 33(1), E7–E15. https://doi.org/10.1097/cnj.0000000000000244

Article Google Scholar

Roy, A. (2018). Discord in matrilineality: Insight into the khasi society in Meghalaya. Society and Culture in South Asia, 4(2), 278–297. https://doi.org/10.1177/2393861718767238

Article Google Scholar

Ruggles, S. (2015). Patriarchy, power, and pay: The transformation of American families, 1800–2015. Demography, 52(6), 1797–1823. https://doi.org/10.1007/s13524-015-0440-z

Article Google Scholar

Sadiq, S., & Khan, A. (2015). Khappanchayats in India: precepts and practices. International Journal of Current Research, 7(1), 11753–11757.

Seltzer, J. A. (2019). Family change and changing family demography. Demography, 56(2), 405–426. https://doi.org/10.1007/s13524-019-00766-6

Article Google Scholar

Sen, A. (1990, 12/20/1990). More than 100 million women are missing, The New York Review of Books.

Sev'er, A. (2008). Discarded daughters: The patriarchal grip, dowry deaths, sex ratio imbalances & foeticide in India. Women's Health and Urban Life, 7(1), 56–75.

Google Scholar

Sharma, U. (1980). Women, work and property in North-west India. Tavistock Publications Ltd.

Google Scholar

Singh, R., & Talwar, U. K. (2014). Culture of missing girls: Anthropological insight in culture, medical technologies and medicine. Anthropology, 2(3), 2–10. https://doi.org/10.4172/2332-0915.100012

Article Google Scholar

Sopher, D. E. (1980a). The geographical patterning of culture in India. In D. E. Sopher (Ed.), An Exploration of India: Geographical perspectives on society and culture (pp. 289–326). Cornell University Press.

Google Scholar

Sopher, D. E. (1980b). Sex disparity in Indian literacy. In David E. Sopher (Ed.), An Exploration of India: geographical perspectives on society and culture (pp. 130–188). thaca, N.Y.: Cornell University Press.

Subba, T. B., & Ghosh, G. C. (2003). The anthropology of north east india. New Delhi: Orient Longman.

Szołtysek, M. (2016). Rethinking East-Central Europe: Family systems and co-residence in the Polish-Lithuanian Commonwealth (Vol. 1). Peter Lang Press.

Book Google Scholar

Szołtysek, M., & Poniat, R. (2018a). Historical family systems and contemporary developmental outcomes: What is to be gained from the historical census microdata revolution? The History of the Family, 23(3), 466–492. https://doi.org/10.1080/1081602X.2018.1477686

Article Google Scholar

Szołtysek, M., & Poniat, R. (2018b). The power of the family: New data reveal the role of the historical family as the instigator of disparate and lasting developmental trajectories. World Values Research, 10(1), 1–39.

Google Scholar

Thomas-Slayter, B., & Rocheleau, D. E. (1995). Gender, environment, and development in Kenya: a grassroots *perspective. Boulder: L. Rienner.*

UNDP. (2019). Gender development index human development report 2019. New York, USA: United Nations Development Programme.

Unnithan, M. (1991). Caste, tribe and gender in south Rajasthan. Cambridge Anthropology, 15(1), 27–45.

Google Scholar

Van de Putte, B., Van Poppel, F., Vanassche, S., Sanchez, M., Jidkova, S., Eeckhaut, M., Oris, M., Matthijs, K., & Teachman, J. (2009). The rise of age homogamy in 19th century western Europe. Journal of Marriage and Family, 71(5), 1234–1253.

Article Google Scholar

Van Ham, P., & Stirn, A. (2000). The seven sisters of India : Tribal worlds between Tibet and Burma. Prestel Mapin Publishing Pvt. Ltd.

Google Scholar

Vishwanath, J., & Palakonda, S. C. (2011). Patriarchal ideology of honour and honour crimes in India. International Journal of Criminal Justice Sciences (IJCJS), 6(1 & 2), 386–395.

Google Scholar

Vishwanath, L. S. (2000). Female infanticide and social structure: A socio-historical study in Western and Northern India. Hindustan Publishing Corporation.

Google Scholar

Vishwanath, L. S. (2001). Female foeticide and infanticide. Economic & Political Weekly, 35(36), 3411–3412.

Google Scholar

Vishwanath, L. S. (2004). Female infanticide: The colonial experience. Economic and Political Weekly, 39(22), 2313–2318.

Google Scholar

Walby, S. (1989). Theorising patriarchy. Sociology, 23(2), 213–234.

Article Google Scholar

Weber, M., Henderson, A. M., & Parsons, T. (1947). The theory of social and economic organization. Oxford University Press.

Google Scholar

CHAPTER 4

Adair, J. R. (2008). Introducing Christianity. New York: Routledge.

Ankerberg, J., & Weldon, J. (2008). The facts on world religions. Eugene, OR: Harvest House Publishers.

Aron, R. (1968). Democracy and totalitarianism (V. Ionescu, Trans.). London: Weidenfeld & Nicolson. (Original work published 1965)

Brague, R. (2003). The wisdom of the world: The human experience of the universe in Western thought (T. L. Fagan, Trans.). Chicago: University of Chicago Press.

Brague, R. (2007). The Law of God: The philosophical history of an idea (L. G. Cochrane, Trans.). Chicago: University of Chicago Press.

Comfort, R. (2008). World religions in a nutshell. Alachua, FL: Bridge-Logos.

Cowan, D. E., & Bromley, D. G. (2007). Cults and new religions: A brief history. Malden, MA: Blackwell.

D'Amato, S. E. (2006). Myths and mythology. In H. J. Birx (Ed.), Encyclopedia of anthropology (Vol. 4, pp. 1657–1661). Thousand Oaks, CA: Sage.

Eliade, M. (1959). The sacred and the profane: The nature of religion. New York: Harcourt, Brace. (Original work published 1957)

Geertz, C. (1975). The interpretation of cultures: Selected essays. London: Hutchinson.

Geertz, C. (2008). Religion. In P. A. Moro, J. E. Myers, & A. C. Lehmann (Eds.), Magic, witchcraft, and religion: An anthropological study of the supernatural (7th ed., pp. 6–15). New York: McGraw-Hill.

Guardini, R. (1998). Eternal life: What you need to know about death, judgment, and life everlasting. Manchester, NH: Sophia Institute Press. (Original work published 1940)

Hick, J. (2005). An interpretation of religion: Human responses to the transcendent (2nd ed.). New Haven, CT: Yale University Press.

Johnson, P. G. (1997). God and world religions: Basic beliefs and themes. Shippensburg, PA: Ragged Edge Press.

Jones, R. R. (2006). Religion and anthropology. In H. J. Birx (Ed.), Encyclopedia of anthropology (Vol. 5, pp. 2003–2006). Thousand Oaks, CA: Sage.

Kant, I. (1998). *Religion within the boundaries of mere reason and other writings*. Cambridge, UK: Cambridge University Press. (Original work published 1793)

Lamb, R. (2006). Religious rituals. In H. J. Birx (Ed.), *Encyclopedia of anthropology* (Vol. 5, pp. 2011–2014). Thousand Oaks, CA: Sage.

Lévi-Strauss, C. (1983). *Structural anthropology* (M. Layton, Trans.). Chicago: University of Chicago Press.

Maier, H. (Ed.). (2004–2007). *Totalitarianism and political religions* (3 vols; J. Bruhn, Trans.). New York: Routledge.

McGrath, A. E. (2007). *Christian theology: An introduction* (4th ed.). Malden, MA: Blackwell.

Meister, C., & Copan, P. (Eds.). (2007). *The Routledge companion to philosophy of religion*. New York: Routledge.

Mitchell, D. W. (2008). *Buddhism: Introducing the Buddhist experience* (2nd ed.). New York: Oxford University Press.

Moro, P. A., Myers, J. E., & Lehmann, A. C. (Eds.). (2008). *Magic, witchcraft, and religion: An anthropological study of the supernatural* (7th ed.). New York: McGraw-Hill.

Morris, B. (2006). *Religion and anthropology: A critical introduction.* Cambridge, UK: Cambridge University Press.

Nigosian, S. A. (2008). *World religions: A historical approach* (4th ed.). Boston: Bedford/St. Martin's.

Otto, R. (1925). *The idea of the holy: An inquiry into the nonrational factor in the idea of the divine and its relation to the rational.* New York: Oxford University Press. (Original work published 1917)

Rodrigues, H., & Harding, J. (Eds.). (2008). *Introduction to the study of religion.* New York: Routledge.

Schleiermacher, F. D. E. (1996). *On religion: Speeches to its cultured despisers.* Cambridge, UK: Cambridge University Press. (Original work published 1967)

Segal, E. (2008). *Introducing Judaism.* New York: Routledge.

Seitschek, H. O. (2006). Religion. In H. J. Birx (Ed.), *Encyclopedia of anthropology* (Vol. 5, pp. 1998–2003). Thousand Oaks, CA: Sage.

Tillich, P. (1988). *Main works: Writings on religions* (Vol. 5). Berlin: de Gruyter. (Original works published 1955, 1961)

Troeltsch, E. (1981). *The social teaching of the Christian churches. With an introduction by H. Richard Niebuhr (O. Wyon, Trans.). Chicago: University of Chicago Press. (Original work published 1912)*

Voegelin, E. (1999). Modernity without restraint. Edited with an introduction by Manfred Henningsen. Baton Rouge: Louisiana State University Press. (Original work published 1938)

Williams, J. (2008). Islam: Understanding the history, beliefs, and culture. Berkeley Heights, NJ: Enslow.

Wittgenstein, L. (2001). Philosophical investigations (G. E. M. Anscombe, Trans.). Oxford, UK: Blackwell. (Original work published 1953)

Young, S. (2007). New York: Marshall Cavendish Benchmark.

CHAPTER 5

Arvind Sharma, "On Hindu, Hindustan, Hinduism and Hindutva", Numen 49, no. 1 (2002): 1–36.

Jaithirth Rao, The Indian Conservative: A History of Indian Right-Wing Thought (New Delhi: Juggernaught Books, 2019);

Shashi Tharoor, Why I Am a Hindu (New Delhi: Aleph Book Company, 2018); The Hindu Way: An Introduction to Hinduism (New Delhi: Aleph Book Company, 2019);

Walter K. Andersen and Shridhar D. Damle, The Brotherhood in Saffron: The Rashtriya Swayamsevak Sangh and Hindu Revivalism (New Delhi: Penguin, 2019);

Walter K. Andersen and Shridhar D. Damle, Messengers of Hindu Nationalism: How the RSS Reshaped India (London: C. Hurst and Company (Publishers) Ltd., 2019);

A.P. Chatterji, T. Blom Hansen, and Christophe Jaffrelot, eds., Majoritarian State: How Hindu Nationalism Is Changing India (New Delhi: Harper Collins, 2019);

Swapan Dasgupta, Awakening Bharat Mata: The Political Beliefs of the Indian Right (New Delhi: Penguin, 2019)

CHAPTER 6

GUPTA, CHARU. "Hindu Women, Muslim Men: Love Jihad

and Conversions." *Economic and Political Weekly*, vol. 44, no. 51, 2009, pp. 13–15. *JSTOR*, *http://www.jstor.org/stable/25663907*.

Aga, Aniket, Ka Shaji, and Chitranganda Choudhury. 2021. 'Love Jihad': Made in Kerala, Exported Nationwide. Article 14. March 30. Available online: https://www.article-14.com/post/love-jihad-made-in-kerala-exported-nationwide (accessed on 20 August 2021).

Ahmad, Talmiz. 2020. How Hindutva Hatred Is Jeopardising India's Gulf Ties. The Wire. April 27. Available online: https://thewire.in/diplomacy/hindutva-india-gulf-ties (accessed on 1 June 2021).

Ahuja, Rajesh. 2018. NIA Ends Kerala Probe, Says There's Love but No Jihad. Hindustan Times. October 18. Available online: https://www.hindustantimes.com/india-news/nia-ends-kerala-probe-says-there-s-love-but-no-jihad/story-wlpWR7BMNcdJHkb1MUso4J.html (accessed on 25 June 2021).

Al Jazeera. 2019. Anger over India's Diplomat Calling for 'Israel Model' in Kashmir. Al Jazeera. November 28. Available online: https://www.aljazeera.com/news/2019/11/28/anger-over-indias-diplomat-calling-for-israel-model-in-kashmir (accessed on 8 June 2021).

Anand, Dibyesh. 2011. *Hindu Nationalism in India and the Politics of Fear*. London: Palgrave Macmillan. [Google Scholar]

ANI. 2021. *'Love Jihad': ISIS targeting Hindu, Christian Girls in Kerala, Says BJP State Chief*. ANI News. March 31. Available online: https://www.aninews.in/news/national/general-news/love-jihad-isis-targeting-hindu-christian-girls-in-kerala-says-bjp-state-chief20210331151850/ (accessed on 29 July 2021).

Barman, Priyanka. 2020. *Tripura Hindu Outfit Seeks Nationwide Law to Curb 'Love Jihad'*. Hindustan Times. November 28. Available online: https://www.hindustantimes.com/india-news/tripura-hindu-outfit-seeks-nationwide-law-to-curb-love-jihad/story-hdXgAEZOBXS29YLO38ImzO.html (accessed on 10 July 2021).

Banerjee, Sikata. 2003. *Gender and Nationalism: The Masculinization of Hinduism and Female Political Participation in India*. Available online: https://www.infona.pl/resource/bwmeta1.element.elsevier-33fac876-1b22-3d3a-a006-0b5a1f5f893c (accessed on 29 July 2021).

Bauman, Chad M. 2015. *Pentecostals, Proselytization, and Anti-Christian Violence in Contemporary India*. Oxford: Oxford University Press. [Google Scholar]

Bergmann, Eirikur. 2016. *Nordic Nationalism and Right-Wing Populist Politics: Imperial Relationships and National Sentiments*. Berlin and Heidelberg: Springer. [Google

Scholar]

Bhardwaj, Ananya. 2020. 'We Step in When Our Women Step out with Muslim Men': How up Law Empowers Hindu Bully Groups. The Print. December 26. Available online: https://theprint.in/india/we-operate-freely-now-how-hindu-groups-are-driving-ups-crackdown-on-love-jihad/574368/ (accessed on 25 June 2021).

Bhaumik, Anirban. 2020. India getting to know its real friends: S Jaishankar on flak from a section of international community. Deccan Herald. March 7. Available online: https://www.deccanherald.com/national/national-politics/india-getting-to-know-its-real-friends-s-jaishankar-on-flak-from-a-section-of-international-community-811495.html (accessed on 22 July 2021).

Brass, Paul R. 2003. The Production of Hindu-Muslim Violence in Contemporary India. Washington, DC: University of Washington Press. [Google Scholar]

Chandra, Kanchan. 2019. How Hindu Nationalism Went Mainstream. Foreign Policy. June 13. Available online: https://foreignpolicy.com/2019/06/13/how-hindu-nationalism-went-mainstream/ (accessed on 26 June 2021).

Chaudhuri, Subhasish. 2020. Matuas Flight, Plight and Fight for Citizenship. Telegraph India. January 24. Available online: https://www.telegraphindia.com/west-bengal/matuas-flight-plight-and-fight-for-citizenship/cid/1739411 (accessed on 5 June 2021).

Das, Veena. 2010. *Engaging the life of the other: Love and everyday life*. In *Ordinary Ethics: Anthropology, Language, and Action*. Edited by Michael Lambek. New York: Fordham University Press, pp. 376–99. [Google Scholar]

Das, Gaurav, and Gorky Chakraborty. 2021. *In Assam, Crimes by Muslims of East Bengal Origin Renews Opportunity for Targeted Communalism*. The Wire. June 21. Available online: https://thewire.in/communalism/in-assam-crimes-by-muslims-of-east-bengal-origin-renews-opportunity-for-targeted-communalism (accessed on 24 June 2021).

Davey, Jacob, and Julia Ebner. 2019. 'The Great Replacement': *The violent consequences of mainstreamed extremism*. Institute for Strategic Dialogue 7. [Google Scholar]

Khattak, Daud. 2021. *Inside Pakistan's 'Conversion Factory' for Hindu Brides*. Gandhara. April 20. Available online: https://gandhara.rferl.org/a/pakistan-hindu-brides-conversion-sindh/31205637.html (accessed on 25 July 2021).

Deb, Debraj. 2018. *Tripura: Migrant Workers from Assam, Bangladesh Involved in Love Jihad, Cow Slaughter, Claims VHP*. The Indian Express. November 9. Available online: https://indianexpress.com/article/north-east-india/tripura/tripura-migrant-workers-assam-bangladesh-love-jihad-cow-slaughter-vhp-5439460/ (accessed on 3 July 2021).

Deka, Kaushik. 2021. *Can BJP Survive the Demographic Disadvantage in Assam? India Today.* March 29. Available online: https://www.indiatoday.in/india-today-insight/story/can-bjp-survive-the-demographic-disadvantage-in-assam-1784851-2021-03-29 (accessed on 21 June 2021).

Frydenlund, Iselin, and Evian Leidig. Forthcoming. Introduction: "Love Jihad": Sexuality, Reproduction and the Construction of the Predatory Muslim Male. *Religions.*

Gökarıksel, Banu, Christopher Neubert, and Sara Smith. 2019. Demographic fever dreams: Fragile masculinity and population politics in the rise of the global right. *Signs: Journal of Women in Culture and Society* 44: 561–87. [Google Scholar] [CrossRef]

Gupta, Charu. 2001. *Sexuality, Obscenity, Community: Women, Muslims, and the Hindu Public in Colonial India.* Hyderabad: Orient Blackswan. [Google Scholar]

Gupta, Charu. 2009. Hindu Women, Muslim Men: Love jihad and conversions. *Economic and Political Weekly* 44: 51. [Google Scholar]

India Today. 2021. *Mood of the Nation Poll: 54% See a 'Love Jihad' Conspiracy to Convert Hindu Women to Islam. India Today.* January 22. Available online: https://www.indiatoday.in/mood-of-the-nation/story/majority-of-indians-see-love-jihad-conspiracy-to-convert-hindu-women-to-islam-mood-of-the-nation-poll-1761707-2021-01-22 (accessed on 25 June 2021).

Jaffrelot, Christophe. 2019. *Modi's India: Hindu Nationalism and the Rise of Ethnic Democracy*. Princeton: Princeton University Press, pp. 194–211. [Google Scholar]

Jaffrelot, Christophe, and Gilles Verniers. 2020. The BJP's 2019 election campaign: Not business as usual. *Contemporary South Asia* 28: 155–77. [Google Scholar] [CrossRef]

Jaffrelot, Christophe, and Haider Rizvi. 2020. Muslim countries with which India had increasingly good relations have become less friendly. *Carnegie Endowment International*, April 22. [Google Scholar]

Karthikeyan, Suchitra. 2021. Assam CM Says 'Jihad also When Hindu Man Marries Girl by Cheating'; Backs Love Jihad Law. *Republic World*. July 11. Available online: https://www.republicworld.com/india-news/politics/assam-cm-says-jihad-also-when-hindu-man-marries-girl-by-cheating-backs-love-jihad-law.html (accessed on 29 June 2021).

Karvy, Insights. 2021. Mood of the Nation Poll January 2021: Methodology. *India Today*. Available online: https://www.indiatoday.in/mood-of-the-nation/story/mood-of-the-nation-poll-january-2021-methodology-1761450-2021 01-21 (accessed on 25 July 2021).

Khan, Fatima. 2021. They're Taking Our Girls to ISIS: How Church Is Now Driving 'Love Jihad' Narrative in Kerala. *The Print*. April 2. Available online: https://theprint.in/india/theyre-taking-our-girls-to-isis-how-church-is-now-driving-love-jihad-narrative-in-kerala/632324/ (accessed on 17 June 2021).

Khatun, Nadira. 2018. Love-Jihad' and Bollywood: Constructing Muslims as 'other'. Journal of Religion & Film 22: 8. [Google Scholar]

Kumaraswamy, P. R. 2019. Modi transforms India's approach to the Middle East. East Asia Forum, October 11. [Google Scholar]

Lahiry, Sujit. 2019. Conflict, Peace and security: An international relations perspective with special reference to India. Millennial Asia 10: 76–90. [Google Scholar] [CrossRef]

Langa, Mahesh. 2021. Gujarat Assembly Passes 'Love Jihad' Law. The Hindu. April 1. Available online: https://www.thehindu.com/news/national/other-states/ gujarat-assembly-passes-love-jihad-law/ article34217780.ece (accessed on 30 July 2021).

Leidig, Eviane. 2019. Immigrant, nationalist and proud: A Twitter Analysis of Indian diaspora supporters for Brexit and Trump. Media and Communication 7: 77–89. [Google Scholar] [CrossRef]

Mahanta, Siddhartha. 2014. India's Fake 'Love Jihad'. Foreign Policy. September 4. Available online: https://foreignpolicy.com/2014/09/04/indias-fake-love-jihad/ (accessed on 25 June 2021).

Majid, Burhan. 2020. *The unconstitutionality of 'love jihad' laws. The India Forum, December 4.* [Google Scholar]

Malik, Ahmed. 2020. *Future of citizenship laws in India with special reference to Assam. Journal of Legal Studies and Research 6: 2455–37.* [Google Scholar]

Mayer, Tamar, ed. 2012. *Gender Ironies of Nationalism: Sexing the Nation. Abingdon-on-Thames: Routledge.* [Google Scholar]

Melegh, Attila. 2016. *Unequal exchanges and the radicalization of demographic nationalism in Hungary. Intersections East European Journal of Society and Politics 2: 87–108.* [Google Scholar] [CrossRef][Green Version]

Methri, Gloria. 2021. *Amit Shah Lists '3 Types of Citizens In Bengal', Says Mamata's Favourites Are Infiltrators. Republic World. Available online:* https://www.republicworld.com/india-news/politics/amit-shah-lists-3-types-of-citizens-in-bengal-says-mamatas-favourites-are-infiltrators.html *(accessed on 4 July 2021).*

Minj, Bijay Kumar. 2019. *Church Worried about 'Love Jihad' in India Again. Union of Catholic Asian News. September 27. Available online:* https://www.ucanews.com/news/church-worried-about-love-jihad-in-india-again/86198# *(accessed on 29 June 2021).*

Mishra, Anand. 2020. *Four BJP-Ruled States Promise Law on Love Jihad; Legal Experts Find the Move*

Unconstitutional. *Deccan Herald*. November 3. Available online: https://www.deccanherald.com/national/four-bjp-ruled-states-promise-law-on-love-jihad-legal-experts-find-the-move-unconstitutional-910937.html (accessed on 16 June 2021).

Mukherjee, U. N. 1909. *Hindus: A Dying Race*. Calcutta: M. Banerjee & Co. [Google Scholar]

Nayak, Priyam. 2021. *How "Love Jihad" Is Being Used to Influence Elections in West Bengal*. Logically. February 8. Available online: https://www.logically.ai/articles/exclusive-love-jihad-elections-west-bengal (accessed on 25 June 2021).

Omer, Atalia, and Jason A. Springs. 2013. *Religious Nationalism: A Reference Handbook*. Santa Barbara: Abc-clio. [Google Scholar]

Pakrasi, Susmita. 2021. *Will Enact Laws to Prevent Love Jihad, Land Jihad, Promises Amit Shah in Assam*. Hindustan Times. March 26. Available online: https://www.hindustantimes.com/elections/assam-assembly-election/will-enact-laws-to-prevent-love-jihad-land-jihad-promises-amit-shah-in-assam-101616747655727.html (accessed on 25 July 2021).

Panday, Chandan. 2020. *Now, Hindu Group Blocks National Highway in Tripura, Demands Law against 'Love Jihad'*. EastMojo. November 28. Available online: https://www.eastmojo.com/news/2020/11/28/now-hindu-group-blocks-national-highway-in-tripura-demands-law-against-love-jihad/ (accessed on 1 September 2021).

Pandey, Alok, and Mariyam Alavi. 2020. *No Conspiracy, Foreign Funding in Inter-Faith Marriages, Say Kanpur Cops*. NDTV. Available online: https://www.ndtv.com/india-news/no-conspiracy-foreign-funding-in-inter-faith-marriages-say-kanpur-cops-2329238 (accessed on 15 June 2021).

Parashar, Utpal. 2021. *Assam Marriage Bill Will Check 'Love Jihad' of all Kinds: CM Sarma*. Hindustan Times. Available online: https://www.hindustantimes.com/india-news/assam-marriage-bill-will-check-love-jihad-of-all-kinds-cm-sarma-101625945309058.html (accessed on 25 June 2021).

Piedalue, Amy, Amanda Gilbertson, and Manas Raturi. 2021. A majoritarian view of 'gender justice' in contemporary India: Examining media coverage of 'triple talaq' and 'love jihad'". *South Asia: Journal of South Asian Studies* 44: 739–55. [Google Scholar] [CrossRef]

Press Trust of India. 2019. *Hindu, Buddhist, Sikh, Jain refugees won't have to leave India: Amit Shah*. Business Standard. Available online: https://www.business-standard.com/article/pti-stories/nrc-must-for-national-security-will-be-implemented-shah-119100101129_1.html (accessed on 24 June 2021).

Press Trust of India. 2020. Amid 'Love Jihad' Row, Himachal Pradesh Implements Act against 'Forced Conversions'. Outlook India. December 20. Available online: https://www.outlookindia.com/website/story/india-news-as-bjp-states-mull-love-jihad-laws-himachal-pradesh-implements-act-against-forced-conversion/367850 (accessed on 14 June 2021).

Press Trust of India. 2021a. Madhya Pradesh Assembly Passes 'Love Jihad' Bill. The Wire. March 8. Available online: https://thewire.in/communalism/madhya-pradesh-assembly-passes-love-jihad-bill (accessed on 8 July 2021).

Press Trust of India. 2021b. Karnataka 'Love Jihad' Law Likely in Next Legislature Session: BJP. The Week. February 17. Available online: https://www.theweek.in/news/india/2021/02/17/karnataka--love-jihad--law-likely-in-next-legislature-session--b.html (accessed on 8 July 2021).

Press Trust of India. 2021c. Haryana Will Bring 'Love Jihad' Law 'as Soon as Possible': Home Minister. The Wire. February 12. Available online: https://thewire.in/government/haryana-love-jihad-law-as-soon-as-possible-home-minister-anil-vij (accessed on 7 July 2021).

PRS Legislative Research India. 2020a. The Madhya Pradesh Freedom of Religion Ordinance, 2020. Available online: https://prsindia.org/bills/states/the-madhya-pradesh-freedom-of-religion-ordinance-2020 (accessed on 22 July 2021).

PRS Legislative Research India. 2020b. The Uttar Pradesh

Prohibition of Unlawful Conversion of Religion Ordinance, 2020. Available online: https://prsindia.org/bills/states/ the-uttar-pradesh-prohibition-of-unlawful-conversion-of- religion-ordinance-2020 (accessed on 22 July 2021).

Putnam, Robert D. 1988. Diplomacy and domestic politics: The logic of two-level games. International Organizations 42: 427–60. [Google Scholar] [CrossRef][Green Version]

Rajeshwar, Yashasvini, and Roy C. Amore. 2019. Coming home (Ghar Wapsi) and going away: Politics and the mass conversion controversy in India. Religions 10: 313. [Google Scholar] [CrossRef][Green Version]

Rana, Yudhvir. 2011. Not just White girls, Pak Muslim Men Sexually Target Hindu and Sikh Girls too. Times of India. January 10. Available online: https://timesofindia.indiatimes.com/world/pakistan/Not- just-White-girls-Puk-Muslim-men-sexually-target-Hindu- and-Sikh-girls-as-well/articleshow/7254035.cms (accessed on 29 June 2021).

Rao, Mohan. 2011. Love Jihad and demographic fears. Indian Journal of Gender Studies 18: 425–30. [Google Scholar] [CrossRef]

Ray, Meenakshi. 2020. From 5-Year Jail Term to Non- Bailable Offence: What States Say on Ordinance against Love Jihad. Hindustan Times. November 21. Available online: https://www.hindustantimes.com/india-news/ frlom-5-year-jail-term-to-non-bailable-offence-what-states- say-on-ordinance-against-love-jihad/ story-0JwKeeXzMFCTZBA38OVU5H.html (accessed on 6

July 2021).

Roy, Rajiv. 2018. *Scrap Long-Term Visas to B'deshi Muslims: Assam MLAs to Centre. Northeast Now. April 9. Available online: https://nenow.in/north-east-news/scrap-long-term-visas-to-bdeshi-muslims-assam-mlas-to-centre.html (accessed on 14 June 2021).*

Sabarwal, Harshit. 2020. *Love Jihad' Funded by Foreign Nations, Conspiracy against India: MP Minister". Hindustan Times. November 26. Available online: https://www.hindustantimes.com/bhopal/love-jihad-funded-by-foreign-nations-conspiracy-against-india-mp-minister/story-tQNBwKIHcLtYa8KbJXGQ1N.html (accessed on 14 June 2021).*

Saha, Abhishek. 2021. *BJP Will Tackle 'Love Jihad', 'Land Jihad': Amit Shah in Assam. The Indian Express. March 21. Available online: https://indianexpress.com/elections/amit-shah-love-land-jihad-elections-7246974/ (accessed on 25 June 2021).*

Sahu, Manish. 2021. *1 Month of UP 'Love Jihad' Law: 14 Cases, 49 in Jail, Woman 'Victim' Complainant in Only Two. Indian Express. January 9. Available online: https://indianexpress.com/article/india/love-jihad-law-up-police-7124001/ (accessed on 2 July 2021).*

Seth, Maulshree. 2020. *Explained: Uttar Pradesh's 'Love Jihad' Law, and Why It Could Be Implemented Vigorously. The Indian Express. December 5. Available online: https://indianexpress.com/article/explained/explained-uttar-pradeshs-love-jihad-law-and-why-it-could-be-*

implemented-vigorously-7066156/ (accessed on 5 June 2021).

Sethi, Manisha. 2002. *Avenging angels and nurturing Mothers: Women in Hindu nationalism. Economic and Political Weekly* 37: 1545–52. [Google Scholar]

Shah, Amit. 2020. *Speech 25 July 2020, Kolkata, India.* Available online: https://www.hindustantimes.com/india-news/will-give-hindu-refugees-citizenship-expel-infiltrators-says-amit-shah-in-bengal/story-GPnV0ke9adJbSaJ7kOsQBK.html (accessed on 3 June 2021).

Shah, Ajit Prakash. 2021. *'Love Jihad' Ordinance Is Symbolic of Social Fabric Being Aggressively Changed: Justice A.P. Shah'. The Wire.* January 31. Available online: https://thewire.in/law/love-jihad-ordinance-communal-rhetoric-divisive-justice-ap-shah (accessed on 1 June 2021).

Siddique, Iram. 2021. *3 Months of MP 'Love Jihad' Law: 21 Cases, Couple Knew Each Other in over Half. The Indian Express.* March 20. Available online: https://indianexpress.com/article/india/mp-love-jihad-law-7236429/ (accessed on 15 June 2021).

Singh, Sinderpal. 2009. *"Border crossings and Islamic terrorists": Representing Bangladesh in Indian foreign policy during the BJP era. India Review* 8: 144–62. [Google Scholar] [CrossRef]

Social Attitudes Research for India (SARI). 2016. *Available* online: https://riceinstitute.org/blog-post/social-attitudes-research-india-sari-data-is-available/ (accessed on 25 June 2021).

Strohl, David James. 2019. Love jihad in India's moral imaginaries: Religion, kinship, and citizenship in late liberalism. Contemporary South Asia 27: 27–39. [Google Scholar] [CrossRef]

Sufian, Abu. 2020. Geopolitics of the NRC-CAA in Assam: Impact on Bangladesh–India relations. Asian Ethnicity 1–31. [Google Scholar] [CrossRef]

The Sentinel Assam. 2018. Victim of Love-Jihad Be Brought Back from Bangladesh. The Sentinel Assam. April 19. Available online: https://www.sentinelassam.com/news/victim-of-love-jihad-be-brought-back-from-bangladesh/ (accessed on 6 July 2021).

The Tribune. 2017. Hadiya Case: BJP Slams Kerala Government. The Tribune. October 17. Available online: https://www.tribuneindia.com/news/archive/nation/hadiya-case-bjp-slams-kerala-government-478728 (accessed on 21 June 2021).

The Wire. 2020a. "Following domestic concern, Indonesia summons Indian envoy over Delhi riots". The Wire. March 1. Available online: https://thewire.in/diplomacy/following-domestic-concern-indonesia-summons-indian-envoy-over-delhi-riots (accessed on 14 July 2021).

The Wire. 2020b. Less than a month after UP's 'Love Jihad'

ordinance, a spate of FIRs. The Wire. December 21. Available online: https://thewire.in/law/uttar-pradesh-love-jihad-firs (accessed on 20 June 2021).

Times of India. 2020. Two Years after 'Love Jihad' Law, Uttarakhand Books Four. Times of India. December 31. Available online: https://timesofindia.indiatimes.com/city/ dehradun/4-booked-in-first-case-under-ukhand-anti-conversion-law/articleshow/80032397.cms (accessed on 7 July 2021).

Times of India. 2021. MP's 'Love Jihad' Law Comes into Force. Times of India. January 21. Available online: https://timesofindia.indiatimes.com/city/bhopal/mps-love-jihad-law-comes-into-force/articleshow/ 80194309.cms (accessed on 1 July 2021).

Tyagi, Aastha, and Atreyee Sen. 2020. Love-Jihad (Muslim sexual seduction) and ched-chad (sexual harassment): Hindu Nationalist Discourses and the Ideal/Deviant Urban Citizen in India. Gender, Place & Culture 27: 104–25. [Google Scholar]

Van Evera, Stephen. 1994. Hypotheses on nationalism and war. International Security 18: 5–39. [Google Scholar] [CrossRef]

Verma, Lalmani. 2021. Will Take Steps to Stop 'Love Jihad', Says Uttarakhand CM Tirath Singh Rawat. The Indian Express. April 10. Available online: https://indianexpress.com/article/india/uttarakhand-cm-says-will-take-steps-to-stop-love-jihad-7267000/ (accessed on 5 July 2021).

Wæver, Ole. 1993. Securitization and Desecuritization. Copenhagen: Centre for Peace and Conflict Research. [Google Scholar]

Warner, Michael. 1991. Introduction: Fear of a queer planet. Social Text, 3–17. [Google Scholar]

Yilmaz, Ihsan, and Galib Bashirov. 2018. The AKP after 15 years: Emergence of Erdoganism in Turkey. Third World Quarterly 39: 1812–30. [Google Scholar] [CrossRef][Green Version]

Zee News. 2020. Deshhit: Pakistan Is Funding the Love Jihad Conspiracies in India. Zee News. September 3. Available online: https://zeenews.india.com/video/india/deshhit-pakistan-is-funding-the-love-jihad-conspiracies-in-india-2307362.html (accessed on 15 June 2021).

Ziegfeld, Adam. 2020. A new dominant party in India? Putting the 2019 BJP victory into comparative and historical perspective. India Review 19: 136–52. [Google Scholar] [CrossRef]

CHAPTER 7

Oberoi, H., 2001. The Construction of Religious Boundaries. Delhi: Oxford Univ. Press.The Hindu. 2020.

RAW Chief Consulted MI6 In Build-Up to Operation Bluestar.   [online]   Availableat: <https://www.thehindu.com/news/national/RAW-chief-consulted-MI6-in-build-up-to-Operation-Bluestar/ article11497124.ece> (PDF)

The Khalistan Movement of 1984: A Critical Appreciation. [online]Available   at:<https://www.researchgate.net/ publication/ 326368349_The_Khalistan_Movement_of_1984_A _Critical_Appreciation>

International Journal of Refugee Law, 1997. 2. RefWorld on CD-ROM reaches third edition. 9(1),pp.83-84.Van Dyke, V., 2009.

The Khalistan Movement in Punjab, India, and the Post-Militancy Era:Structural Change and New Political Compulsions. Asian Survey, 49(6), pp.975-997.Ipcs.org. 2021. [online] Available at:<http://www.ipcs.org/ issue_briefs/issue_brief_pdf/17871321811PCS-ResearchPaper12-SimratDhillon.pdf>

CHAPTER 8

J. I. Packer, Rediscovering Holiness

John MacArthur, "The Call to Repentance," in The Gospel According to Jesus: What is Authentic Faith?

Paul Helm, The Beginnings: Word & Spirit in Conversion

CHAPTER 9

Bunsha, D. (2004) 'Developing doubt', Urban Development, Frontline, Vol. 21, No. 12, Availableat: http://www.hindu.com/2006/10/06/stories/ 2006100602341200.htm.Burra, S. (2005)

'Towards a pro-poor framework for slum upgrading in Mumbai, India',Environment and Urbanization, Vol. 17, pp.67–88.

Collins, H. and Champy, J. (1995) *Re-Engineering Management*. New York: Harper BusinessBooks.

Crain's Chicago Business (2007) 'A land of many contrasts', April 30, Vol. 30, No. 18, p.33.

Davis, M. (2006) *Planet of Slums*. London: Verso.Desai, V. (1988) 'Dharavi, the largest slum in Asia: development of low income urban housing inIndia', *Habitat International*, Vol. 12, No. 2, pp.67–74.

Edwards, S.M. (2001) *The Gazetteer of Bombay City and Island, Reprint. First published in 1909.*New Delhi, Cosmo, 3 Vol., 1396p.

Friedman, T. (2006) *The World is Flat*. New York: Farar, Straus and Giroux.Goering, L. (2007) 'Would you tour a slum?' *Chicago Tribune*, 31 March.

Giridharadas, A. (2007) 'Rumbling across India to a new life in the city', *The New York Times*, 25November.

Gupchup, V. (1993) *Bombay: Social Change, 1813–1857.* Mumbai, India: Popular Book Depot.

Hammer, M. and Stanton, S. (1995) *The Re-Engineering Revolution.* London.

Jacobson, M. (2007) 'Dharavi: Mumbai's shadow city', *National Geographic Magazine*, May.

Lancaster, J. (2007) 'Next stop, squalor: in poverty tourism, 'poorism' they call it exploration orexploitation?' *Smithsonian Magazine*, March. Available at: http://www.smithsonianmag.com/people-places/ Next_Stop_Squalor.html?page=2.

Mahalingam, T.V. (2007) 'A foggy castle in the toxic air', *Business Today*, 1 July, p.84 (1) (PDF)

McDougall, D. (2007) 'Waste not, want not in the £ 700 m slum', *The Observer*, 4 March.Available at http://observer.guardian.co.uk/world/story/

0,,2026024,00.html#article_continue.

Mukhija, V. (2002) 'An analytical framework for urban upgrading: property rights, property valuesand physical attributes', Habitat International, Vol. 26, pp.553–570.

Mukhija, V. (2003) Squatters as Developers? Slum Redevelopment in Mumbai Burlington. VT:Ashgate Publications.

Neuwirth, R. (2005) Shadow Cities: A Billion Squatters. A New Urban World, New York:Routledge.

Patel, S. and Jockin, A. (2007) 'An offer of partnership or a promise of conflict in Dharavi,Mumbai?' International Institute for Environment and Development, Vol. 19, No. 2,pp.501–508.

Patel, S. and Thorner, A. (Eds.) (1995) Bombay: Metaphor for Modern India. Mumbai, India:Oxford University Press.

Perry, A. (2006) 'Life in Dharavi: inside Asia's biggest slum', Time Asia, 12 June. Abvailable at:http://www.time.com/time/asia/covers/501060619/slum.html.

Prahalad, C.K. and Hammond, A. (2002) 'Serving the World's poor profitably', Harvard BusinessReview, Vol. 80, No. 9, pp.48–57.

Prahalad, C.K. and Hart, S. (2002) 'The fortune at the bottom of the pyramid', Strategy + Business,Vol. 26, pp.2–14.

Roy, A.N., Jockin, A. and Javed, A. (2004) 'Community police stations in Mumbai's slums',Environment and Urbanization, Vol. 16, No. 2, pp.135–138.

Sachs, J. (2005) The End of Poverty: Economic Possibilities of Our Time. New York: The PenguinPress.

Sanyal, B. and Mukhija, V. (2001) 'Institutional pluralism and housing delivery: a case ofunforeseen conflicts in

Mumbai, India', World Development, Vol. 29, No. 12, pp.2043–2057.

Sharma, K. (2000) Rediscovering Dharavi: Story from Asia's Largest Slum. Penguin Books.

Subramanian, L. (1996) Indigenous Capital and Imperial Expansion: Bombay, Surat, and the WestCoast. Delhi: Oxford University Press.

The Economic Times (2007) 'Organized retailing in slums! Biyani makes it possible', 12 August.

The Times (United Kingdom) (2003) 'Prince crowns India trip with slum visit', 6 November, p.15.Tindall, G. (1992) City of Gold. Penguin Books.

Whitehead, J. and More, N. (2007) 'Revanchism in Mumbai? Political economy of rent gaps andurban restructuring in a global city', Economic and Political Weekly, June 2007 (1) (PDF)

CHAPTER 10

G. P. D. "Dalit Literature." *Economic and Political Weekly*, vol. 17, no. 3, Economic and Political Weekly, 1982, pp. 61–62,

Bama, and M. Vijayalakshmi. "Dalit Literature." *Indian Literature*, vol. 43, no. 5 (193), Sahitya Akademi, 1999, pp. 97–98.

Balagopal, K. "Dalit Literature." *Economic and Political Weekly*, vol. 17, no. 6, Economic and Political Weekly, 1982, pp. 177–177.

Bhoite, Uttam, and Anuradha Bhoite. "The Dalit Sahitya Movement in Maharashtra: A Sociological Analysis." *Sociological Bulletin*, vol. 26, no. 1, Indian Sociological Society, 1977, pp. 60–75.

Webster, John C. B. "Understanding the Modern Dalit Movement." *Sociological Bulletin*, vol. 45, no. 2, Indian Sociological Society, 1996, pp. 189–204.

Baudh, Sumit. "Invisibility Of 'Other' Dalits and Silence in The Law." *Biography*, vol. 40, no. 1, University of Hawai'i Press, 2017, pp. 222-243.

Kavitha, K. Dalit Literature in India Social Science. 2014.

Thiara, Nicole, and Judith Misrahi-Barak. "Editorial: Why Should We Read Dalit Literature?" The Journal of Commonwealth Literature, vol. 54, no. 1, 15 Sept. 2017, pp. 3–8.

"Significance of Dalit Literature in Indian Context - Ignited Mind Journals." Ignited.in, ignited.in/I/a/89630.

Mandavkar, Pavan. (2016). Indian Dalit Literature Quest for Identity to Social Equality. Humanities & Social Sciences Reviews. 3. 42-48.

Buwa, Mr. Vilas Rupnath. "Dalit Literature: A Contemporary Perspective." International Journal of English Literature and Social Sciences, vol. 4, no. 3, 2019, pp. 895–899.

Kumar, Soumya Nair Anoop. "Indian Dalit Literature — a Reflection of Cultural Marginality." International Journal of

Languages, Literature and Linguistics, vol. 2, no. 4, Dec. 2016, pp. 209–212.

Kumar, Sukrita P, Vibha S. Chauhan, and Bodh Prakash. Cultural Diversity Linguistic Plurality and Literary Traditions in India. Delhi: Macmillan India, 2005.

Moon, Vasant, Gail Omvedt, and Eleanor Zelliot. Growing Up Untouchable in India: A Dalit Autobiography. Lanham, Md: Rowman & Littlefield Publishers, 2001. Print.

Kamble, B (2008) The Prisons We Broke (Translated from the Marathi). Hyderabad: Orient Blackswan.

Giri, Dipak. (2020). Perspectives on Indian Dalit Literature: Critical Responses.

CHAPTER 11

Goldstein, Joshua S. 200 I. War and Gender: How GenderShapes the War System and Vice Versa. Cambridge:Cambridge University Press.

Hays, Sharon. 1996. The Cultural Contradictions ofMotherhood. New Haven: Yale UniversityPress.

Kimmel, Michael S. 1996. Manhood in America: ACultural History. New York: Free Press.

Kanter, Rosabeth Moss. 1977. Men and Women of the Corporation. New York: Basic Books.

Lippa, Richard A. 2002. Gender, Nature, and Nurture.

Mahwah, NJ: L. Erlbaum.Oakley, Ann. 1972. Sex, Gender, and Society. New York:Harper and Row.

Thorne, Barrie. 1993. Gender Play: Girls and Boys in School. New Brunswick, NJ: Rutgers UniversityPress.

Williams, Christine. 1995. Still a Man's World: Men Who Do "Womens Work." Berkeley: University of California press.

Williams, Joan. 1999. Unbending Gender: Why Family andWork Conf/ict and What To Do About It. Oxford:Oxford University Press.

Gender Roles and Society. Available from: https://www.researchgate.net/publication/ 304125569_Gender_Roles_and_Society

AAUW. 1992. Shortchanging Girls/Shortchanging America. Washington DC: American Association of University Women.

Andersen, Elaine Slosberg. 1990. Speaking With Style: The Sociolinguistic Skills of Children. London: Routledge.

Bellinger, D. and Gleason, Jean Berko. 1982. Sex differences in parental directives to young children. Journal of Sex Roles, 8:1123–1139.

Biernat, Monica; Manis, Melvin; and Nelson, Thomas. 1991. Stereotypes and standards of judgment. Journal of Personal and Social Psychology, 60:485–499.

Blackless, Melanie; Charuvastra, Anthony; Derryck, Amanda; Fausto-Sterling, Anne; Lauzanne, Karl; and Lee, Ellen. 2000. How sexually dimorphic are we? Review and synthesis. American Journal of Human Biology, 12:151–166.

Nochlin, Linda. 1992. Why have there been no great women artists? Heresies, 7:38–43. Ortner, Sherry 1990. Gender hegemonies. Cultural Critique, 14:35–80.

Ortner, Sherry. 1996. Making Gender: The Politics and Erotics of Culture. Boston: Beacon Press.

Ortner, Sherry and Whitehead, Harriet. 1981. Sexual Meanings: the Cultural Construction of Gender and Sexuality. New York: Cambridge University Press.

Patsopoulos, Nikolaos A., Tatsioni, Athina and Ioannidis, John P.A. 2007. Claims of sex differences: An empirical assessment in genetic associations. Journal of the American Medical Association, 298.880-93.

Poole, J. 1646. The English Accidence. Menston, England: Scolar Press Facsimile. Richardson, Sarah. forthcoming. Sex itself: Male and female in the human genome. Chicago: University of Chicago Press.

Rose, Robert; Gordon, Thomas; and Bernstein, Irwin. 1972. Plasma testosterone levels in the male rhesus monkeys: influences of sexual and social stimuli. Science, 178:634–645. 21:35–51.

Rubin, J. Z.; Provenzano, F. J.; and Luria, Z. 1974. The eye of the beholder: parents' view on sex of newborns. American Journal of Orthopsychiatry, 44:512–519.

Rudman, Laurie A. and Glick, Peter. 2008. The social psychology of gender: How power and intimacy shape gender relations: Texts in Social Psychology. New York and London: The Guildord Press.

Morgan, and M. Pollack, 325–263. Cambridge, MA: MIT Press. Staples, R. 1973. The Black Woman in America: Sex, Marriage and the Family.

Chicago: Nelson Hall. Thorne, Barrie. 1993. Gender Play. New Brunswick, NJ: Rutgers University Press. Valian, Virginia. 1998. Why So Slow?: Women and Professional Achievement. Cambridge, MA: MIT Press.

West, Candace and Zimmerman, Don. 1987. Doing gender. Gender and Society, 1:125–151.

Whiting, B. B. and Edwards, C. P. 1988. Children of Different Worlds: The Formation of Social Behavior. Cambridge, MA: Harvard University Press.

Wilson, T. 1553. Arte of Rhetorique. Gainsville: Scholars Facsimiles and Reprints, 1962

CHAPTER 12

M. Keizaburo, "Kotoba To Wa Nanika Natsumeshobou", 1995.

G. Ritzer and D. J. Goodman, "Sociological Theory Modern", translated by Aliman. Jakarta: Kencana, 2012.

M. Konosuke,"Thoughts About Men", Jakarta: Pustaka Jaya, 1997.

P. W.J. Nababan, "Sosiolinguitik: An Introduction", Jakarta: Gramedia, 1984.

I. W. Jendra, "Sociolinguistic Theory and Practice", Surabaya: Paramita, 2007.

F. de Saussure, "Course de Lingustique Generale",Translated into Indonesian by Rahayu S. Hidayat and edited by Harimurti Kridalaksana. Yogyakarta: Gadjah Mada University Press. 1996.

L. Bloomfield, "Language", New York: Holt, Rinehart and Winston, 1933.

A. Chaer, dan A. Leonie, "Sosiolinguitik", Jakarta: Rineka Reserved, 2004.

Agbaje, A.A.B. (1992) The Nigerian Press, Hegemany and the Social construction ofLegistimacy: The Edwin Melien Press Ltd. Lamp eter (uic).

Adewumi, F. (1994) "Government - Media Relations in nigeria: A general Overview" WorkshopPaper.

Crokhire, G., Communication and Awareness Philippines: Conimngs Pub. Co. Inc. 1976.

McQuall, D. (1969); Towards A Sociology ofMass Communication, Cotlier: Maomollian Press.

Marx & Engels (1976) The German Ideology Moscow: Progress Publishers: PP.65. - 71.

Silberman, A. "The Sociology of Mass-Media and Mass Communication" in ISST Vol XIX No.4 1967 and Vo1XX No.4. 1969

Language, Society and Culture. Available from: https://www.researchgate.net/publication/ 341926007_Language_Society_and_Culture

CHAPTER 13

Akhundov, M. D. 1986. Conceptions of Space and Time. Cambridge, MA: The MIT Press.

Bull, W. 1968. Time, Tense and the verb: A Study in the Theoretical and Applied Linguistics, with Particular attention to Spanish. Berkeley/Los Angeles: University of California Press.

Choi, Y. H. 2000. Language and Time. Seoul: Park-i-Jung Publishing Company Croft, W. and D. Alan Cruse. 2004.

Cognitive Linguistics. Cambridge: Cambridge University Press Fauconnier, Gilles. 1997. Mappings in Thought and Language. Cambridge: Cambridge University Press.

Fauconnier, Gilles and Sweetser, Eve E. (eds.) 1996. Spaces, Worlds and Grammar. Chicago: Chicago University Press.

Hopper, P. (ed.) 1982. Tense and Aspect: between Semantics and Pragmatics. John Benjamins Publishing Company. Jakel, O. 1995.

The mental Concept of mind: 'Mental activity is manipulation'. In Taylor, J.R. & R.E. MacLaury(eds). Language and Cognitive Construal of the World. Berlin/ New York: Mouton de Gruyter, 197-227. Jhee, I. 2012.

A Cognitive Analysis on Time and Space: Spatial

Expressions used for Time. Korean Journal of English Language and Linguistics 12-4, 977-999. Seoul: The Korea Association of English Language and Linguistics. Kövecses, Z. 2002.

Metaphor; a practical introduction. Oxford: Oxford University Press. Lakoff, G. and Johnson, Mark. 1980. Metaphors we live by. Chicago: Chicago University Press. Lakoff, G. 1987.

Women, Fire and Dangerous things. Chicago: Chicago University Press. Langacker, Ronald W. 1987. Foundations of cognitive grammar, vol.1: theoretical prerequisites. Stanford: Stanford University Press.

Langacker, Ronald W. 1991. Concept, Image, and Symbol. The Cognitive Basis of Grammar.

Mouton de Gruyter. Sarrazin, J.-C., Giraudo, M. -D., Pailhous, J., & Bootsma, R. J. 2004. Dynamics of balancing space and time in memory: Tau and kappa effects revisited. Journal of Experimental Psychology: Human Perception and Performance, 30-3. 411- 430.

Smart, J. J. C. 1949. *The river of time.* Mind 58:483-494.

Talmy, L. 1983. *How language structures space. In H. Pick and L. Acredolo(eds), Spatial Orientation: Theory, Research and Application. 225-82. New York: Plenum Press.*

Traugott, E. C. 1978. *On the expression of spatio-temporal relations in language. In J. H. Greenburg(ed.), Universals of human language: Vol. 3. Word structure. pp. 369-400. Stanford, CA: Stanford University Press.*

Wierzbicka, A. 1996. *Semantics: Primes and Universals. Oxford: Oxford University Press.*

Yu, N. 1996. *The Contemporary Theory of Metaphor: A Perspective from Chinese. University of Arizon*

CHAPTER 14

Ambady, N., Shih, M., Kim, A., & Pittinsky, T. L. (2001). *Stereotype susceptibility in children: Effects of identity activation on quantitative performance. Psychological Science, 12, 385-390.*

Aronson, J., & Good, C. (2003). *The development and consequences of stereotype vulnerability in adolescents. In*

F. Pajares & T. Urdan (Eds.), *Adolescence and education: Vol. 2. Academic motivation of adolescents* (pp. 299-330). Greenwich, CT: Information Age.

Aronson, J., & McGlone, M. (2009). Stereotype and social identity threat. In T. Nelson (Ed.), *The handbook of prejudice, stereotyping, and discrimination*. New York: Guilford.

Baron-Cohen, S. (2004). *Essential difference: Male and female brains and the truth about autism*. New York: Basic Books.

En ligneBeilock, S. L., Rydell, R. J., & McConnell, A. R. (2007). Stereotype threat and working memory: Mechanisms, alleviation, and spillover. *Journal of Experimental Psychology: General, 136,* 256-276.

En ligneBenbow, C. P., & Stanley, J. C. (1980). Sex differences in mathematical ability: Fact or artifact?. *Science, 210,* 1262-1264.

En ligneBrosnan, M. J. (1998). Spatial ability in children's play with Lego blocks. *Perceptual and Motor Skills, 87,* 19-28.

Chan, N. H. W., & Rosenthal, H. E. S. (2014). Working memory moderates stereotype threat effects for adolescents in Hong Kong. *International Review of Social Psychology / Revue Internationale de Psychologie Sociale, 27,* 103-118.

En ligneCheng, Y. L. & Mix, K. S. (2014). Spatial training improves children's mathematics ability. Journal of Cognition and Development, 15(1), 2-11.

En ligneCimpian, A., Mu, Y., & Erickson, L. C. (2012). Who is good at this game? Linking an activity to a social category undermines children's achievement. Psychological Science, 23(5), 533-541.

En ligneCunningham, S. J., & Macrae, C. N. (2011). The colour of gender stereotyping. British Journal of Psychology, 102, 598-614.

En ligneDavies, P. G., Spencer, S. J., & Steele, C. M. (2005). Clearing the air: Identity safety moderates the effects of stereotype threat on women's leadership aspirations. Journal of Personality and Social Psychology, 88, 276-287.

En ligneFeng, J., Spence, I., & Pratt, J. (2007). Playing an action video game reduces gender differences in spatial cognition. Psychological Science, 18(10), 850-855.

En ligneFrome, P. M., Alfeld, C. J., Eccles, J. S., & Barber, B. L. (2006). Why don't they want a male-dominated job? An investigation of young women who changed their occupational aspirations. Educational Research and Evaluation, 12(4), 359-372.

En ligneGaldi, S., Cadinu, M., & Tomasetto, C. (2014). The roots of stereotype threat: When automatic associations disrupt girls' math performance. Child Development, 85(1), 250-263.

En ligneGanley, C. M., Mingle, L. A., Ryan, A. M., Ryan, K., Vasilyeva, M., & Perry, M. (2013). An examination of stereotype threat effects on girls' mathematics performance. Developmental Psychology, 49(10), 1886.

En ligneGoble, P., Martin, C. L., Hanish, L. D., & Fabes, R. A. (2012). Children's gender-typed activity choices across preschool social contexts. Sex Roles, 67, 435-451.

En ligneHuguet, P., & Régner, I. (2007). Stereotype threat among schoolgirls in quasi-ordinary classroom circumstances. Journal of Educational Psychology, 99(3), 545-560.

En ligneHuguet, P., & Régner, I. (2009). Counter-stereotypic beliefs in math do not protect school girls from stereotype threat. Journal of Experimental Social Psychology, 45(4), 1024-1027.

Hyde, J. S. (2005). The gender similarities hypothesis. American psychologist, 60(6), 581-592.

En ligneJahoda, G. (1979). On the nature of difficulties in spatial-perceptual tasks: Ethnic and gender differences. British Journal of Psychology, 70, 351-363.

Liben, L. S., & Bigler, R. S. (2002). The developmental course of gender differentiation: Conceptualizing, measuring, and evaluating constructs and pathways. Monographs of the Society for Research in Child Development, 67, (2, Serial No. 269).

En ligneLytton, H., & Romney, D. M. (1991). Parents' differential socialization of boys and girls: A meta-analysis. Psychological Bulletin, 109(2), 267.

En ligneMa, L., & Woolley, J. (2013). Young children's sensitivity to speaker gender when learning from others. Journal of Cognition and Development, 14(1), 100-119.

McNally, M. (2013). Successful LEGO strategy delivers continued strong growth. Retrieved April 8, 2014 from http://aboutus.lego.com

En ligneMiller, D. I., & Halpern, D. F. (2013). Can spatial training improve long-term outcomes for gifted STEM undergraduates?. Learning and Individual Differences, 26, 141-152.

Mix, K. S., & Cheng, Y. L. (2012). The relation between space and math: Developmental and educational implications. Advances in Child Development and Behavior, 42, 197-243.

En ligneMoè, A. (2009). Are males always better than females in mental rotation? Exploring a gender belief explanation. Learning and Individual Differences, 19, 21-27.

En ligneMoè, A., & Pazzaglia, F. (2006). Following the instructions! Effects of gender beliefs in mental rotation. Learning and Individual Differences, 16, 369-377.

En ligneMoore, D. S., & Johnson, S. P. (2008). Mental rotation in human infants a sex difference. Psychological Science, 19(11), 1063-1066.

En ligneNeuburger, S., Jansen, P., Heil, M., & Quaiser-Pohl, C. (2012). A threat in the classroom: Gender stereotype activation and mental-rotation performance in elementary-school children. Zeitschrift für Psychologie, 220(2), 61.

En ligneNeuville, E., & Croizet, J.-C. (2007). Can salience of gender identity impair math performance among 7-8 years old girls? The moderating role of task difficulty. European Journal of Psychology of Education, 22(3), 307-316.

En ligneQuinn, P. C., & Liben, L. S. (2008). A sex difference in mental rotation in young infants. Psychological Science, 19, 1067-1070.

En ligneRégner, I., Smeding, A., Gimmig, D., Thinus-Blanc, C., Monteil, J. M., & Huguet, P. (2010). Individual differences in working memory moderate stereotype-threat effects. Psychological Science, 21(11), 1646-1648.

Régner, I., Steele, J. R., Ambady, N., Thinus-Blanc, C., & Huguet, P. (2014). Our future scientists: A review of stereotype threat in girls from early elementary school to middle school. International Review of Social Psychology / Revue Internationale de Psychologie Sociale, 27, 13-51.

Ruble, D. N.; Martin, C. L., & Berenbaum, S. A. (2006). Gender development. In: Eisenberg, N., (Ed.), Handbook of Child Development. New York: Wiley.

En ligneSchmader, T., Johns, M., & Forbes, C. (2008). An integrated process model of stereotype threat effects on performance. Psychological Review, 115, 336-356.

En ligneSerbin, L. A., Poulin-Dubois, D., & Eichstedt, J. A. (2002). Infants' response to gender-inconsistent events. Infancy, 3, 531-542.

Shelvin, K. H., Rivadeneyra, R., & Zimmerman, C. (2014). Stereotype threat in African American children: The role of Black identity and stereotype awareness. International Review of Social Psychology / Revue Internationale de Psychologie Sociale, 27, 175-204.

En ligneShih, M., Pittinsky, T. L., & Ambady, N. (1999). Stereotype susceptibility: Identity salience and shifts in quantitative performance. Psychological Science, 10, 80-83.

En ligneSmith, J. L., & White, P. H. (2002). An examination of implicitly activated, explicitly activated, and nullified stereotypes on mathematical performance: It's not just a woman's issue. Sex Roles, 47, 179-191. doi:10.1023/ A:1021051223441

En ligneSpelke, E. S. (2005). Sex differences in intrinsic aptitude for mathematics and science?: A critical review. American Psychologist, 60(9), 950-958.

En ligneSpencer, S. J., Steele, C. M., & Quinn, D. M. (1999). Stereotype threat and women's math performance. Journal of Experimental Social Psychology, 35, 4-28.

En ligneSteele, C.M., & Aronson, J. (1995). Stereotype Threat and the intellectual test-performance of African-Americans. Journal of Personality and Social Psychology, 69(5), 797-811.

En ligneTomasetto, C., Alparone, F. R., & Cadinu, M. (2011). Girls' math performance under stereotype threat: the moderating role of mothers' gender stereotypes.Developmental Psychology, 47(4), 943.

En ligneWolfgang, C. H., Stannard, L. L., & Jones, I. (2001). Block play performance among preschoolers as a predictor of later school achievement in mathematics. Journal of Research in Childhood Education, 15, 173-180.

CHAPTER 15

P. Brey, "The politics of computer systems andthe ethics of design," in Computer Ethics: Philo-sophical Enquiry , J.v.d. Hoven, Ed. Rotterdam,The Netherlands: Rotterdam Univ. Press, 1998.

B. Friedman and P.H. Kahn, "Humanagency and responsible computing: Implica-tions for computer system design," in HumanValues and the Design of Computer Technolo-gy, B. Friedman, Ed. Stanford, CA: CSLI Pub-lications, 1997, pp. 221-235.

B. Friedman and L.I. Millet, "Reasoningabout computers as moral agents: A researchnote," in Human Values and the Design ofComputer Technology, B. Friedman, Ed. Stan-ford, CA: CSLI Pubs., 1997, pp. 205.

D. Grossman, On Killing. Boston, MA: Lit-tle Brown & Co, 1995

D. Grossman, "The morality of bombing: Psy-chological responses to "distant punishment," pre-sented at the Center for Strategic and InternationalStudies, Dueling Doctrines and the New AmericanWay of War Symp., Washington, DC, 1998.

D. Grossman, "Evolution of weaponry,"Encyclopedia of Violence, Peace, and Conflict.Academic Press. 2000.

P.R. Helft, M. Siegler, and J. Lantos, "The riseand fall of the futility movement," New EnglandJ. Medicine, vol. 343, no. 4, pp. 293-296, 2000.

D.G. Johnson, Computer Ethics , 3 ed.Upper Saddle River, NJ: Prentice Hall, 2001.

H. Jonas, The Imperative of Responsibility:In Search of an Ethics for the TechnologicalAge. Chicago, IL: Univ. of Chicago Press, 1979.

S. Milgram, Obedience to Authority. NewYork, NY: Harper and Row, 1975.

K.L. Mosier and L.J. Skitka, "Human deci-sion makers and automated decision aids: Madefor each other?," in Automation and Human Per-formance: Theory and Applications, R. Parasur-aman and M. Mouloua, Eds. Mahwah, NJ:Lawrence Erlbaum Assoc., 1996, pp. 201-220.

C. Nass, J. Steuer, and E.R. Tauberm,"Computers are social actors," presented at theCHI'94: Human Factors in Computing Sys-tems, Boston, MA, 1994.

W.V. O'Brien, The Conduct of Just andLimited War. New York, NY: Praeger, 1981.

R. Parasuraman, and V. Riley, "Humans and Automation: Use, misuse, disuse, abuse," HumanFactors, vol. 39, no. 2, pp. 230-253, 1997.

R. Parasuraman, T.B. Sheridan, and C.D.Wickens, "A model for types and levels ofhuman interaction with automation," IEEETrans. Systems, Man, and Cybernetics, vol. 30,no. 3, pp. 286-297, 2000

B. Reeves and C. Nass, The Media Equa-tion: How People

Treat Computers,Televisionand New Media Like Real People and Places .Stanford, CA: CSLI Pubs., and New York. NY:Cambridge Univ. Press, 1996.

T.B. Sheridan, "Speculations on futurerelations between humans and automation," inAutomation and Human Performance, M.Mouloua, Ed Mahwah, New Jersey: LawrenceErlbaum Assoc., 1996, pp. 449-460.

L.J. Skitka, K.L. Mosier, and M.D. Bur-dick, "Does automation bias decision-mak-ing?" Int. J. Human-Computer Studies, vol. 51,no. 5, pp. 991-1006, 1999.

D.L. Wells, "Opening remarks," presentedat the Swarming: Network Enabled C4ISR,McLean, VA, 2003. (1) (PDF) Digital identity. Available from: https://www.researchgate.net/publication/ 3226811_Digital_identity

CHAPTER 16

Craik, J. (1993). The face of fashion. New York: RoutledgeCrane, D. (2000). Fashion and its Social Agendas: Class, Gender, and Identity in Clothing. Chicago: University of Chicago Press.

Curle, R. (1949). Women, An Analytical Study. London:Watts & Co.Davis, F. (1988). Clothing, fashion and the dialectic of identity. In: Maines, D., & Couch, J. (Eds.). Communication and social structure.Springfield, USA: Charles & Thomas.

Davis, F. (1989). Of Maids' Uniforms and Blue Jeans : The Drama of Status Ambivalences in Clothing and Fashion. QualitativeSociology, 12, 337 – 354.

Davis, F. (1992). Fashion, Culture and Identity. Chicago: University of Chicago Press.

DeLong, Â., Salusso-Deonier, C. & Larntz, K. (1983). Use of Perceptions of Female Dress as an Indicator of Role Definition. HomeEconomics Research Journal, 4, 327 – 336.

Dodd, C., Clarke, I., Baron, S., & Houston, V. (1998). Lo oking the part: Identity, meaning and culture in clothing purchasing —Theoretical considerations. Journal of Fashion Marketing and Management, 4, 41 – 48.

Entwistle, J. (2000). *The Fashioned Body: Fashion, Dress and Modern Social Theory.* Cambridge: Polity.

Flügel, J. (1930). *The Psychology of Clothes.* London: Hogarth.Giles, H., & William, C. (1975). Communication Length as a Function of Dress Style and Social Status. *Perceptual and Motor Skills, 40,*961 – 62.

Holman, H. (1981). Product use as communication source. In: Enis, Å., & Roering, Ä. (Eds.). *Review of marketing.* Chicago: AmericanMarketing Association.

Hughes, J. (2004). 'Zivil Ist Allemal Schadlich' Clothing in German – Language Culture of the 1920s. *Neophilologus, 8,* 429 – 445.

Kawamura, Î. (2005). *Fashion-ology: An Introduction to Fashion Studies.* Oxford: Berg.

Lloyd, B., & Duveen, G. (1993). *Gender and education.* Hemel Hempstead: Harvester Wheatsheaf.

Lurie, A. (1981). The language of clothes. London: Heinemann.

Mayer, R., & Belk, R. (1985). Fashion and impression formation among children. In Solomon Â. (Ed.). The psychology of fashion.Lexington : Lexington Books.

Rodnitzky, J. (1999). Feminist Phoenix: the rise and fall of a feminist counterculture. London: Greenwood Publishing GroupSawyer, C. (1987). Men in Skirts and Women in Trousers, from Achilles to Victoria Grant: One Explanation of a Comedic Paradox. TheJournal of Popular Culture, 21, 1 – 18.

Schor, N. (1987). Dreaming Dissymet ry: Barthes, Foucault, & Sexual Difference. In Jardine, A. & Smith, P. (Eds). Men in Feminism,London: Methuen.

Solomon, Â., & Douglas, S. (1987). Diversity in Product Symbolism: The Case of Female Executive Clothing. Psychology & Marketing,4, 189 – 212.

Steele, V. (1989). Men and Women: Dressing the Part. Washington: Smithsonian Institution Press.

Tseelon, E. (1989). Communicating via clothes. Unpublished paper. Department ofExperimental Psychology, University of Oxford.

9 7 9 8 8 8 9 0 9 6 7 4 0